HOW TO GET HEALTHY ACCORDING TO GEORGE (AND VOLTAIRE)

RANDY FORDE

HALLARD PRESS

Published by Hallard Press LLC.
www.HallardPress.com 352.460.6099
Cover Art by Miblart
Back Cover Photograph by Anita Bitterman

Library of Congress Control Number: 2023922556

Publisher's Cataloging-in-Publication

Names: Forde, Randy, author.
Title: How to get healthy according to George (and Voltaire) / Randy Forde.
Description: The Villages, FL: Hallard Press, 2024.
Identifiers: LCCN: 2023922556 | ISBN: 978-1-962326-22-3 (hardcover) | 978-1-962326-21-6 (paperback) | 978-1-962326-23-0 (ebook)
Subjects: LCSH Older people--Health and hygiene--United States--Popular works. | Nutrition. | Health. | Self-care, Health. | Longevity. | Exercise. | BISAC HEALTH & FITNESS / General | HEALTH & FITNESS / Diet & Nutrition / Nutrition | HEALTH & FITNESS / Exercise / General | HEALTH & FITNESS / Longevity
Classification: LCC RA776 .F67 2024 | DDC 613--dc23

ISBN: 978-1-962326-22-3 (HARDCOVER)
ISBN: 978-1-962326-21-6 (PAPERBACK)
ISBN: 978-1-962326-23-0 (EBOOK)

NOTICE

CONTENTS

INTRODUCTION

Many, many centuries ago (or were they decades?), when I was but a young lad entering the third grade, a new kid showed up at school that year. I still steadfastly remember him because he was such an anomaly in those days. He was severely overweight, or obese, as professional medical people describe the condition today. Though several of our other classmates were also carrying a few extra pounds, he was by far the biggest kid in our class, and perhaps even in the entire school, which included sixth graders.

Being such an irregularity among our classmates, he possessed an extremely low level of self-esteem. He cried easily and often, particularly out on the playing field during P.E. class when he couldn't do what the other kids were doing. I also recall him being on a special diet way back then, and again, crying because he wanted more to eat. Even at such a youthful age, I understood the value of being healthy and I felt so sorry for that poor kid.

I don't know if he had some type of medical condition, or if he just had an extremely poor diet for whatever reason that limited his physical mobility. And I would wager that when he got home from school, he did not go outside and run around all over the place, playing with his friends like I did for a couple of hours before dinner. As memory serves, that was the only year he attended our school, and I have no idea whatever happened to the unfortunate lad.

Sadly, though (at least to me), he would just be one of the gang in grade school these days, as approximately one in five of his classmates would be obese like him, and another 20% of his peers would be overweight. This phenomenon genuinely saddens me because I now know the damage accruing inside the bodies of these children even at their young age and a significant percentage will never live to see as many years on this planet as I have been blessed with.

And you parents and grandparents of these youngsters, and all you other adults out there, are in much worse physical shape than these children. Three out of every four of you are obese or harboring way more weight than you should. I also know from a not-so-secret source that 60% of you are suffering from some type of chronic illness, such as a cardiovascular disease, type 2 diabetes, cancer, or other ongoing syndrome that most likely could have been avoided. And only one out of every four of you engages in the recommended level of physical activity.

Several years after moving on into middle school, a stark moment occurred in my life one Saturday afternoon while watching the Major League Baseball game of the week. Yes, the light bulb and television had been invented when I was a young adolescent. During that broadcast, an image appeared on the screen, and like a red-hot iron upon a steer's backside, that scene was seared into my brain. I have never forgotten that moment, and I promised myself that very day so long ago that I would always keep myself as healthy as best I could, for as long as I could. And to this day, I have succeeded reasonably well all these centuries—I mean *decades*—later.

I felt so sorry for that poor kid back in the third grade, and moving through the years to now, I have also felt sorry for countless people along the way who have had (or have) less-than-stellar health. And I have always had a deep desire to help people improve their health because I know how wonderful being fit feels, and oh by the way, how fleeting well-being can be if proper attention is not exercised to preserve that blessing.

But full disclosure here, I am not one of those people who can stand in front of an aerobics class whooping and hollering to get people moving and excited (that's so eighties), nor one of those people spinning on one of those fancy new stationary bikes, acting all enthused and animated hoping to garner a million clicks and going viral. No, I am just a decent senior athlete who likes to live mainly in the real world.

Also, I do not have a secret taco sauce to consume every Tuesday evening to make you feel like you are twenty again, nor any new and improved lizard lubricant (or was it snake oil?) to revitalize you. However, improving your health is doable for practically everyone, including you, and I graciously invite you to come aboard and begin your journey to better well-being.

Now notice I said that improving your health is achievable, and that is the pertinent objective of our mission. I did not say anything about losing weight. You may lose ample weight as you proceed on our excursion through this book, or only a limited amount. Or you may even gain weight if you add enough muscle to help facilitate enhanced body movement, thus rendering common everyday tasks easier to perform. In my humble opinion, Americans need to focus away from how their bodies appear and focus more (much, much more) on what their bodies can do.

Again, I desire to encourage you and help you improve your overall health. In addition, I want to clearly and emphatically stress to you that athleticism is most definitely not required toward achieving that goal of cultivating your well-being. However, and this is most exceedingly important, a devoted participation in this vital endeavor of resuscitating and then maintaining your health and enjoyment of life is essential.

Thus, if like that spy person from long ago, you choose to accept this most important and rewarding mission of improving your health (and I sincerely hope you do), welcome aboard! And even if you are fairly healthy, you can always improve your well-being. No one is perfectly healthy, including me.

Yes, I have been blessed with good health and I have always had a deep sense of appreciation for my well-being. However, and again this is of the utmost importance, the real-world reason for my long-term health is not because I am better than anyone, or more athletic, or prettier (I'm certainly not that!), but that I have always reasonably, persistently, and fairly consistently worked at keeping myself fit, healthy, and socially engaged. And as I mentioned above, devotion to the mission is most essential and all I will ask of you during our expedition toward improving your health.

So please come aboard so we can begin your long-anticipated expedition to Healthyville!

CHAPTER 1: BEFORE WE BEGIN

BEFORE WE BEGIN, let's go on a bike ride, a serious bike ride, a Tour de France-like bike ride. Don't worry, for you it will be virtual. For me, it will be full-on real life.

We will ride about 30 miles today with roughly 20 other cyclists, and it looks like we have some especially stout riders here. This little excursion should be fun, and exciting, and dangerous, and lung-searing, and thigh-burning, and exhilarating, but seriously not boring! The weather looks good, perhaps a bit breezy, but no rain in sight. The course is hilly, but you will manage it. I promise.

Are you ready? Okay, we're rolling out.

00:01

We are about a minute into the ride now. Notice several of the riders casually chatting as our heart rates are rising and our muscles are warming up. As the pace quickens in a few minutes, the chatter will slowly subside, and the only sounds you will hear is the wind rushing by and an occasional shout of warning or request. So, please pay attention.

Also, watch for any hand signals that I give. If I'm pointing in some direction to the ground, slightly steer away from that direction, because something is lying on the pavement such as a pinecone, a rock, or other obstacle that you want to avoid. And I may wave you to get directly behind me because of approaching riders, runners, or hikers. Fortunately, we will ride on a closed course today, meaning no automobiles are allowed on the trail, but there may be a few deer, turkeys, and bears loitering along the trail. Just stay in your seat. The deer and turkeys won't hurt you. Nor will the bears, unless, of course, you get between momma bear and baby bear. Got all that?

Here's a tip. Stay as directly and as closely behind me as possible, say 18 to 24 inches. Yes, it's scarily close, but not only does it keep you out of the line of fire from oncoming people, it's the most efficient way to ride. Those NASCAR people figured out that drafting deal a long time ago over in Daytona, and we will do the same thing today, though we will not be going quite as fast as they normally do.

You see, the person riding up front, breaking the wind, is working about 30% harder than the rest of us. When the leader gets tired, that person will give a signal and move over. The next person will then dictate the pace. I'll let the former leader back in front of me in our peloton of riders. Everyone here knows me and my Medicare rule. Of course, back here, we will have to deal with the accordion effect; but never mind, I don't want to complicate this for you. You're going to have enough to think about.

Just relax and feel your mind and body coming alive!

00:10

Okay, we are about three miles out now and we're starting to cook. Comfortable yet? Good, but just so you know, it is about to get considerably faster! By the way, I put two bottles filled with an electrolyte drink in your bottle cages below your seat. Keep drinking; it's hot today. Your muscles and brain are devouring carbohydrates, and you need to replace them on the fly but try to do that as safely as possible. Just watch when I retrieve my bottle and you do the same. You should go through an entire bottle on the way out. As I said, it gets hot down here on the peninsula.

In case you don't have enough to think about, here is something else to ponder. The wind will be behind us at just a slight angle going out, so it's near optimal. However, coming back after the turn around, it will be in our face. I know, I know, there is a great deal to think about, but your brain can manage all of these decisions. I promise.

Here we go! Game time! We're ramping up! Just let it happen. Just let it flow. Your mind, your body, and your bike will all become one. You will experience life at full throttle! And you will not believe the feeling that comes over you. We'll be riding on the wind!

00:15

We're flying now! I would guess we are moving about 22 miles per hour. While on this bike flying at these speeds with all these people, prudent mindfulness is highly recommended. Stay focused! And keep your cadence high, about 80-90 times a minute. Sorry, that's how many times you turn the pedals over. Let the gearing do most of the work depending on the terrain.

You should notice your brain in a much higher gear, too. It's accepting and processing data at a rate you probably didn't know it could achieve. And yes, your vision is extremely busy deciphering out non-essential information, so you have a better chance of staying upright. Trust me, you don't want to hit the deck right now. Just take my word for it on that one.

If we were not busy enough, we are going to have to think about something else. At these speeds, gaps could open between riders, and we will have to decide rather to cross the gap or follow the rider falling back. Like right now!

Hammer down!

Come on! Come on! Come on!

Well, that was fun! Now we're back with the main group.

00:24

We are about halfway out to the turnaround now, and this pace is getting ridiculous. I suppose I forgot to tell you the format of today's ride. It is championship Thursday. I didn't want to scare you away before we got started. If we can keep up, we keep up. If we can't, we get dropped from the peloton like those two riders a few minutes ago.

Another gap! Hammer down! Wait, wait, wait, executive decision time here. We are in a good group now. Two more of my friends up ahead have decided to drop back. They're waiting for us. Yes, we can work with this group. We're down to about 20 miles per hour now, a good pace. The ride will be a bit more relaxed now, but don't lose your focus. And drink some more fluid.

Like I said, this is a good group, so I am going to make another executive decision and wave my Medicare rule now and help pull the group from up front when it's my turn. Just stay behind me and when we do get up front, watch for me to flick my elbow after riding up there for a few minutes. That signal means I'm pulling off the front of the group. Pull off with me and we'll drift back to the end of the line. It's demanding work, but it's a great feeling contributing to the group. I am more than happy to do it when I can.

00:46

Okay, slow it down. We're approaching the turnaround point. We are halfway through the ride, so now would be a suitable time to eat something. Check your back pocket. I put an energy gel pack in there. As I said earlier, your brain and muscles are burning through the carbohydrates in your body and the gel will help replace them. You have been drinking from your bottle, haven't you? I can assure you that you do not want to run out of fuel. Race cars, jets, and tractors do not go far without fuel, and neither will you. I know, just one more item to think about.

Speaking of things to think about, it now looks like we're going to have a rain shower up ahead. Welcome to Florida in the summertime.

Those weather people did say there was a 10% chance today, so they did cover themselves. However, they also said the showers would be scattered, so hopefully, we will miss it.

00:54

The wind is seriously kicking up now. And right on cue, here comes the rain, but no matter what happens, we can deal with it. Let's just hope there is no lightning, because out here, there is no place to hide. The more immediate issue will be the spray coming off our tires. Ride just slightly to one side and not directly behind me so the spray doesn't hit you in the face. Turn on your windshield wipers if you have any. Just kidding, a little levity goes a long way on a bike ride and in life.

01:02

Okay, the shower is over and here comes the sun again. The humidity should really be amusing now. Nothing like a five-minute Florida rain shower to provide an instant outdoor sauna, so keep drinking from your water bottle. We have less than 20 minutes to ride at this speed, so enjoy these last few miles, sweat and all. You will be rewarded at the end of the ride if you haven't already been. I promise.

01:24

Twenty-eight miles in about 84 minutes. Not a bad ride! Let's pull out of the group now. We're going to cool down over these last couple of miles by riding at a leisurely pace. Still pay attention, but now we can take in the scenery a bit more instead of just focusing on the back wheel of the rider in front of us.

"Hi, how are y'all doing today?"

Sorry, we are in the south. We say y'all down here. That was a couple of people I've seen a hundred times out here walking. And look at those little kids up there. Aren't they cute? I just love seeing all these people out here enjoying the outdoors after I'm done with a robust ride.

01:36

Here we are, at the end of the trail. We rode thirty miles in 96 minutes. Not bad, just under twenty miles per hour, including our cool down time. How do you feel? All warm and alive, huh? Kind of like being bathed in the firelight. The afterglow of the flow! Stress is gone. Tranquility base here.

Not only did we work our bodies today, but our brains as well. Our bodies will be building our muscles back even stronger, and our brains will be building new neurons and connections, and maintaining and strengthening memory, attention, and other cognitive skills. Not to mention feeling the fun of experiencing the wind rushing by and being with our friends.

Back here in the parking lot, you can see most of them are still around reliving and retelling their personal moments from the ride, socializing, bonding, basking in the glow. In a few minutes, we will all go our separate ways back to our separate lives; but be assured, in a day or two, we will be back here again to strap on our helmets and ride once again on the wind!

DID you enjoy that virtual ride? I participated in that ride in real life a couple of weeks ago, well except for the rain part. I made that up for effect, but it's not like that hasn't happened while riding with my friends, like last Monday, for instance! We started riding with sunny skies overhead, but after the turnaround, the skies darkened and before long, we were riding through a torrential downpour, a veritable monsoon. But I was having a blast! Granted, I may not be entirely sane, but I do enjoy life, and fortunately, I am still able to do so.

Remember I mentioned the Medicare rule during our ride. That's my decree stating that a rider who owns a Medicare card doesn't have to get on the front and do a lot of work breaking the wind that we spoke of. We have a hall pass when riding with younger riders to sit protected in the peloton. A healthy quantity of riders on the ride could easily have been my children, and one young man could have been my grandson. As I write this chapter, I'm staring down both barrels of my seventieth birthday. How did that happen?

So, what is my secret? How can an ancient athlete like me (no, it's not true that I participated in the original Olympic Games in Greece back in 776 BCE) still perform at this level? I have no idea. I'm an athlete, not a doctor, nor a dietitian. But as an athlete, I have learned a few things over the years, and I would like to share them with you. I can assure you; my secret is not rocket science. I'm not that smart. And truth be told, it's not even a secret. I'm not saying it's easy to do, but it's not hard to understand how to be healthier, happier, and more appreciative during your life. However, it does involve getting off the couch; that is, putting forth a little effort.

Will you ever be able to feel the rush of riding in a peloton? Probably not. But promise me; *please* promise me that you will not get discouraged by that fact. Zooming around on a bicycle is great for some people, but it is highly dangerous. In fact, it has nearly gotten me killed. Yes, I have stared death straight in the headlights of oncoming vehicles twice (which I chronicle later in this book if you stick around, and I sincerely hope you will). And honestly, having the ability to ride that fast is like anabolic steroids for the egos of many riders. You don't need to go there.

So many people are unhealthy, unhappy, and bored these days. They have no meaningful purpose in their lives, and sadly, very little hope for better days ahead. To paraphrase an old saying, life is *fill in the blank* and then you die. I went by one of our local big box stores the other day where several homeless people struggling for survival can often be seen, and one of those poor souls had painted on a wall, "A long life is a slow death." Life doesn't have to be that way. There is a difference between living and merely existing.

Like all of us, I have made my share of mistakes (plenty) in my life. I have had my disappointments (numerous). And I have my share of weighty baggage that most of us collect as we proceed through our lives. But I do still have my health which allows me to continue being a (mostly) fully participating member in this one life that I have been blessed with here on the planet.

Somehow, I stumbled upon some answers early on, continued to pay attention and found many more, and overall, have had a decent, meaningful ride through life which I hope will continue for some time. Like all of us, it could have been much better, but it could have been much worse—much, much worse. And even though my life could end tomorrow, I hope I have many decades left, as I am confident you do, too. And that's why I want to share those answers I found along the way with you.

I don't have a magic pill for you, or a 30-day crash diet plan, nor a five-minute a day, super exercise routine to craft you into an ace athlete, give you abs of steel, and fashion you into a good-looking (but of course, pure and modest) creature of lure and lust.

But I do have a solid strategy and game plan to keep you in your game of life much longer so you can enjoy your grandkids, and an active, gratifying lifestyle as an elder citizen. And all you millennials and zoomers out there, trust me on this one, that becoming a senior citizen event will be upon you before you know it. Like that famous singer-sailor guy once said, we are not really here all that long, and from my vantage point, he is right.

So, I sincerely hope you will continue your journey with me through this book. I want you to be healthy enough to feel the rush of taking your granddaughter (maybe even your great-granddaughter) to the park, or your granddaughter and great-grandson to the ball game. Or land that big one that didn't get away this time. Or run in a 5k race for charity, or just for fun. Or restore that old car that you brought home on a trailer last evening. Or walk through your local park or along the beach and enjoy the aliveness and beauty of the natural world. Or retire when you want to instead of your poor health dictating when you must stop working. These activities are doable and much more enjoyable when you are healthy. Athleticism is not required!

So, please stay with me on this journey as we work our way back to Chapter 12 when it will be showtime for you to embark upon your own journey to healthier days through the rest of the one life you are blessed with. You can even perform short rehearsals as we progress through these hopefully helpful and entertaining pages.

And come back and visit anytime you want to resharpen your skills. I genuinely want you to live long and prosper. Oh dang, that slogan has already been used. Sorry, Mr. Spock. Wait a minute. Mr. Spock will live in the future. So technically, I can use that phrase. Is that correct? Are there any copyright lawyer people that can help me out here?

Possessing a higher level of health and well-being genuinely gives us the best opportunity to experience that most precious gift of life to its fullest. Of course, there are exceptions to all things, but no matter where you are along your path, or where your physical or mental state lies now, or what talent level you happen to possess, improvements most often can always be made. And please remember, for as long as you still have it, life is truly a gift! Let us go out there and live!

CHAPTER 2: MY STORY

So why listen to a dumb athlete for your health and well-being advice? I'm not even a world-class athlete like that gentleman that lives down the road a piece. I think his name is Tom Brady. You know, that quarterback guy that has played football since before the turn of the century and has won more Super Bowls than any team in the National Football League's century-plus existence. While my story may not be as exciting as Mr. Brady's (spoiler alert: I do not have a supermodel wife), it has been an interesting journey.

Let me take you back into a far eon, although the dinosaurs had all died out by that time. I was just a young lad, and according to a reliable source (my mom) I was trying to walk by the time I was eight months old. A month later, she said I had that walking thing down, and one can always rely on moms to accurately reflect their child's accomplishments. Right, moms?

I cannot honestly say I remember all that, but I do recall the first time I rode a bicycle without training wheels. I think Orville and Wilbur still had their bike shop up on the mainland somewhere before they decided to go do that flying thing. Maybe I'm not quite that old (it's not true that my parents bought my first bike from their shop), but I was barely five years old when I accomplished that riding with no training wheels feat. What a feeling that was—I had done it! I rode all the way around the house to the pasture gate where my grandfather's cows grazed on the other side. I have always had a robust sense of balance.

Back then, my uncle was a very good baseball player. I remember going to the ballpark at an early age when the family went to see him play. The only thing I ever wanted to be was a ballplayer, a Major League Baseball player. My mom has videos of me when I was three years old throwing a ball in the air, swinging for the fences, only to miss and fall to the ground with the inertia of the swing. To have had such good balance, I sure did fall down a lot when I was a kid. My sister can tell you about the time I rode my bike into a pine tree and knocked myself out. Come to think of it, that could explain a great deal, at least to my friends.

I started playing T-ball (they called it Mighty Mites back then) when I was five years old. I so loved it! I still remember those searing, muggy Florida mornings when sweat began dripping from my body as soon as I stepped out of my mom's air-conditioned (by all four windows being rolled down as we sped along at 55 miles per hour) car. I played first base because I was the only kid on the team that could catch the ball. After all, I had been practicing almost half of my life.

A couple of years later, my mom, or it could have been my dad, taught me how to read the Major League Baseball (MLB) standings. Believe it or not, the Pittsburgh Pirates had a very good team that year and met the mighty New York Yankees in the World Series. The Yankees outscored the Pirates by about a thousand runs in that seven-game Series. However, with the score tied in the bottom of ninth inning in the winner-take-all Game 7, Bill Mazeroski hit his famous walk-off home run over Yogi Berra's head to win the Series. I think that was the game where Yogi, who was playing left field that day, came up with his famous saying, "Well, it ain't over 'til it's over my head." I think that's what he said. It's been a long time ago.

As a typical kid back then, I collected baseball cards. I can still remember going to the store and buying those nickel (half my allowance) packages with six paperback cards and one piece of "paperback" gum inside. I was like all those people you see in the grocery store, furiously scratching away at their just purchased lottery tickets. With great excitement and anticipation, I would open the pack, pop the gum into my mouth careful not to cut my gums as my teeth tried to break the rock-hard gum down, and see if I got a card of one of my heroes.

Eventually, I grew out of collecting baseball cards because of other interests, and somewhere during that time as a young teen, I saw one of my former boyhood baseball heroes who had retired a couple of years earlier on television while watching the MLB game of the week. I don't remember who he was, but my word, had he put on weight since his recent playing days. Lots of it. I could not believe how different he looked. I vowed right then to never let myself go there. I didn't know how yet, but I was determined to always be fit and healthy.

Early in 1970-something, my baseball dream was over. I came to realize that while I was decent at the game, I would never turn pro. I wound up working at a grocery store in Gainesville, the same town where Tom Petty was perfecting his rock and roll gig. I was on my own for the first time, depressed, searching for direction. Even listening to Mr. Petty playing live couldn't cheer me up because first of all, I had no idea who he was, and second, I was too young to get into the bar where he played back then.

While working one morning, I found a book regarding the benefits of consuming dietary fiber in one's diet on the bookshelf that was near the frozen food section that I was supposed to be stocking. No, I wasn't goofing off. My work was done for the day. I had a couple minutes before the end of my shift, and I was "leisurely" walking to the time clock. I promise. Ironically, across the aisle from the bookshelf containing that dietary fiber book was the bakery with all its fiber-challenged pastries.

I don't specifically remember purchasing and reading the book—after all, it's been more than a decade or two...okay *five* since then—but it was a resident on my bookshelf for many years. And my diet began transforming during those early grocery store days.

I remember having a small brown paper sack of fiber that I apparently purchased from a health food store. That stuff was nasty. I tried putting it into yogurt, but that wasn't much better. Soon, however, I discovered the benefits of steaming fresh vegetables. So, by the sheer random luck of finding that book, I had stumbled across my first gem of nutrition and had begun my long road toward mastering basic healthy living.

As a kid, I had grown up on carrots. They were my go-to snack food. My mom claims she doesn't remember her limited purchases of snack food back then; but as I recall, she would normally bring home one regular bag of potato chips and one package containing six little cream pies or Swiss rolls on her Friday trips to the grocery store. And just so you know, growing up in a family of six, those items usually didn't survive the weekend, so carrots it was until the next Friday. By the end of the Carter administration, those carrots had found their way into salads for lunch which became a daily fixture in my diet.

In 1972, I watched Frank Shorter win the Olympic marathon gold medal. I was mesmerized. Shorter had come to Mr. Petty's town to pursue a law degree and train with the legendary Florida Track Club, who sent three of their runners, including Shorter, to the Olympics that year. Shorter's victory helped launch the running boom in America, and Gainesville became a mecca for world-class runners and joggers alike.

I dabbled with running during that time and received a pair of real running shoes (those old black and white sneakers were so not cool anymore) as a Christmas gift, a pristine pair of Nike waffle trainers. But those beautiful blue and yellow Nikes got very little use during the middle of the decade.

I was still struggling with figuring life out and what I was going to do with mine. I went back to school at the University of Florida, got a degree, and got a job that barely paid more than the grocery store. Meanwhile, those Nikes spent more time in the closet than they did on the road. Fortunately, my diet, while not pristine, was not getting any worse. Those steamed vegetables and salads were still around.

Toward the end of seventies, I rebooted my life. I went back to the university in Gainesville with a serious plan this time, a mission. I bought a used bicycle to get to my classes, and in the process of riding around campus, I realized how much I missed being an athlete. I started riding that bike just for the fun of it.

And with Gainesville having so many runners all over the place, those Nikes started seeing the light of day more often. I began tracking my running milage and becoming a serious runner. I bought a couple of books on how to train and devoured them. I subscribed to a couple of running magazines, which usually had an article or two on nutrition which contributed to the improvement of my diet.

Six weeks before the end of the decade, I entered my first 5k race which is 3.1 miles in distance. I finished that race in 18:14 (18 minutes and 14 seconds), and a month later I ran another 5k finishing under 18 minutes. Twelve days into the new decade, I ran an ordinary, open-to-the-public 15k (9.3 miles) race, and Marty Liquori was in the field that day. If you have watched track and field events during the Olympic Games this century, you probably know who he is. He's that announcer guy.

He was the third American high school kid to run a mile in less than four minutes. Very few people can even ride a bicycle for a mile in that time. When he was 19, he made it to the Olympic 1500m (about a mile) finals in Mexico City. But here is the amazing fact, on that day we both ran in the same 15k race in Gainesville (a decade after his Olympic performance), he didn't even win. He was third. I finished 21st, "only" 12 minutes behind him. Yes, the kids in Gainesville could run back then. Incidentally, I am quite sure Tom Petty wasn't in the race that day because he had already moved to California singing about some American girl. I never did find out who she was.

OKAY, let's call our first timeout here and look back at my first decade as an adult, although I use the term adult rather hesitantly (all you young zoomers pay particular attention here). I haven't even mentioned the fact that during that decade I gave up a baseball scholarship, dropped out of two universities, and had at least five different jobs that I can remember. But as the 1980s began and with my thirties on the horizon, I finished school again, got a real degree, and landed a professional job back in my hometown that I kept for nearly 40 years after yet another false start in a big oil town.

For most people, including me, that first decade-long foray into adulthood can be compared to our first decade in life when, through the process of trial and error, we are rapidly growing physically and mentally, exploring, learning, and yes, making mistakes and getting into trouble because our brains are still maturing. Perhaps you have already landed in places you did not want to go, and perhaps your health is less than stellar. But do not despair! Most often, you still have time to change the road you're on especially toward improving your health no matter how far along in life you are.

We all have our issues, self-doubts, challenges, etc., and granted, some of us have more profound obstacles to overcome than others for any number of reasons and circumstances. We all have different combinations of nature and nurture within us to manage. However, we are all human beings and share more than 99.6% of our DNA. Though none of us will start in the same place, and we are not all going to get to the same destination, we can all move closer toward improving our health and well-being by employing this same exploratory, empirical process of trial and error once we absorb some genuine guidance which I hope to provide over the forthcoming chapters. That is my mission here.

So again, just as in your first decade in life, don't panic (or give up), and use that trial-and-error process of starting, stopping, moving forward, backward, experimenting, sometimes making gross mistakes and sometimes meaningful accomplishments on your journey toward becoming healthier, happier, and more appreciative of life. And hopefully, once you learn the basics from this book and other reliable sources, you will land in those proverbial greener pastures of health, well-being, and happiness. Just never stop trying to get there. Please make that your mission. You are worth it!

————

OKAY, so getting back to my story, I now had a decent job and a physical activity to replace baseball, but I should have listened to that great group of philosophers. No, not Socrates, Plato, and Aristotle although I hear those guys were pretty good (not sure who their lead singer was), I'm talking about The Who when they said too much of anything was too much for them, and apparently too much running was too much for me.

During the fall before I got that real job, I ran a marathon which is 26.2 miles long in 2:43 something (two hours and 43 minutes). It wasn't in the Frank Shorter stratosphere (he ran a 2:12 in those 1972 Olympics), but the time wasn't that bad. I then put everything I had into running. I worked my way up to where I was running over 100 miles per week and ran over 4,000 miles in 1981. During the Thanksgiving weekend, I ran my next marathon in 2:37 something. All of that for just a six-minute improvement. But I wasn't discouraged.

After the race, I never genuinely allowed my body to fully recover. The following month after the race, I averaged 85 miles per week and ran 100 miles during the first week of 1982. And then, I got sick. I took it easy for a week and then started building my milage back up only to get sick again in February. March was a replay of the previous two months.

With spring well sprung, my running began to re-bloom in April. And then, on the second day of May, I went on a run that I will never forget. Normally here on the peninsula, it starts getting hot in May and the humidity returns, but on that day, it was still pleasantly cool and crisp. I can't remember how far I had planned to run, probably something like 18 to 20 miles, but I only finished nine. I can still take you to the place where my body made me stop running because it hurt so badly. I can't remember how I got home that day, probably through a combination of jogging and walking. Although I bounced back during that week and the next one, by the end of the month, I couldn't run anymore.

And I had no idea why. Neither could an assorted array of doctors. During that last marathon a few months earlier, I remember smelling something like ammonia apparently coming from my body about 24 miles into the race. It was hot that day and I didn't properly hydrate. I know now that my body had started burning its protein because it had run out of glucose. Perhaps that had something to do with not being able to run any longer without my body saying no. I still do not know.

Nevertheless, over the course of the next two years, my body slowly recovered. I tried to start back running a time or two, but this time, I actually listened to my body, and it was still saying not yet. In early 1984, I joined the fancy new health spa in town which featured not only an indoor swimming pool and racquetball courts, but those newfangled Nautilus weight machines designed for ordinary people to begin a weight training program. The fitness craze was full-on back then. Who can forget Richard Simmons, aerobics, leotards, and legwarmers? Okay granted, you millennials and zoomers may not, and honestly, don't even look that up, unless, of course, you want a big laugh. It was the age of *Flashdance*, and we boomers were coming of age!

Anyway, I didn't do a lot of dancing, but I did start using those weight machines. And because they were so easy to use, the habit stuck. Arnold Schwarzenegger didn't have to worry about me in his Mr. Universe competitions, but I was getting stronger. Over the summer, I began to run again, and by fall, I was back up to 60 to 70 miles a week again.

And then, something happened, but for the life of me, I don't remember what it was. On October 12, my running records stopped. I did a speed workout that day. After a two-mile warm up, I did six one-mile repeats averaging 5:47 per mile. Again, I can't remember why my records stopped that day. I can only surmise that something was wrong.

However, the first week of December, I apparently felt well enough to run my first race in over two years, our annual Reindeer Run, but I didn't race again until the following May. During that period, I evidently gave up on the effort to become a world-class runner as I had grudgingly given up my effort to become an MLB player many years before when I gave up that baseball scholarship.

From the middle of July in 1985 when my records picked back up, until the end of the year, I averaged 25 miles a week, slightly above the sweet spot of exercise recommended by the Physical Activity Guidelines for Americans issued by the US Department of Health and Human Services. And I averaged running about 20 miles per week for the next 25 years. I also started playing baseball again that year, sort of. The only game in town remotely resembling baseball was slow-pitch softball, but as Mr. Petty once said, that was good enough. I played the game for the next 15 years and have a full vault of cherished memories of the good times spent with my teammates and opponents, not to mention some of the umpires. We were all family.

The following year, now in my physical prime and having my health back, I set most of my major personal records, fondly known as PRs to runners. My best performance came in sauna-like conditions on a sweltering June afternoon in Jacksonville, Florida. Now if you know anything about the summer months in Florida, you know that afternoon thunderstorms often roll in, dump heavy amounts of rain, and 30 minutes later, the blazing sun comes back out in all its glory like I mentioned on our virtual ride in the last chapter. I call it our 90-90 weather pattern with temperatures well above 90 degrees and the humidity also well above 90%, not exactly the best conditions to run in. But we were on fire that day.

The race was the famous (to me) Run for the Pies 5k. Granted, it may not be as famous as the Boston Marathon, but they still have that race annually on those same sweltering Saturday afternoons in June. In 1986, they had an invitational and an open race. The 1996 Olympic marathon team member, Keith Brantley, won the invitational race that day in just under 14 minutes, the first time that had ever been done on an open road course. I finished third in the open race with a time of 15:34. Now just so you know, the average male runner in his twenties completes a 5k today in about 33 minutes these days, women in about 38 minutes.

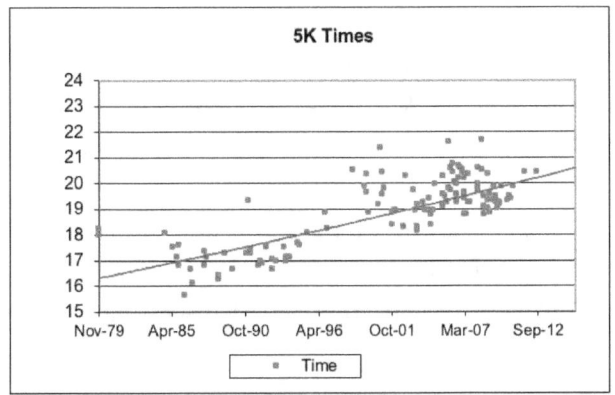

Figure 1 – My 5k Times

The following year, I turned 34, and my inevitable physical decline began. I still ran those same 20 miles a week with the same intensity, but my race times gradually crept higher over the next 25 years. One can run, but cannot hide, from Father Time. But I was determined that he was going to have to fight for every tenth of every percentage point of my physical decline as long as I was alive on Mother Earth.

Over the next decade, I continued my healthy diet and weight training. I also continued to race and play softball. Running is a steady-state activity with one foot following the other in essentially the same pattern. Softball is not. It's often a series of sudden, random movements depending on circumstance and where the ball goes. As players move into their forties, strained and pulled muscles happen more frequently due to the loss of muscle elasticity. Even the great Nolan Ryan, who was baseball's version of football ironman Tom Brady, could not overcome this reality, and neither could I. Reluctantly, I had to give up the game I loved.

As I moved into my fifties, the gym I was frequenting offered a yoga class just as I arrived there from work, so I began participating. I can't say how much enlightenment I absorbed over the following 18 months, but I certainly got my range of motion and flexibility back.

And let me say this, from class to class, I did not get much of a sense of improvement. It felt like I was just going through the same routine from week to week with nothing happening. Then one day, a couple of months after beginning those classes, I was walking through my garage, saw a piece of trash on the floor, and nonchalantly reached down and scooped it up as I was passing by. Then I stopped dead in my tracks. I could not have done that simple task so easily before those classes. Despite the lack of discernment of improving, I had.

With my continued strength training, running those 20-mile weeks, maintaining my nutritional diet, and newfound flexibility, I ran more than 100 races in my fifties and won my age category in over 90% of them. Approaching my sixties, I qualified for the Florida Senior Games in Fort Myers in late fall of that year. The 10k race was held in conjunction with the annual River Run that I had run 25 years before. The iconic feature of the race was that the course crossed over two extensive bridges over the Caloosahatchee River. I can't remember those bridges' road surfaces way back when, but in 2010, the surface was mostly comprised of concrete. You wouldn't think running on concrete would be much different than running on asphalt, but trust me on this one, it most definitely is. Perhaps it's just me, but every time I ran on concrete throughout my running career, the next day my calf muscles would be extremely sore.

However, I had a great race that day. The weather that Saturday morning was perfect, and I ran the 10k (6.2 miles) in under 40 minutes winning my age category (which qualified me for the National Senior Games) and breaking a Florida Senior Games record that had stood for over 30 years. And I'm not totally sure how this happened, but shortly after the awards ceremony, I found myself below deck on a $3 million boat. The owner told me he would sell it to me for less than $2 million, but I was a little short of cash that day.

I didn't run the next two days to rest my anticipated sore calves. The Senior Games 5k race was the following Saturday. Tuesday after the 10k race, I had planned to do an easy four-mile run, but I only made it two. Midway through the run, an arrow of angry pain pierced the inside of my right knee and, having already been a veteran of two knee operations, I knew something was seriously wrong. And after 30,000 miles of running, I could recognize when to shut down a run and when to run through the pain.

Two days later, I evaluated the knee on a short run and found that it hurt when I started, stopped, and turned a corner, but as I approached running speed in a straight line, it was more or less fine. That Saturday, I won the Senior Games 5k race outright, but nowhere near record time. I was just glad I finished with my knee still in one piece. However, I didn't run again for over six months due to that knee hurting so badly when I did, and I missed those National Senior Games that were held the following year.

Over the course of the next three years, life became more difficult than I had ever experienced. I felt like a professional bull riding cowboy being unceremoniously slammed to the ground over and over again by a rank bull. I occasionally made it through eight seconds of life's ride, only to be slammed to the ground again. My grandmother always said hard times were coming, and for me, they had arrived.

I was faced with some profound domestic issues. I had to take a second job. And I had to give up running, my go-to anxiety relief endeavor, due to the increasingly unbearable pain. As those race car people say, you only have so much 'goody' in a set of tires, and apparently in a set of hips, ankles, and knees. The 'goody' in my lower extremities that allowed my running wore out in 2011, and I had to give up the activity that had provided me with so much gratification and stress alleviation over the years. After a brief comeback attempt after the Senior Games, I had to give up the activity I loved.

I had every reason to be miserable, but I also realized that life could be much, much more sinister. With all the discipline I had learned from being an endurance athlete, I got up every day and did what I had to do. Sometimes not very well, sometimes atrociously, but nevertheless, I persevered. Sometimes you don't know how resilient you are until you are fraught with life's direst confrontations.

I continued frequenting the gym and employing those weight machines, practicing my now abbreviated yoga routine, and riding my old fat tire bike through an adjacent neighborhood. There is just something about moving through time and space that the fancy aerobic machines at the gym cannot provide, although I continued using them to ramp up my endorphin and dopamine flows, providing me with some semblance of well-being however fleeting. I went for long walks in the park where I used to run and allowed my mind to roam at will, sometimes delivering me to pleasant places, sometimes not.

The grocery business is deeply engrained in my genes and was the source of my second income. Filling empty shelves with cans all perfectly aligned with labels forward is, for whatever reason, appealing to my simple brain comparable with that perfectly mowed lawn that looks so attractive—the simple sense of accomplishment. And I loved the interactions with my customers...well, most of them. But combined with my real job, I was working 60 or more hours each week. In 2013, I had 14 days off the entire year.

One of the managers at the store was a big guy, who, like me, was enamored with endurance sports. He talked me into pursuing cycling. After striking out at the first cycling shop I visited, I walked into a second store and my gorgeous bicycle was there waiting for me. Mind you, there was some sticker shock going on. That bike was just a bit more expensive than a basic bicycle at one of those big box stores by a factor of about 20. But that marvelous machine was worth every penny I paid. I was again able to pursue my deep passion of being an endurance athlete, and now had a much more enjoyable axiety relief activity than using those indoor aerobic machines.

I almost immediately began racing again and was rather humbled, but not humiliated. That bike had a lot more talent than I did, and so did my competitors. But I had my sights set on those National Senior Games that I had been denied as a runner because of my knee which was not an issue on the bike. I joined my burly friend on several weekly group rides that included many stout riders. I quickly improved.

In the fall of 2015, I qualified for the Florida Senior Games and had no idea what to expect. Running a race on foot and racing a bicycle are two entirely different affairs due to the draft, as I explained on our virtual ride. If you still can't quite grasp this concept, imagine you are casually driving down the Interstate and one of those huge semi-trucks comes roaring past you. Just as the truck completes the pass, you feel that huge surge of wind from behind pushing you down the highway. That is the draft effect, and that is why most bicycle races usually end in a bunch sprint and running races do not.

I finished in the sizable lead group of riders that day, but like in running, I was never an accomplished sprinter, so I didn't come close to winning. But now I knew I could race with these people. The next year, with my daughter watching, I managed a fourth-place finish in my fourth and last race at the state level to qualify for the National Senior Games. And the following summer, with my son watching this time, I again finished with the large lead group at the National Senior Games, but in 19th place. I did at least beat two riders in the sprint that day. I wouldn't be lying by saying I have finished in the top twenty at a national race, but with that, and five or ten dollars, I might be able to get a cup of coffee at a coffee shop.

But let me tell you this, I saw horrific and unabashed ugliness that day. I saw riders throwing elbows at each other during the race, cutting each other off in corners, and in the second race I participated in the next day (I finished 16th in that one), virulent arguments erupted between the top finishers over the race results which nearly led to fisticuffs. And all of that for a stupid piece of metal painted gold.

I went to the Alabama Senior Games the next year and won the state championship and a "gold" medal, but with no family or friends there, it was meaningless, and egos were epidemic there, too. I did, however, get to race with Tarzan that day, so at least that was cool. However, on the way back home and despite having qualified for the National Senior Games a second time, I decided to never race my bike again.

So here we are today, just a little while since our virtual ride, and now you know my simple story which does not exactly resemble epic legends of superhuman strength, valor, and otherworldly powers. No, I'm just a dude with bowed legs that's never been in a rock and roll band like that singer-sailor guy I mentioned after our ride. He probably wouldn't trade places with me. I hear tell he's been to a rodeo or two, and I'm not talking about the ones with horses, bulls, and such. And I'm sure Mr. Brady wouldn't swap places with me either with all his Super Bowl rings. But that's okay. I'm not sure I would want to be all that famous anyway. Sounds like too much infrastructure to maintain to me.

So, now you know how I stumbled upon a lifelong mission to maintain my health and well-being thanks to the sheer random happenstance of seeing my former boyhood baseball hero (whoever he was) who had let himself go after retiring and never wanting to go there. Fortunately for me, that event occurred during my adolescence.

I can only imagine how the rest of my hero's life proceeded, but I have a fairly decent idea concerning his health if he continued down the same path he had chosen since his retirement from baseball. And in the next chapter, we will examine what probably happened to my long-ago hero over the next 20, 30, or 40 years if he even lived that long, assuming he continued down the same path he was on when I last saw him.

Without proper maintenance and preservation, our physical and mental health will deteriorate more rapidly than it has to whether we are great athletes or not. I genuinely do not want that hasty deterioration to happen to you wherever you are along your life's voyage. Nonetheless, if it already has, most of you can still improve your situation.

So please, stick with me here, and let us now go look at what can and probably will happen if you ignore your precious life's health.

CHAPTER 3: THE FACTS

As I TOLD YOU, the grocery business is deeply engrained in my genes. My grandmother ran a little country store back in the day and my dad was a grocery store manager for over 30 years. So, when I turned 16, I went to work for my father bagging groceries, making $1.60 an hour because like all 16-year-old kids, I wanted a car. It was the era of muscle cars and if you wanted to be the big man on campus, you had to have a Pontiac GTO, Chevy Chevelle, Ford Mustang, or any of the other brawny coupes back then. You didn't even have to play on the football team.

I worked hard, and in a few months, I got my first car. It wasn't exactly a Pontiac Trans Am like Burt Reynolds drove in *Smoky and the Bandit*; it was a 1940-something Jeep that my dad thought was cool. I'm fairly certain General Eisenhower didn't ride in it during World War II, but it was certainly within the realm of possibility. The speedometer went all the way to 60, that's six-zero, not 160. I can say this out loud now, but I used to peg that needle all the way over to six-zero. That may have had something to do with the engine blowing after a couple of years. I don't know, I'm an athlete, not a mechanic. Anyway, I never did get a date with the homecoming queen.

Speaking of the homecoming queen, when I went to my 50-year (plus one due to COVID-19) high school reunion, I didn't see her. At least I don't think I did; my how people change after 51 years, including me with my new hair color! I'll let you guess what color it is now; but fortunately, I do still have most of it, despite the lack of its original color. It was good to see them again, and even though for the most part, I expected how they would look; it was still very sad to see how many were in such poor health. And sadly, about one out of six of our former classmates had already died. Honestly, it breaks my heart.

Now far be it from me to throw my erstwhile classmates under the proverbial bus; I do want to see these people again and not be thrown under an actual bus. If it's any solace to them, they are not alone in experiencing less-than-stellar health. According to the 2020-2025 *Dietary Guidelines for Americans*, three out of every four American adults are overweight or obese which is a prominent contributing factor to chronic illness. Six out of every ten Americans now live with at least one diet-related chronic disease, such as cardio-vascular disease, type 2 diabetes, liver disease, and some types of cancer, costing trillions of dollars in medical cost and lost productivity every year.

And it's not just us boomers, either. You Gen Xers and millennials are right there with us, and you zoomers are already catching us quickly in this "race" to poor health, misery, and medical bills. And sadly, most of this suffering and expense can be (or could have been) avoided or at least mitigated. Before we look at how these mounting chronic diseases can be largely avoided and lessened, let us look at generally why all of this misery abounds.

NUTRITIONAL WASTELANDS

More concerning these poor health outcomes in a moment, but getting back to my dad's grocery store, I soon worked my way from bagging groceries to helping the stock crew replenish the store with merchandise. What a cast of characters they were! I'm not sure where my dad found all of those offbeat and wonderful people, but we were a tight band. We could put some groceries on those empty shelves starving for merchandise.

I was often assigned to replenishing the fastest selling items in the store, such as bags of sugar. We had a four-foot section stacked with hundreds of five-pound bags of sugar stacked five feet high. Today, sugar is packaged in four-pound bags, which perplexes me. As the bags of sugar are shrinking, people are getting larger. How does that math work?

In my last tour of duty in a grocery store, the section containing those now four-pound bags of sugar was a small fraction of the literal ton of sugar I used to put on the shelf at my dad's store. I asked my assistant manager why that was. He said that's easy because no one cooks real food anymore, they just microwave [insert four-letter word].

He may have exaggerated a bit, but today's abundant ultra-processed food (think frozen pizza, sandwich meat, corn chips, etc.) with all its added sugar, salt, saturated fat, artificial color, artificial flavor, and preservatives that most of us cannot pronounce, makes up a healthy (or should I say unhealthy) majority of the calories Americans consume today. Our kids are eating even more of that [insert four-letter word]. And research shows consuming higher levels of ultra-processed foods leads to numerous chronic health issues including obesity, diabetes, cardiovascular disease including stroke, and many others.

I'm not going to say Americans are getting lazy with their food choices today, but just like electricity, many (or most) people take the path of less resistance to satisfy their hunger for themselves and their families in this hurry-up world. And truth be told, if asked if I ever consume any ultra-processed food, my hand would reluctantly be raised. It's just so dang easy today.

And, with more than 80% of us living in urban areas, sit-down and fast-food restaurants seem to be just around every corner. Americans today spend more money eating out than they do in grocery stores. And I get it. The food is delicious with its added salt, sugar, fat, artificial flavors, etc., and it's just too convenient. Convenient and delicious, yes, but not necessarily your healthiest choice.

And we just about can't buy gasoline for (or plug in) our automobiles anymore without an attached convenience store enchanting us inside with its ever-expanding selection of mega-drinks, chips, snacks, and troves of other nutritionally barren, ready-to-eat food. Can you even find a carrot in those places? Perhaps in those ready-made salads with those orangey-stick things that resemble carrots and taste just like preservatives? Thank goodness for pay-at-the-pump!

READY, SET, SIT

Way back in elementary school, when Abe and I used to walk uphill to and from the log cabin in four feet of snow in Florida before global warming kicked in, we had P.E. every morning with some type of planned outdoor activity.

Then in the afternoon, we had 30 minutes of unstructured free play. That was absolutely my favorite time of the day. However, after that mid-afternoon recess period, I have specific memories from the fifth grade of coming back inside for the last period of the day and being authentically focused on the material being presented after being allowed to be a kid and run around a bit. Our teacher was more focused also because he was often out there playing ball with us.

Today, only one out of four adults in the US implements the recommended level of physical activity according to the Centers for Disease Control (CDC). So, let's see, one out of four gets enough exercise and three out of four are overweight or obese. Well, at least that math works, sadly enough. And oh, by the way, high school students are getting even less exercise. Only one in five meet the guidelines and these kids are the future.

Now I'm not Nostradamus, Jean Dixon, or any other famous fortune teller, but I can look into the future of you young zoomers and see what many of you are destined for: problems with your weight leading to chronic disease, diabetes, cardiovascular disease, regimens of medication that hopefully won't get out of control, physical and mental misery, and many of you will (or will want to) die long before you ever envisioned.

And with the never-ending life extending medical breakthroughs, all that misery and living with little or no quality of life could go on for decades as that famous singer-sailor guy pontificated about. I saw my grandmother and dad still living while they were basically dead, but mind you, they were in their late eighties, early nineties when they passed and didn't suffer much until the end. Dad was still climbing ladders into his mid-eighties. Most of you fledgling zoomers more than likely won't be so lucky unless you get on board toward a healthier lifestyle now. And, neither will you Gen X people and millennials, as many of my boomer buddies are finding out these days.

DEFINITIONS

Before we move on to additional damaging behaviors Americans are inflicting upon themselves, let's introduce a couple of terms. We all know what our **lifespan** is: the time between our initial appearance on the stage of life until we take our last breath. Another term that you may not be familiar with is your **healthspan**. A precise definition has not been agreed upon for this term, but assuming that you were born healthy, it is the length of time between your birth and the point in your life where your quality of life has eroded to living in pain, misery, or incoherence (or all of the above), and generally caused by some sort of chronic illness or disability due to an accident, aging, or not taking care of yourself.

Let's take my dad as an example. As I said, he was still climbing ladders when he was 85. Then, he tripped over a root, fell, and broke his hip. He recovered from that episode fairly well and had a few more good years (though he didn't climb ladders any longer). So, let's say his healthspan was 88 years. He died at 92, so his healthspan-to-lifespan ratio was well over 95%. Best I can tell, that is a remarkable number, as the soundest estimate I could find out there was around an 80%-85% healthspan ratio for the average person. Thanks for the genes, Dad!

MENTAL (AND SOCIAL) RETIREMENT

So back to the damaging behavior business. In addition to bad nutritional choices and participating in little or no physical activity, is there anything else bad for you out there? I'm not exactly an expert in this field, but when I went to see my primary care doctor for my annual well check appointment a few years ago and divulged to her that I was preparing to retire (from my nearly 40-year real job) in a year or so, a profound expression of concern cascaded over her face.

She anxiously asked me if I had things to do when I retired. I told her I was booked until I was 132 if I was going to get everything done I wanted to do. Relieved, she told me that was good because if I retired to the couch and watched television all day, I would soon be defunct (that means being dead, I had to look it up) before my time. She was telling me to use my body and brain, or I would lose them.

RISKY BEHAVIOR

Jumping out of an airplane without a parachute is risky and could be detrimental to your health unless the plane was actually sitting on the ground and even then, you might want to have one of those bouncy things that kids have at their birthday parties to land on. My dad was training to be a paratrooper when World War II ended, and I am fairly certain he always had his chute on during his training jumps; hence my existence materializing several years later. My dad, as all of us do, didn't always avoid risky behavior, but in this case, I'm glad he did. Risk assessment can be a good thing which we will explore later.

THE RATS ALWAYS WIN

Back when my parents were rearing my siblings and me, the expression keeping up with the Joneses was quite popular. We didn't know who the Kardashians were back then. They probably were not even born yet. Anyway, it meant striving to have the same material things the Joneses next door had. If they acquired a shiny new car, well then, you had to acquire a shiny new car. Life for many people was an endless anxiety-filled obsession for the acquisition of material loot to impress neighbors, friends, family, or whomever. Sound familiar? Incidentally, I'm not sure who the Joneses tried to keep up with back then.

But Americans are much more sophisticated these days. Yes, as humans have always done, they still vainly engage in pursuing material obsessions to impress others but keeping up with the Joneses—and the Kardashians—has now also migrated to the virtual world. Squarespace, the website building and e-commerce company, performed a survey and found that roughly 60% of millennials and zoomers feel their online presence is more important than their appearance in real life. Yikes!

This past summer, I was relaxing on a non-virtual beach with the sound of authentic waves crashing to shore, when a beautiful young lady suddenly appeared. Now before your imagination drifts to uncultivated domains, she was as totally oblivious of my presence as she was of the pelicans flying by in formation, the high-strung sandpipers chaotically running around in random directions, and the shy community of Atlantic Ghost crabs peeking out of their burrows periodically. She was there for only one reason: taking glamorous selfies.

She even had a selfie stick! After taking 843 selfies in various glitzy poses, she vacated the seashore.

I have no idea what this young lady was doing, and I learned long ago to never judge anyone until you walk in their shoes. However, if I had to guess, her seaside mission had something to do with social media accounts and her online virtual aura. Just like when the boomers were trying to keep up with the Joneses, too many people today are caught up in the endless fret-filled obsession to impress others not only in the real world but also in the social media universe and in the computer-generated, metaverse world. I hear you can now buy virtual clothes for your avatar. Seriously? This modern-day rat race for wealth, status, and online opulence, combined with always-on addictive digital connectivity, has so many snarled in stress and self-defeating behaviors that are rampantly guzzling their real lives away.

———

So, let us call our second timeout here and review. We've discussed how the consumption of today's delicious, ultra-processed food is leading to epidemic levels of human weight proliferation leading to chronic disease and exacerbated by a famine of physical activity among Americans. We spoke of putting one's brain out to pasture, undertaking perilous risk, and being enveloped in the incessant stress of keeping up with those Kardashian people. Is your hand raised from being guilty of any of these behaviors? Let me just say: relax, breathe, and call a timeout.

In our first timeout back in the last chapter, I told you of my mistake-prone journey through my first adulthood decade and how through the process of trial and error (with some guidance), making mistakes and experiencing a few achievements, I eventually moved toward improving my life. Thus, if you now carry a few extra pounds (or more), feel trapped and stressed out on the hamster wheel of the grind, suffering from a chronic illness, or wandering aimlessly through life, or all of the above, again, call a timeout and just breathe.

For the most part, you still have time to change the road you're on, contemplate a new strategy moving forward (which we will cover in the next chapter), come up with a new game plan (Chapter 5), and make a few (or numerous) adjustments in your life toward improving your health and well-being. But now is the time to get on board! Now is the time to cross the start line. Even if you are late, late in your game of life, you can still rally toward improving your health for at least a respectable moral victory, and live several more days, weeks, months, or more to enjoy those last precious morsels of your life.

Again, my mission for writing this book is for you to streamline your journey toward better health and eliminate some of your potential blunders along the way. But full disclosure here: enjoying better health, well-being, and happiness requires effort. Again, I do not have a miracle pill created in Dr. Jekyll's lab that will make you feel 20 again (or like Mr. Hyde). Desire better health and pursue it.

I will give you that strategy, a game plan, and some guidelines, and by using that trial-and-error method, you can then find your most enjoyable methods toward meeting those guidelines and improving your health. So again, if you find yourself not in good health, don't beat yourself up, just relax and pursue a course change. Life is not a race; it is a journey. Improvements can usually always be made. Okay, feel better? Let's move on.

ASSESSING OUR HEALTH

So, how do we know if we are overweight like three out of four of our fellow Americans? We all know the answer to that. We can just look in the mirror or step on the scale, and we all have a fairly adequate idea. Not much rocket science required there. But if you want a more scientific definition, according to the CDC, being overweight means your weight is higher than what is considered healthy for your height. Granted, that doesn't help us much more than looking in the mirror, but they have a simple-to-use Body Mass Index (BMI) calculator on their website (CDC.gov) and a plethora of sound health advice.

BMI	Weight Status
Below 18.5	Underweight
18.5 – 24.9	Normal
25.0 – 29.9	Overweight
30.0 and Above	Obese

Figure 2 – Body Mass Index

Your BMI is the ratio of your weight divided by your height and indicates whether or not you are overweight, sort of. The BMI ratio has its issues. I am 5'10" (and apparently shrinking as I used to be taller) and weigh 162-ish, so my BMI ratio is 23.2 which is a lot closer to the overweight category (see chart) than the underweight category. Very few people would say that I am anywhere near being overweight as I am often referred to as being "skinny."

And then there is that movie star guy, Dwayne "The Rock" Johnson. He has muscles on top of muscles and something like minus 6% body fat, but with his 6'5" height and 260 pounds, he has a BMI of 30.8 which is in the obese category. Now, the CDC can call Mr. Rock obese, but I'm certainly not! Heck, even Tom Brady at 6'4", 225 pounds and a BMI of 27.4 is squarely in the overweight category. Perhaps he still had his helmet on when they weighed him.

But all jesting aside, a cubic inch of muscle weighs more than a cubic inch of fat, so the ratio doesn't work as well for people with a lot of muscles. And though, the BMI ratio is a simple, inexpensive surrogate measure of body fat to estimate whether your level of weight has the potential to lead to obesity-related disease, the measure has many other scientific and ethical issues, and at best is an imperfect way to measure your body fat given it doesn't account for differences across gender, age, and ethnic groups.

The CDC also offers another simple method for assessing

whether or not you are carrying more weight than you should. If you are a normal guy and have a waist circumference of more than 40 inches (unless you are 8'9" tall), you may want to make some changes in your lifestyle, go see your healthcare provider, and most definitely read the rest of this book. And ladies, if you are not pregnant and have a waist circumstance of 35 inches or more, same advice.

If you seriously want to assess your body fat percentage, you could go see those Harvard people who say the Computerized Tomography and Magnetic Resonance Imaging methods and the Dual Energy X-ray Absorptiometry method are extremely accurate. I'll take their word for it. Sounds really expensive and too much like rocket science to me, although I do deeply appreciate the scientific research they, and many other fine universities, government agencies, and corporations, do. We have come a long way from the days of the bubonic plague, smallpox, and more recently, polio, not to mention measles, mumps, rubella, and many other diseases.

THE UNFORTUNATE FACTS

Speaking of research, I went to the CDC website to find out if, and how, being overweight increases the risk of serious diseases and health issues. I found a 262-page report. The Executive Summary was 20 pages long. I commend them for being thorough.

I'm not going to bore you with all the details, but the short answer is yes, people with excess weight are at an increased risk for many serious and chronic diseases such as type 2 diabetes, coronary heart disease and stroke, osteoarthritis, various types of cancer, and many other sicknesses. I have seen what many of these diseases, especially cancer, can do to a human body.

With chronic diseases, the increase of pain, the decrease of physical function, and the disorders such as depression and anxiety become a real possibility. The quality of your life declines to the point where your healthspan declines, leaving you with pain, misery, and despair.

I don't want you to go there, because when you approach my age, you will have enough increased pain and decreased physical function, even if you don't have one of those diseases. And if you are already suffering from one or more chronic diseases, I want to encourage you to move toward mitigating some of your suffering. It's doable.

Chronic disease is broadly defined as conditions that last a year or more, require ongoing medical intervention, and limit daily living activities. Six out of every ten Americans suffer from a chronic disease and four out of ten have two or more. These chronic diseases are the leading causes of death and disability every year in the United States and are some of the main reasons health care costs trillions of dollars every year.

Many of these diseases are caused by the behaviors we've talked about above: poor nutrition, lack of physical activity, and risky activities such as using tobacco (and exposure to secondhand smoke) and excessive alcohol use. The CDC didn't specifically mention jumping out of airplanes without a parachute, but I'm assuming if you did somehow survive that event, you would have a chronic disease. Just guessing.

THE HAUNTING TRUTH

So, you are a 30-something millennial in the prime of your life and you are thinking, "Yes, I know I am carrying way more weight than I should, but I still feel great, so what's the big deal?" Being in the prime of one's life suggests that it will be followed by a stage where you are in less than the prime of your life. Aristotle would be proud of me for that salient bit of logic.

But as a reminder, as the chart of my 5k racing times (Figure 1) from the previous chapter illustrated, your physical prime starts to erode somewhere in your thirties. I ferociously fought Father Time, but in the end, my race times continued to rise even though I was training with the same intensity. And trust me on this, he is setting his sights squarely on you now.

The abuse you are doing to your body today will come back to haunt you when you are past the prime of your life. Back when I was in my late thirties (and no, it wasn't back in the 1930s), I was playing shortstop one evening and the batter hit a fly ball to shallow leftfield. The shortstop is supposed to run back and try to catch the ball until the left fielder vocally proclaims responsibility for the catch. I never heard an utterance from him, and running back at full speed, just as I reached out to corral the ball, we violently collided. My left hip took the brunt of the blow and I crashed nastily to the ground. Apparently, I finished the game, but looking back at my records, I had another collision around second base affecting the same hip sometime later. That collision interrupted my regularly scheduled running, and combined, those two collisions would come back to haunt me later in life.

I mentioned in the last chapter that I had to give up running because of the pain. Yes, my knees were the center of the acute discomfort (due to one ill-advised tactic I employed to win one my 5k races), but somehow, I knew the real issue was somewhere deep down inside that hip. My knees felt fine after shutting the running down, but the latent ache in my hip gradually progressed until, by the time COVID-19 emerged, I could not walk without pain emanating from that left hip.

As the second wave of the COVID surge began to wane and hospitals were beginning elective surgeries again, I went to see my orthopedic surgeon for some relief. The X-ray his talented technician captured showed the head of my left femur in a deep bone-on-bone embraced with my pelvis. I'm not sure what they were doing down in there with the lights turned off, but I knew those collisions had come back to haunt me. And the abuse you are putting your body through in your prime, particularly if you are overweight, will come back to haunt you.

A few weeks after the loving (and extremely painful) bond

between my femur and pelvis was exposed, I found myself lying in pre-op at six o'clock one morning waiting for a total hip replacement. Little did I know, the next COVID-19 wave had begun in earnest. I heard someone walk into the area outside my little curtained-off room, when the lady behind the desk asked her, "What are you doing here? You just left at four!"

The lady walking through the area apparently had worked all night, gone home, taken a shower, drank a cup of coffee, and was back two hours later to work another shift due to all the staff out ill with COVID-19. The lady behind the desk confirmed they had three people from her department out for the same reason. Nevertheless, the operation went as planned, and I got my new hip. But so it is said, those people were definitely heroes during the pandemic, and are truly heroes every day.

After arriving back home the next day, I went through five days that I would rather not experience again. Even though I was a highly trained endurance athlete, I felt like a lethargic mollusk, and it wasn't because of my hip. My non-opioid pain medication alleviated that discomfort. No, a ubiquitous malaise had pervaded my consciousness. In plain English, I felt really bad.

On the fifth night, I went to bed and could not get comfortable for more than a few seconds. I tossed and turned for hours, and with a four-inch gash in my hip, those maneuvers were not pleasurable. Somewhere in the three o'clock hour, I drifted off to sleep and four hours later, I awoke. Astonishingly, I felt basically normal, although drained. It was like when a rabid fever finally breaks.

Two days later, I was tested for COVID-19, and sure enough, I had contracted the virus. I'm not blaming the hospital as I had been to the grocery store the day before the surgery. It doesn't matter where I was infected with the virus; the point is, due to my good overall health, I simultaneously survived a case of COVID, and a total hip replacement fairly unscathed despite having possessed a Medicare card for several years. Three weeks later, I was back on the bike, new hip and all, and I felt so good on my first post-ordeal voyage,

I rode twice as far as I had planned, although the total ride was only eight miles.

A few days after my positive COVID test, a lady from the Health Department called. She was mundanely, though professionally, working her way through her script of questions concerning my case. Then she asked me if I had experienced any diarrhea. I told her, "Well, yes, but it was voluntary." I think she fell out of her chair.

After she finally stopped laughing, she asked me if I could please elaborate on my answer. So, I explained to her that I had just had a hip replacement and that the non-opioid pain medication I was prescribed had gummed up the plumbing a bit, which I was warned about. One of my riding buddies who you will meet later told me to go get a little bottle of magnesium citrate, otherwise known as liquid dynamite. Just so you know, that stuff will clean you out. If you've ever had a colonoscopy, you know what I'm talking about. Anyway, after a few more questions, she merrily thanked me for my time. I think I made her day.

I can laugh and tell my stories about that whole affair now, but the point is what you do in the prime of your life can and probably will come back to hang out with you when you are 60- something or younger, for better or worse. Will it be a healthy diet that comes back to haunt you, or will it be excess weight you are carrying around? Those softball collisions most definitely came back to plague me, but so did all of those carrots, cardiovascular exercise, flexibility movements, and muscle-strengthening workouts, which is why I can still ride my bicycle for 150 to 200 miles each week.

TEAM EFFORT

So, you are the spouse of that 30-something millennial above, but you are right in the middle of the normal range on the BMI scale. Good for you, sort of. Being thin doesn't give you a hall pass to a long life. In 1967, Jim Fixx was 35 years old, weighed 220 pounds or so, and smoked two packs of cigarettes a day, but since his dad had died at age 43, he decided to take up running to get back in shape and improve his chance for a longer life. Ten years later, he had lost 60 pounds, quit smoking, and published a best-selling book about the virtues of running. His BMI was firmly in the normal range. While on a ten-mile run seven years later, he died of a heart attack at 52.

He died? While running? Yes, the guy who literally wrote *The Complete Book of Running* died while he was out for a run. You can only imagine how the non-exercising world responded to that event. However, despite being in "shape" to run ten miles a day, Fixx was not as fervently attentive in other areas of his life. His diet was not exactly vegan, and legend has it that he once pounded down four doughnuts just before a speech saying he had forgotten to eat breakfast. Fast food and excess amounts of sugar were reported to be staples in his diet. He had a stressful job before his fame, and I can only imagine the stress he experienced after his fame. And, despite his family's history of cardiovascular disease, he did not have a regular doctor when he died.

But let's look at the lessons from his relatively short life. First of all, we now know running single-handedly (that is, exercise in general) is not the panacea for a long healthy life as he thought it was, no one thing is, and we must have a broader approach to good health. Although borderline obesity and smoking for several years causes permanent damage to your body, he lived nine years longer than his dad after he lost the weight, exercised, and quit smoking. So, if you are one of the 60% of Americans who now suffer from chronic disease, a path toward improving your life and well-being exists, and you don't even have to run a marathon. But you do have to improve your health habits—all of them.

You probably already know that you should eat healthier, exercise more, and text less while driving, but you can't seem to find that healthy path or stay on it. I remember all those Januarys in the gym when there were about nine million new people there, and by February, everything was back to normal. If you were one of those January gym rats only to never see the inside of the gym for the rest of the year, it's okay. As I said in our second timeout, don't beat yourself up; just breathe.

And here is some good news for you. If you have made it this far in this book, you've moved past the "I'm not going to do it" and the "I can't do it" stage, and you are now thinking "maybe I can" get healthier. That's a good sign. That's half of the battle, and you are probably now trying to figure out how to motivate yourself toward a better and healthier lifestyle this time. Good for you and welcome aboard!

Over the next two chapters, we're going to go over that strategy and game plan I mentioned just after our virtual ride to keep you in the game of life for as long as possible and approach my dad's outstanding healthspan ratio and longevity. Reaching the age of 92 with a healthspan ratio over 95% is pretty good and I hope we both get there.

Life is truly a gift and possessing a higher level of health and well-being gives you the best opportunity to experience that most precious gift to its fullest. No matter where you are along your path through life, or where your physical or mental state lies, or what talent level you possess, improvements in your life can most always be made, just like my marigold did. I promise I will tell you my marigold story later.

Are you ready to begin improving your health? Let's go do this.

CHAPTER 4: THE FOUR CORNERS OFFENSE

Rumor has it around these parts, that a while ago some guy in a conquistador outfit landed here in Florida in a big sailboat and was looking for the fountain of youth. No, it was not Tom Brady. He landed on the other side of the peninsula and another rumor has it that he truly found said fountain. The conquistador guy was named Ponce de León.

He was born into Spanish nobility back in 1474, and when his dad asked him what he wanted to do when he grew up, the young lad said he aspired to be a conquistador because he didn't want to go around, and fight bulls all day. So, his dad hooked him up with this Italian dude named Christopher Columbus. You may have heard of him. He was looking for a western route to China and ran into America.

Mr. Columbus and Ponce were indeed brave explorers, but I'm not sure about their eyesight, however. Legend has it that when they got here in the "new" world, they saw a bunch of manatees swimming around and thought they were mermaids. Just so you know, manatees are not beautiful creatures if you have never seen one. Gentle and loveable, yes; beautiful, no, unless, of course, you are another manatee.

Anyway, about 20 years later, when governing Puerto Rico, Ponce heard from the indigenous natives there about an island that had a magical spring whose waters would rejuvenate anyone who drank it, so he set sail. As they watched him sail off into the sunset, they were chuckling among themselves, not believing that he actually fell for such lunacy as the existence of a fountain of youth. He was not popular on the island.

As legend has it, a few weeks later, he landed here on the peninsula somewhere near Saint Augustine, thought it was a lovely place, so he named the new land Florida, which he thought was an island. When he asked the locals if they had seen the fountain of youth around, they told him no, not here, but if he got back in his boat and sailed south, he would find it somewhere on the other side of the "island."

Somehow, Mr. Brady found out he was headed his way, so he sent a bunch of his buccaneers down to encourage Ponce that he didn't really want to sail any further. I'm not sure how all that turned out, but I think Mr. Brady threw four touchdown passes in that battle. Anyway, Ponce reluctantly sailed back to Puerto Rico, but decided to return to Saint Augustine several years later to look for the fountain of youth again and colonize the territory.

That didn't turn out too well for him, but he got a natural spring named after him over here on the east coast of the peninsula. It's a serene little spring, and yes there are mermaids, I mean manatees, occasionally swimming around during the winter, but I haven't seen a dude walking around in a conquistador outfit the several times I have visited the spring, so apparently Ponce never did find the mythical fountain of youth.

Poor Ponce should not feel too bad though, for many people before and after him have searched for a mystical elixir to provide eternal youth. There once was an ancient Chinese emperor who, on the astute advice of his medical sages, thought drinking liquid mercury would give him eternal life. Just so you know, that didn't turn out so well for him. Do *not* try that at home.

Even today, billionaires, biotech companies, and start-ups, not to mention our government, are investing heavily in anti-aging and human longevity studies. However, even if these organizations and billionaires come up with a magic concoction that provides Youth Potion No. 9, I'm quite positive us common folks won't be able to afford it for decades, if ever.

So, what do we do in the meantime to increase and maintain our level of health (and longevity), which the WHO (the World Health Organization, not the rock band) defines as a state of physical, mental, and social well-being and not merely the absence of disease? Like I said after our virtual ride, I don't have a magic pill, or a 30-day crash diet plan, nor a five-minute a day, super exercise routine to make you feel like you are 25 again and live forever, but I do honestly want to help you get healthier and I do have a strategy.

First, an apology. As I told you, I am an athlete, and having watched (and participated in) my share of sports events in my life, I do frequently use sports terms and analogies. Okay, quite often. And I will use a sports analogy to lay out our strategy, but I promise a sports-neutral analogy for my non-sports fan readers in a couple of chapters from now, so hopefully you will hang in there until then.

I may be an endurance athlete, but I am not a basketball player. I am sure there are plenty of ten-year-old kids out there who can handily destroy me in a game of Horse. Is that still a thing? I do not know a lot about the obscure details of the game either, but I watched a lot of high school, college, and pro basketball during the last century.

In one game back in 1960-something, the mighty UCLA Bruins were playing the Little Haven kindergarten team. I think Kareem was on that UCLA team. Back then, there was no shot clock. In today's basketball world, when a team gets the ball, they have to take a shot at the basket within a certain number of seconds which the shot clock counts down. If they don't shoot the ball toward the basket before the shot clock runs down, they have to give the ball back to the other team.

The Little Haven team was a bunch of scrappy little kids, but since their average height was about four feet shorter than the UCLA team, their legendary coach, Shorty Turner, who was 4'11", with no shot clock to worry about, employed the four corners offense to keep UCLA from getting the ball and scoring.

The four corners offense is basically a game of keep-away. The other team cannot score if they don't have the ball. It was to be executed when playing a formidable foe or to run the clock out when holding a small lead in a game. Four of the team's five players would position themselves in each corner of the offensive end of the court, and the fifth player, usually the best ball handler, would be in the middle and pass the ball around to keep the other team from stealing it. If they got an easy shot, they would take it; otherwise, they would just keep passing the ball around since they didn't have to deal with a shot clock.

So, back to the game. The kids from Little Haven were great ball handlers and kept the ball away from UCLA most of the first half. Kareem, who was about 8'3", got the ball one time, but he dunked the ball into the basket, which was not allowed back then. Just before the buzzer to end the first half, Tiny Zeller, the Little Haven point guard, heaved the ball up toward the basket with all her might. Kareem managed to partially block the shot, but the ball careened off his hand and went into the basket. So, Little Haven went into the locker room with a 2-0 lead at halftime.

I am not exactly sure how that game turned out, but I think somewhere in the second half, the Little Haven kids finally ran out of gas, and UCLA went on a scoring run. As I remember, Kareem perfected his famous sky hook shot in that game and wound up with something like 132 points.

Anyway, Kareem, being the genuine human being that he is, held up the little 3'6" Little Haven center to the basket in the closing seconds, and the kid slammed home a dunk that rattled the rafters.

But of course, that was illegal, and the basket did not count. But again, Kareem being Kareem negotiated with the referees into letting the basket stand by invoking the unwritten no harm, no foul basketball rule. I think I'm remembering this game correctly, though some details are a little foggy now. I think the final score was something like 228-4.

The Little Haven kids gave it all they had, but in the end, the mighty UCLA Bruins got the better of them. And in our game of life, we are all on the Little Haven team, but the other team is not UCLA. The other team is composed of Father Time and his teammates, who are all those insidious blokes of bad health outcomes we talked about in the last chapter, like cardiovascular disease, diabetes, Alzheimer's disease, etc. You know as well as I do, Father Time's team always wins every single time, and we will eventually lose in our game of life.

Pretty depressing if you let it be. But like me, you can make that band of bummers earn every stinking point and assure that they know when the game is over, they were in a ball game. A hard-fought ballgame. What we are really fighting for is a long life and high healthspan ratio like my dad's.

I was recently riding my bicycle with a young zoomer friend of the family, and she was telling me that she had recently had a quarter-life crisis, but she was fine now. She was 25. So, let's use her delineation for the length of our potential lives as being 100 years. It's a doable number as there are over 80,000 Americans alive today that have passed the century mark. Of course, there was that French lady Jeanne Calment, who was born in 1875. Apparently, she was a plucky lady because she lived to be 122. And incidentally, it's not true that I am her son. I can't speak French.

In that Little Haven game, those little guys and gals made a game of it well into the second half, so if we say they lived to be 86 and their healthspan ratio was 90%, they finally ran out of gas early in the fourth quarter when they were 77, when UCLA finally took over the game. Not bad for a little team, against such long odds and arduous challenges. Jeanne went deep into overtime in her lifespan, so she must have been particularly scrappy before she finally threw in the towel. Not sure what her healthspan ratio was.

———

WE NEED to take a time out here, but this is not one of our ordinary timeouts when we review some material, or I give you a word of encouragement. No, this is a timeout for me. I need to take this pause in the action here because of a bike crash. A Tour de France worthy bike crash. Yes, when I got to this point writing this book for you, I had a tumultuous encounter with a stretch of non-forgiving tarmac after hitting a pothole while riding my bicycle. And trust me, it was not a virtual ride. This wreck was most definitely full impact, real life!

I had actually finished my ride, but since it had rained during my outing, I swung through the parking lot headed to the bike wash area. I never made it. During the rain shower, a puddle had accumulated on the pavement and had impeccably camouflaged an enormous pothole just inside the puddle's edge. As I recall, as soon as I hit the stealthy cavern, I began falling to my left and hit with a thud. I was only going eight, maybe ten, miles per hour.

Ironically, that very morning, my sister had come to visit me. I was telling her that it had been about five years since I had last wrecked. I even knocked on some real wood. In that wreck back then, I was riding alone before a scheduled group ride. I came through a slightly downhill turn to the left at 22 miles per hour when I lost my balance and went overboard, hitting the pavement on my right side, rolling and tumbling, and then skidding off into the grass.

Despite bleeding from both elbows, both knees, and a serious contusion on my right femur, I got up, got back on the bike, and rode for another 24 miles with the group. My orthopedic surgeon said one time that apparently, I had a high pain threshold. However, when I hit that pothole, there was no skidding, no rolling, no tumbling. I was slam dunked straight to the pavement, landing on my left scapula (shoulder blade), and high pain threshold or not, I was in some serious anguish! My head did slightly smack the ground, but of course, I was wearing my helmet, and I fortunately never lost consciousness.

I tried to get up, shake it off, and head home, but that was not my fate for that evening, nor my destination. My destination was the hospital where I would, unknowingly, camp out for six long, uncomfortable days. In the wee hours of that evening, I was finally wheeled to my room with a broken clavicle (collar bone), a broken scapula, and four fractured ribs. A mysterious pain also emanated from my groin area where the new hip had been installed, and although the X-rays and MRI came back negative, I could not walk. As long as I remained perfectly still, the discomfort was virtually non-existent, but with the slightest movement, the pain intensity would register about a magnitude six or seven on the Richter scale of agony.

And let me say this, even though I was a highly trained endurance athlete, that near weeklong stay in the hospital was difficult. First, you get very little sleep. Alarms go off at all hours of the day and night for whatever reason, people moaning, some being belligerent and rude, nurses and staff waking you up every couple of hours to stick yet another needle into you, and I could go on. I can only imagine going through that ordeal in less-than-stellar health.

But now after a ten-day timeout, I am finally back in front of my computer again literally typing with one hand because I seriously want to motivate you to get out there on the floor in your game of life and improve your healthspan, your well-being, and help you stay out of the hospital for as long as possible. Despite the heroic efforts of the entire hospital staff, a stay in that place is arduous and difficult at best. You just want to go home.

———

OKAY, so what were we talking about before my lengthy timeout? Oh yes, the strategy we need to employ for the rest of our lives if we want to stand up to Father Time deep into the fourth quarter, or perhaps even into overtime, as Jeanne did. Like the legendary coach Shorty Turner and his Little Haven phenoms, we are going to use the four corners offense to battle Father Time and his insidious colleagues to live as healthily as possible and for as long as possible with the least amount of pain, and without taking many prescription drugs, expensive elixirs, and the forthcoming magical (and probably beyond our budget) longevity pills the biotech companies are working on.

You are the point guard on this team staring into Father Time's eyes, but don't be intimidated. Now, for my non-sports fan readers, the point guard is the court commander who accepts the responsibility for connecting with teammates and orchestrating the offense. Your main job is to distribute the ball to your colleagues and let them make healthy plays. And, you have a great group of teammates, although they have some rather weird names, but just go with it. They are Fuel, Hardware, Software, and the renowned Repair Shop.

Your teammates will only be as good as you, the team leader, let them be, so embrace them and their particular talents. Work with them, encourage them, and motivate them to play up to their potential. Yes, as team leader, you have a serious responsibility, but you can do this. Your healthspan will grow longer, as your lifespan should, thus minimizing the misery in your final years. Hopefully, you will approach my dad's outstanding 95% healthspan instead of the normal 80% where you suffer the last fifth of your life.

We are going to examine the game plan in the next chapter, then we are going to spend an entire chapter getting to know each of your teammates in-depth individually, but let me give you a brief introduction to each one here.

Fuel is your diet and your nutrition. There is an old saying in the computer world: garbage in, garbage out. The same holds true with your diet. If you eat a garbage diet, garbage will be produced inside your body. I don't have a specific diet plan for you, such as, "Eat 43 apples a day and you will be fine." Instead, our nutritional plan is grounded in science and in the basics, what you can and should eat, what you should avoid for the most part, and how much you should consume.

Your second teammate, Hardware, is your physical body. To survive back in the saber-toothed tiger days, humans evolved to move so as not to be sitting ducks for an easy feline meal. We don't have any saber-toothed tigers running around these days (I don't think), but we still have to move to keep our bodies functioning efficiently. We need to maintain some level of physical fitness. We don't have to run a hundred miles each week like that famous Olympic marathon guy, but we have to keep our bodies moving.

We all know what happens when you put a vehicle in the shed for two years and then try to drive it. First of all, it probably won't start. But even if it does, it will be a rough ride because the tires will more than likely have flat spots on each of them from sitting in one place for so long. And you probably won't get too far down the road before something breaks because some rubber part on the engine dry rotted and burst under pressure. I'm fairly certain if you sat on the couch for a few years and streamed every episode of *Keeping up with the Kardashians*, and then went out and tried to run a 5k, you'd blow a gasket, too. As the old saying goes, use your body or lose it.

Teammate Software is that magnificent computer between your ears. You probably can't imagine all the wonderful things it does for you without you even realizing it. And, like your body needs to be regularly exercised, so does your brain. It gets easily bored and loves novelty and learning new things. And again, going back to those good old saber-toothed tiger days, our brains evolved to be with other human beings back then for sheer protection. Today, our social connections with family, friends, and work colleagues are vital to our well-being.

Our fourth teammate, the Repair Shop, is a team and fan favorite. When the ball is passed to the Repair Shop, your entire world chills like when you sit down in your favorite chair after a couple of hours on your feet. You know that feeling, what a relief it is. And curling up in bed after a long, taxing day and drifting off to dreamland, that is the Repair Shop's specialty. Your Repair Shop teammate has many other talents, such as resilience, risk assessment, and stress reduction, to name just a few. The Repair Shop can do it all, y'all.

So those are your four talented and dazzling teammates. Hopefully, you will get to know them well, and your confidence will grow in them when you utilize their many talents against those bad troupers led by Father Time. When you and your teammates are seamlessly zipping that ball among yourselves keeping Father Time and his fearsome fiends off balance, your game of life can truly become a thing of beauty, as my dear, late friend (whom you will meet in Chapter 12) used to say.

And I will say this one more time, no matter how well or how poorly you have been playing the well-being derby during your life, you can and will get better by continuing to learn, perform, and work together with your team. Your teammates are extremely essential in increasing both your healthspan and lifespan, and they all have unique talents. And, like my dad's offbeat and wonderful grocery stock crew from way back when, your partners are a tight band of talented colleagues.

Remember, we are most definitely participating in a team sport here, and with our teammates, the glue that keeps us all together is our common purpose, meaning, and hope in our game of life we are playing and living for hopefully 100 years (or more). We will look at how to strengthen this bond with our teammates later in Chapter 10, after we get to know them better.

And who knows, working as a cohesive unit with these colleagues, with a bit of good fortune, you could break Ms. Calment's record and live past 122, although that wouldn't please her. She told me one time she wanted to keep her record of longevity forever. At least, I think she told me that. It could have been Mr. Brady. I can't remember. Anyway, even if you don't break her record, by running the four corners offense with your teammates, you can definitely improve your lifespan and your healthspan ratio. If my dad was still around, he wouldn't have minded a bit if you surpassed his 95% healthspan ratio.

I'm sure you have heard that old saying that if we don't have our health, we don't have anything. All of the money in the world, all the king's horses, and all of the queen's men (is that how that old saying goes?) won't be of much interest to us if we are in perpetual pain. I can promise you, those six painful days lying in the hospital with broken bones were not pleasurable.

And here is another old saying, freedom isn't free, and neither is our health. We have to work at it, maybe not to the level Mr. Brady does, or that Olympic marathon guy did, but we have to put forth a healthy measure of effort. Unlike Mr. Brady, we don't have to approach perfection in our quest for better health and happiness. Although I do truly admire what he and Mr. Shorter did in approaching perfection in their state of health and athletic pursuits, we're not exactly going for a Super Bowl ring or the Olympic gold medal here. We are just trying to improve our well-being and increase our lifespan and healthspan ratio.

I had a friend long ago named George. He was a different individual, I can assure you. He is the only person who I've ever known who had a campfire behind his desk at the widget factory. More on the widget factory in the next chapter. He was my formal mentor at work for a while, and he would say to me, just give him 80%, that's all he needed, just 80%. George was a firm believer in not annihilating the good in pursuit of the perfect, as Voltaire once pontificated.

George expected results, however, and would not be satisfied with that obscure baseball pitcher from a few decades ago. The wives of the players on that team got together and thought it would be a great idea to find out their husband's favorite meal they prepared, compile those recipes together in a book, and sell it to their fans for charity. This pitcher dude wasn't married, so he submitted his beanie-weenie recipe: open can, pour into pot, heat until bubbly. George expected a little more exertion than that, and so does a decent level of health. Incidentally, I'm not sure if the wives included that obscure pitcher's robust cuisine in their final recipe compilation.

I have one more ancient proverb for you before we move on to study the actual game plan in the next chapter. I can teach you, but you will not learn until you do. I think Yoda said. Or maybe it was Shorty Turner, I'm not sure. I'm sure it wasn't Ponce because he didn't know a mermaid from a manatee. In other words, just reading this book will not help you until you get out there on the floor and practice the new skills you will acquire by getting to know and participating with your teammates.

So, we now have a solid strategy to begin our mission toward better health, and I think you will grow to enjoy being with your terrific team. Once we go over the game plan in the next chapter, I think you will be a little more confident in yourself, believe that you can do this, and begin implementing healthier habits into the one precious life that you have. Yoda didn't say this because I'm saying it now. Learn, absorb, do. You will be rewarded!

CHAPTER 5: THE GAME PLAN

As I HAVE STATED, I am an athlete. Let me tell you what I am not. I am not a guitarist. Not a very skillful one anyway. I only started seriously learning the instrument a couple of years ago. But ever since I was a wannabe Royal Guardsmen (channel all of those Snoopy songs) from back in the 1960s, I have wanted to play the guitar. I actually know one of those guys, not that he would own up to that fact. Or maybe he would. I haven't seen him in a while.

The band was from my hometown and the surrounding area. One evening, many years after they had their brief run as genuine rock stars (he has actual gold records hanging up in his house, so I hear), I was shopping at a local market when he approached me. I didn't know what to do. I'm thinking to myself, why is this former rock star coming up to talk to me?

As it turned out, after the Guardsmen's fame faded, he moved back home and began leading a normal life again. He would make appearances around town playing music every now and then, and evidently, he got into running along the way to get into better shape. He began talking to me about how good of a runner I was, and every time he went to a race, he would see me winning a trophy, medal, or whatever for winning the race or my age category.

I don't enjoy talking about myself, so I began expanding the conversation. I must have hinted or spoken of music, and suddenly, with apparent wonder, he asked me if I knew who he was. I told him of course I knew who he was. He then started telling me about recording those Snoopy songs up in New York when they were "just kids," and some of the times they had.

We had a mini-admiration society going on there for a while. I suppose that was my 15 minutes of fame, having a former rock star think I was pretty cool. Just so you know, he is a very nice guy; something this world needs a little more of these days.

Being an athlete always came naturally to me. However, I am most definitely *not* a natural musician like my rock and roll buddy or my boyhood friend that lived across the road when I was growing up. No, trying to play the guitar is extraordinarily difficult and taxing for me, and I have to earn every single note that I produce on the instrument. Don't look for me in a rock and roll band up on a stage near you anytime soon.

So, I know how hard it is to learn and do something that does not come easily to you. And I know how challenging it will be for many of you to begin, and more importantly to continue, rescuing your health and well-being from the clutches of Father Time and keep him at bay for a while. Even for you natural athletes who have just let yourself go like my boyhood baseball hero from old, it's going to be laborious.

Because here is a well-known secret, even for you natural athletes, maintaining your weight (and particularly losing some) becomes more and more daunting as we age. I know because it took me in the neighborhood of a decade to lose 20 pounds, and I know exactly how easily that extra weight can so clandestinely creep upon you.

In the early 1980s, when I was running those marathons, I

weighed about 150 pounds. Fast forward to 2002 when I headed into my fifties, I weighted around 180-182. Where did that 30 pounds come from? It wasn't like I was sitting around watching television and drinking fizzy drinks all day. I had a real job, maintained my healthy diet, lifted weights, kept running those 20 miles a week, and played in hundreds of softball games. Yet, I still gained 30 pounds! I was actually just inside the periphery of the overweight category on the BMI scale.

I lost about a pound a year in the first five years of that ten-year period yo-yoing up and down, down and up; and then I got a little more serious about losing the rest of the surplus weight. I didn't make any drastic changes in my exercise, diet, or lifestyle, but I made a few tweaks and became more vigilant in monitoring my in-between-meal snacks and regularly weighting myself. By 2012, I was down to my current 160-162 weight level.

So, how are we going to get you into better health, help you lose weight (if you need or want to), eat more wisely, improve your body's strength and flexibility, and help your mind be fresher and more alert when you are in there competing against Father Time? And how am I going to become proficient at that six-string instrument I have wanted to play since Snoopy and the Red Baron were in those high-flying dogfights? Before we go over the game plan that will hopefully get us there, let us come face to face with reality. Please pay attention here!

REALITY CHECKS

REALITY CHECK 1: NO QUICK FIXES

We need to stare reality straight in the eye if we are going to have any chance of giving Father Time and his merciless band of misery makers a decent game. As I have already told you several times, I do not have a 30-day whizbang, crash diet scheme to get you svelte and luscious, or a five-second per week routine to give you the abs of Arnold, the Mr. Universe guy.

And, I don't have a secret energizer concoction for you to ingest hourly, nor any old-fashioned snake oil (or lizard lubricant) for that matter to sell you. First of all, my conscience would not let me go there. But as you probably already know, this world is full of people more than willing to sell you the promise that you can easily lose weight, paint the Mona Lisa, or hit a tennis ball like Serena Williams with little or no effort. Don't part with your money.

To put this in the simplest language that I can, at this point in time in our scientific knowledge and abilities, no easy short cuts exist to maintain exemplary levels of health and well-being if you are in a less than satisfactory condition. But you don't have to be a slave to improving your health either. That's not how we evolved. I wasn't quite born yet, but I'm fairly certain those cave people did not make sure they did their sit-ups every day and take their vitamin C pills at night while sitting around the campfire. As with most conundrums, the soundest solution lies somewhere in between.

Your teammates will help here if you let them. In fact, they are essential. And they will work with you for next to nothing. Again, get to know them in the next few chapters, and working together, you can become your own merry band of longevity legends. Now granted, someday, just like Luke, you will walk into a clinic and tell the medical professional that you lost your arm last night in a laser fight, and an hour later walk out with a brand-new arm. But we're not quite there yet.

And if you are on that path of least resistance to poor health I spoke earlier, don't expect your physician to be a miracle worker with a quick, no-pain solution to solve your health issues in your darkest hour. They are good at addressing symptoms, but not necessarily at ferreting out the root cause of your health problem. No time for that. Most people would not be interested, anyway. For example, people go to the doctor because of some agonizing discomfort. Oh, you have a pain there? Here's a pill for that. Oh, you have a pain down there, too? Here's another pill.

I am definitely not blaming physicians and health care providers, it's what their patients expect because of the incessant instant remedy mentality of today. Something for nothing is most everyone's plan today as it always has been. And here is another genuinely distressing matter to me: many, if not a majority of you medical and healthcare professionals (not to mention your staff), are also on that same path of least resistance to poor health.

Somehow, I suspect Ponce is behind all of this quick fix temperament and those serpentine oil sales pitches out there pervading print media, television, the internet, and a metaverse coming near you. I suppose, in a way, that he did find the fountain of youth because we all still know who he was, and we still chase his dream of effortless and eternal youthfulness.

But again, with all due respect to Mr. de León, there are no instant resolutions or paths of least resistance to excellent health, or becoming a decent guitar player, for that matter. That is reality. But do not despair! Hopefully, after we go over the game plan, you will feel confident that you can truly do this and live long in good health, and who knows, perhaps someday you will see me up on stage playing the guitar with my old rock and roll buddy.

REALITY CHECK 2: A LONG AND WINDING ROAD

When you get to know your teammates and start playing in your game of life with them, you will not make steady, straight-line progress toward weight loss, better health, and happiness. Like the Beatles said way back when, it's going to be a long and winding road.

You may lose five pounds the first week, then another two the next week, and then gain a pound in the third week. Ebbs and flows in your progress to better health will color your journey, but remember what Aerosmith taught us so long ago: it's not about the destination, it is all about the journey. Just observe, appreciate, learn, and improvise, just like I did when I lost those 20 pounds. It only took me ten years to get there, and it was a scenic tour. Cherise the journey!

Let's discuss destinations for a moment. Many performance and motivational gurus harp on, pound their clinched fist on the podium, and pontificate that the veritable pathway to success and greatness lies in setting and reaching goals, or in my mind, destinations. Now mind you, I'm not victimizing goals or saying evade them altogether, but concerning our health, let's not look at goals as reaching the end zone. For instance, to get healthy, let's say you set a goal to lose 20 pounds, and with a determination that came from some transitory fortitude, you actually achieved your weight loss goal.

Then what? From my observations, upon reaching their goal (that is, their destination), many people often vacate the journey. Next thing you know, they gain all the weight back they lost plus an additional five pounds. They are back at square one, or square one plus those five extra pounds on board. Yes, their journey toward well-being took the off-ramp to the dusty back roads to the undesirable wasteland of health once they accomplished their "goal." So, in terms of destinations, or goals, getting there and staying there are two entirely different matters. Please keep that in mind.

So how have I kept those 20 pounds off I lost more than a decade ago? Short answer, because I didn't abandon my lifelong journey toward my most appreciated health and well-being once I got to my "goal" weight. I continue to consume those carrots and healthy food I enjoy. Despite losing my ability to run, I switched to riding the bike and continue to enjoy moving through time and space and burning calories. I continue to lift my modest weights and perform my abbreviated yoga routine. I also regularly stay in contact with family and friends, and even though some of them may disagree, I try to keep my brain activated and engaged. And above all, I consistently monitor my health to assure I am not straying too far off my healthy path. Again, the prize is the journey, not the 20 pounds I discarded.

———

SPEAKING OF RIDING BICYCLES, let's take a 30-second timeout here for an update. It's been four weeks now since my bike crash, and when I finally got to weigh myself, I was down to 158 from my usual 162 or so pounds. Obviously being all broken up, I haven't been exercising all that strenuously and my diet hasn't changed, so apparently one's body burns a significant sum of calories when healing bones. But just so you know, I am *not* recommending going out and breaking your bones just to lose weight! Please do not try that at home!

My bike crash also perfectly illustrates the journey being a long and winding road, one full of ebbs and flows. That last particular ebb was rather brutal. After four weeks, I am not even close to contemplating getting back on the bike, but fortunately, my hip has improved, and I am able to go on walks again. And over the last week, I have practiced my guitar again for my normal allotted hour a day.

So again, please stay on the long and winding path toward improving and preserving your health and well-being. Sometimes the scenery may not be too scenic, but just keep moving. And do not be too obsessed with the destination, just stay on the voyage despite the inevitable setbacks and enjoy the ride.

———

REALITY CHECK 3: HOMEOSTASIS AHEAD

To change and evolve toward an improved level of health and vigor is not a comfortable process, especially in the beginning. As the old saying goes, no road is without potholes. I certainly was reminded of that about a month ago! Anyway, developing into a sleeker, sportier individual is so challenging and problematic because your body does not like to change dramatically.

Scientist, professors, and other smart people call this circumstance homeostasis, which works like a thermostat to keep your body in its comfort zone. And yes, you and your homeostasis partner are inseparable for better or worse, but that is not necessarily a dreadful phenomenon. Your body wants and needs stability, and because of your homeostasis spouse, it is just as happy staying in bad shape as in respectable shape. Your body just hates changing radically. In order to move toward being that new sleeker, sportier person, you will need to learn to work with your homeostasis partner's aversion to major modification.

Remember, in the previous chapter, I spoke of blowing a gasket when you attempted to run a 5k after spending a couple of years on the couch watching the Kardashians? That's what your beloved thermostat mate doesn't want to happen (blowing the gasket that is, not watching the Kardashians), so you are going to have to negotiate if you want to move the needle toward improving your health and well-being. Can I run a mile? No, don't even think about it. Can I run a kilometer? Nope. How about a hundred yards? Negative. Can I walk a hundred yards? Maybe. Okay, I'll walk 50 yards. Deal!

I live in an authentic thoroughbred hotbed, but for the life of me, I don't really know what all those horse whisperer people do. I think it has something to do with whispering into the horse's ear, and then getting the horse to let you get on its back when the horse is not necessarily willing, but eventually allows you too anyway after gently persuading the horse that having you there will be okay. That's how you need to collaborate with your homeostasis companion.

Don't be like the old Wild West cowboys who got onboard and rode the bucking bronco until the unfortunate creature was subjugated. And unless you are a professional rodeo person, if you tried that, you would probably wind up in a hospital near you with a bunch of broken bones and a blown gasket or two. And speaking from my experience with broken bones, you don't want to go there.

On the other hand, don't be a wimp either. When told you can't do that 5k just yet, don't go back inside with your tail between your legs and start catching up with the Kardashians again. Go out and walk those 50 yards. Tomorrow, perhaps you will be allowed to walk

60 yards and then continue to increase (through careful negotiation with your homeostasis partner) your training distance until one day, you will be allowed to run in that 5k race.

And remember, there is no shot clock when you get out there and start playing the four corners offense with your teammates. Take your time, don't get in a big rush, and keep whispering to your thermostat softly, gently persuading your partner to allow you two to move to a healthier locality. Like I said, your transformation-abhorring companion will be just as happy in Healthyville as in Miseryville. And above all else, keep whispering and stay on your long and winding journey toward better health and well-being.

REALITY CHECK 4: AWKWARD AND UNWORTHY

When game time rolls around and you get out there on the floor with your teammates for the first time, you are more than likely going to feel dreadfully awkward and unworthy. I can reasonably guarantee it. I know if I got up on stage with my rock and roll buddy and attempted to play in his band, I would most definitely feel awkward and unworthy at this point in my guitar journey. He would probably start me off playing a tambourine rather than a guitar. That is, with something I could handle.

So, you let yourself go a little bit. Okay, you have let yourself trek deep into the dark forest of poor health, and your sense of worth has plummeted. You know that you will face the indignity of looking awkward and clumsy when you get into the game with your team-mates or go for a walk in the neighborhood. Don't mentally let yourself go there. Your journey is not about trying to impress anyone. It's about getting to a healthier neighborhood of well-being. Endeavor to ease up on yourself a modest bit, and by extending some care and attention to your physical body, you can restore your fragile sense of worthiness.

Let me give you a hero to emulate, and no, it's not Ms. Serena or that Super Bowl guy. A while back before my smashing crash, my buddy (the one who recommended the liquid dynamite during my hip replacement/COVID-19 days) and I had just come off the bike trail, and while we were restocking our supplies getting ready to go back out, we met a rather heavy-set gentleman who was unloading an extremely sturdy electric bike. One of those half-ton brown bears up in Alaska could have ridden that bike in the circus, it was so brawny.

He (the gentleman, not the bear) started chatting with us and enlightening us on all the wonderful features of his muscled machine. He was more than blessed with expansive body rolls and folds, but he was a delightful fellow with a prodigious gift of conversation. He gave us the rundown on how much he weighed, how much he had lost, and how much more he had to lose before he could get back on his regular bike. We could have been there an hour if we hadn't politely excused ourselves because we still had another 15 miles to ride.

Our new friend was a smart guy, and he didn't care what other people thought about his girth when he was out riding. I'm not sure if he felt awkward or not, but he certainly did not exude that emotion. He knew he had let himself go, but he had a plan in place, and he was on a mission to execute it.

And let me tell you a secret. If you resemble and relate to this gentleman—let's call him E-bike Mike—be assured that the vast majority of people you see when you are out there walking in the park, riding a bike, or working out in the gym, are on your side. They are happy for you and happy you are out there sharing their experience. Sure, you will come across a few (perhaps even many) ego-laden people who will turn their nose up at you, but don't let them intimidate you. Just be like E-bike Mike and enjoy your ride, walk, or fitness class, and don't let those ego clowns get inside your head.

When E-bike Mike mounts his heavy-duty bike, he may feel awkward, but he gets out there. I've seen him a couple times since we met pedaling away on his robust machine. And, I have seen him riding with his wife who has her own sturdy e-bike. Yes, she is nearly as big as E-bike, but she is just as enthusiastic about getting out there as he. In fact, I have witnessed her urging him to go a few more miles with her.

Again, your journey is not about trying to impress anyone, it's about improving and maintaining your health like those two are trying to do. You, me, E-bike Mike, Mrs. E-bike, and our homeostasis partners are all worthy of our mission to improve and maintain our health.

And oh, by the way, your teammates don't care who you are, what you look like, how much you weigh, what color your skin is, what sex you are, what nationally you are, what political party you belong to, or whatever else you are or represent, it simply doesn't matter to them. They are on your team and are exceedingly adaptable and will work with you and your particular idiosyncrasies. Be kind to them, work with them, and they will take you far into Healthyville and deep into the game of your life.

Okay, have you got all that? You were paying attention, right? Now that we have stared reality straight in the eye, it's time to go over the game plan. Again, please pay attention. There may be a pop quiz somewhere along your journey.

THE GAME PLAN PRINCIPLES

GAME PLAN PRINCIPLE 1: SEEK KNOWLEDGE

Okay, where do you go to seek knowledge concerning how to become healthy and more alive? Just so you know, you don't have to go down to your local travel agency (you millennials and zoomers probably don't even know what a travel agency is, do you?), book a flight to Tibet, climb one of those seriously high Himalayan mountains, and seek out a random guru sitting cross-legged with his arms resting on his knees and both his hands flashing the okay sign. He's thinking to himself, "Oh, good, here comes another sucker." If you choose to go on this expedition in search of true knowledge, make sure your new sage's name is not Guru P. T. Barnum (or Ponce).

Nor do you have to be like the karate kid and go wash and wax that dude's car and paint his house before he even lets you break your first two by four. And by the way, one doesn't become a champion in two hours or a year. It takes a while to go from no physical exercise for a couple of years to running a 5k race without blowing that gasket. Your homeostasis partner can promise you that.

No, truth be told here, you don't have to go out and seek a fitness guru, or a professor of physiology, nor a licensed dietitian to move closer to Healthyville. Living well is not that hard to understand, and if you have ever paid any income tax to Uncle Sam, you have helped pay for all the knowledge you will most likely ever need to know regarding how to become physically healthier. And even if you haven't paid any income tax to him, he is still cool with you perusing that information. We will look at Uncle Sam's not-so-secret accumulated knowledge later.

My fitness and health education began with that book on fiber as I told you and continued with those running books and magazines that I enthusiastically consumed. As far as learning the guitar, I am most definitely taking the scenic route in that endeavor.

Back in the early eighties, when I got my first real job, I met a guy who used to talk about the blue ionic haze. I'm not sure what all that was about, but we both had a mutual desire to learn to play the guitar. YouTube wasn't a thing back then, so off to music store we went for some guidance.

When we got there and talked to the music store guy, he ushered us to the bookshelf where he picked up a book and said in a reverential voice, this is the way to six-string adroitness. I think that's what he said. I may be paraphrasing a bit. Anyway, the book was written by a fellow named Mel Bay who, strangely enough, looked like my boyhood friend with natural musical ability who lived across the street. The book was entitled *Mel Bay's Modern Guitar Method—Grade 1,* and our music store chap proudly proclaimed that he had completed all seven of Mel's grades. So, I bought the book.

My buddy wasn't really impressed with Mel because he wanted to play Beatles songs, so I bought a Beatles songbook, and we began trying to learn some of their songs. But our lives soon diverged in two different directions, so we never became rock and roll legends. I continued to go through Mel's Grade 1 and even made it through Grade 2, but somewhere in Grade 3, apparently life got in the way, and I barely touched the guitar for nearly 40 years.

More on Mel and life getting in the way in a moment, but the point here is to absorb a healthy measure of guidance when you embark upon your journey toward better health. The fact that you are reading this highly serious, academic health book (stop laughing) proves you are already proceeding down that path. Stay the course, and good for you, but just remember what Yoda said about teaching you, but not learning until you do. That is, all the knowledge in the world won't help you unless you put that knowledge into practice, and practice, and then practice some more, and some more. Hence, our next game plan principle.

GAME PLAN PRINCIPLE 2: PRACTICE

So, Yoda, back here in the 21st Century, we don't know what the Force is yet. I can't levitate a pencil, much less Luke's X-wing Starfighter. But fortunately, since we aren't in any battles with any evil Empires or Romulans, I'm not going to practice levitating anything, except hopefully your health and well-being. And, since in this century we do not know how the Force works, the only method I can offer you here is good old-fashioned practice to benefit from what you hopefully learn. I have been telling you that getting healthier requires effort, that is, practice. Sorry *Star Trek War* fans. It's all Yoda's fault.

To maintain the level of improved proficiency you accomplish in your quest to live a healthier life, you must regularly practice what you learn. Being an athlete all of my life, I always loved to practice. I spoke of playing T-ball when I was five and playing first base because I was the only kid on the team that could competently catch the ball, because I had practiced catching for nearly half my life. Improving and maintaining your health and love of life will also require practice, repetitive tasks, and consistent routines.

When I got my real job, I found myself in a manufacturing plant where they made those proverbial widgets. In college, I had studied something called a learning curve and to my surprise, they were, in fact, used at the widget factory. The basic theory behind a learning curve is that the more widgets you make, that is, the more you practice crafting them, the less time it takes to make the next one. On your 138th widget, you discover that if you hold your special widget tool at a different angle, you finish fabricating the widget ten seconds faster than before. Then on your 295th widget, you find that if you hold your tongue on the right side of your mouth instead of the left, you save another five seconds, and so forth.

One of my friends was tasked with painting all those widgets. Day after day, month after month, year after year, he stood there painting widgets one after another until he became an authentic Michelangelo with the airbrush! Talking about always practicing, I wish you could have seen his countless widget masterpieces, not to mention the paint job he did on his truck and motorcycle helmet. Amazing works of art they were simply because he used that airbrush every day, learned the nuances of the tool, and continually honed his technique. That is what practice is all about.

But let me say this, I am most definitely not asking you to spend the same amount of time practicing being healthy as my friend did painting all of those widgets. That was his job. Nor do you have to eat as healthily as Tom Brady (I'm assuming you don't have your own personal chef) and practice as long and tirelessly as he does, because again, more than likely you're not trying to win a Super Bowl against Ponce and his conquistadors. Again, that is his job.

However, consistent practice will be required in your quest

toward better health and also in my quest to play the guitar. I get the fact that I am going to have to spend thousands upon thousands of hours practicing to become respectable when playing the instrument. I am not going to be able to just watch a couple of YouTube videos and take a couple of lessons to become a decent guitar player.

But I am embracing the effort and will keep practicing until I do. I'm not going to practice until my fingers bleed, as the legend goes for so many rock and roll stars. That hour I do practice most every day is sufficient for me. I am not striving to play the blues like Stevie Ray Vaughn used to do. All I want to do is reach George and Voltaire's 80% benchmark. Being pretty good will be just fine with me. I'm not striving to be a virtuoso like my widget-painting friend, Stevie Ray, or Mr. Brady.

And I hope you will promise yourself that you will start (if you haven't already) and continue to learn and to practice with your teammates toward achieving better health and enjoyment of that charming affair we call life. And if you have started down your healthy path, be satisfied (at least for today) that you have begun your journey to better health, but please stay the course, and continue to get healthier. Keep learning and keep practicing to gain and maintain whatever level of improved proficiency you accomplish on your mission toward well-being.

GAME PLAN PRINCIPLE 3: INCREMENTALLY

A couple of years ago, when I picked up the guitar again and told myself I was really going to learn to play this time, I did not start out attempting to play Beethoven's sonatas.

I told you about purchasing Mel's *Modern Guitar Method – Grade 1* back in the eighties, and I have kept that book all those years, so I pulled it out of the closet a couple years ago to restart my journey to guitar proficiency. Mel didn't launch me into Beethoven's Moonlight sonata on day one. He started out by telling me how to hold the guitar on page two and how to hold the pick, which is the little piece of plastic that the guitarist uses to pluck the strings. I have to give Mel some credit here for being a cool guy because back then, all of the snobbish guitar aficionados called it a plectrum, darling. Anyway, on page three, he showed me how to tune the instrument, and so on.

It wasn't until page eight that I finally got to play my first note. He kept allowing me to take baby steps by giving me little incremental bits of knowledge to add to my nascent skill as a guitarist. Your teammates will incrementally help you build your skills too if you keep practicing and performing with them.

What is that old saying about eating that brown bear that rode Mike's e-bike? Do it one bite at the time? Or was it an elephant the old saying was referring to? Mel couldn't remember either, so he just kept giving me more and more petite nuggets of knowledge and increasingly challenging exercises to practice in my effort to expand my guitar prowess in small, incremental steps.

Toward the end of *Grade 1*, Mel included a short piece of music by a famous Spanish guitarist from long ago named Fernando Sor. Mel dumbed the arrangement down for me, but for the life of me, I still haven't been able to play that waltz all the way through without making any mistakes, after almost two years of trying. You, too, will make mistakes on your quest to improve your health. That's what we humans do. Mel told me to just keep practicing, so you do the same. Okay, Mel, I promise I will keep practicing, but just don't listen to whatever I may be muttering underneath my breath.

More on the difficulties of honing a new skill later, but the point here is to begin your journey toward better health and a better life incrementally, step by step. Keep practicing each new culinary skill you learn, continue walking those 50 yards, increase your distance traveled a few steps at a time, and keep whispering to your homeostasis partner that you two can do this. Together, move slowly in the beginning, one increment at a time, toward a healthier life for both of you.

I can almost guarantee that you will become bored with this whole practice/incremental process. Boredom, way more likely than not, will become a part of your expedition to decent health. Babies learn almost everything from their new experiences in their young lives, thus we humans have a strong desire to seek fresh experiences in our nature. That is not necessarily a bad thing, and we will talk about the pluses and minuses of seeking novelty in a later chapter, but for now, let us just accept the fact that you are going to get bogged down and bored from time to time, but just keep saying to yourself, stay the course, stay on your long and meandering expedition.

Now granted, some people can make drastic, sudden changes in their lives. I have a new, short little rotund (is that what they call an oxymoron?) friend that told me recently that I may not have noticed, but he had lost 30 pounds! Let's call him Jolly-man Stan. I was ecstatic for him, but before I could ask how he did it, he launched into how he had cut this out of his diet, and had cut that out, and given the fact that he gets a ton of exercise doing his job, he dropped the weight rather easily.

My dad was the same way. He came of age when smoking was cool and the Marlboro Man was a stud, but when he decided to quit smoking, he quit. No nicotine patches or anything. However, most of you will not be successful with this approach, and that is why I recommend being kind to your homeostasis partner. Take the incremental path, and just know there will be times when you get aggravated and exasperated. Sometimes I look Mel straight in the eye and say, "Mel, what are you trying to do here, kill me?" He just kindly tells me to try playing "Sor's Waltz" one more time.

Again, for most of us (and Mel told me to raise my hand here), we will have to take the well-worn path of practice to gain those little nuggets of incremental health improvement that we seek to accomplish. Keep learning, keep practicing, and keep improving your well-being step by step.

GAME PLAN PRINCIPLE 4: CONTINUOUS IMPROVEMENT

When I first got to the widget factory, it was the Wild West days of manufacturing. Some of the old timers told me stories about how they used to clean the widgets by rinsing them in pans of gasoline. And oh, by the way, smoking was allowed inside the plant back then. What could possibly go wrong with that scenario?

Fortunately, I never witnessed any explosions, but somewhere along the line, the Mothership sent us a guru from high atop the mountain. He was from the Rocky Mountains instead of the Himalayas, but when this guru of continuous improvement was transferred to our plant, within a few years we entered the modern age of manufacturing, thanks to his vision. It was an amazing transformation. Every specific phase of the production process was examined to figure out how each widget could be made more efficiently and more resourcefully. Needless to say, the Mothership people were thrilled with our improvement.

I am using some of these continuous improvement tactics on my guitar journey. After playing a piece of music several times, I look to see if there is a more efficient way to place my fingers on the fretboard to produce the same notes. Most of the time, Mel gives me hints on which fingers to use, but sometimes he doesn't. On one particular piece, I actually use my thumb to hit a note on the top of the fretboard, instead of sending one of my fingers, which are all busy down on the bottom, up there. Mel didn't say I couldn't.

However, making something simpler doesn't necessarily make it better. Remember, throwing [insert four-letter word] into the microwave as my assistant manager at the grocery store spoke of, or heating until bubbly like that bachelor baseball pitcher guy used to do, are definitely simpler methods of cooking, but they may not pave the highway to nutritional wholesomeness in your diet.

You probably will find shortcuts in preparing your recipes without compromising the nutritional value of your dishes. That's another thing we humans do (or should strive to do), continuously improve ourselves like we did at the widget factory. That is what we have always done since our cavepeople ancestors were around, or we would still live in caves. Just be sure you know the difference between simplification and improvement. Sometimes they work together, sometimes they don't.

Let me say one more thing before we move on to our next principle, when you get to a certain reasonable and beneficial level in, for example, your weekly walking distance, you don't have to keep increasing your effort and distance until you can run a marathon (unless of course you want to). As I told you, after nearly killing myself running those 100-mile weeks, I settled on 20 miles per week to maintain my fitness for decades.

If in the culinary arts, you don't want to put in the extraordinary time my friend did to reach his plane of widget-painting proficiency, that's fine. George doesn't expect fancy, gourmet prepared dishes every day to satisfy his appetite for healthy food. And since you probably don't have your own personal chef like Mr. Brady, just dine on your modest menu of simple, healthy, and wholesome recipes that you, George, and Voltaire enjoy.

However, when you hopefully have continuously improved your well-being in incremental actions to an acceptable healthy level, then what? I am most hopeful that you know Father Time and his intimidating teammates are extremely erosive and are incessantly applying those corrosive forces upon your selected plateaus of nutrition, exercise, etc. Thus, in order to inhibit their relentless assault upon your accomplishments and prevent you from sliding back into the dark hollows of ill health and self-dissatisfaction for as long as possible, you must endeavor to always maintain your levels of well-being and know where you are along your path which leads us to our next game plan principle.

GAME PLAN PRINCIPLE 5: MONITOR AND MAINTAIN

Have you, at some point, lost a certain amount of weight and then gained most, all, or more of it back? Building your well-being mansion of glory and maintaining it are two entirely different affairs. That French lady Jeanne, who lived to be 122, told me one time how much maintenance was required to keep the Eiffel Tower from crumbling into disrepair.

But works of beauty of that magnitude and glory, including your own wondrous body and mind, are so worthy of the maintenance they require. I cannot emphasize enough the importance of maintaining your well-being mansion of glory to avoid major, painful, and expensive restoration projects. And you must habitually monitor your well-being manor for signs of deterioration to avoid those major renovations.

On the most fundamental level, our maintenance routines should begin with our daily personal hygiene practices such as bathing, brushing (and flossing) our teeth at least twice a day, regularly washing our hands, etc. In addition, keeping our work (and play) areas and particularly our cooking spaces clean (including our microwave), washing our clothes, assuring our living spaces are as free as possible of falling hazards, etc. are also enormously important not to mention wearing our seatbelts when driving (or riding in) a vehicle.

These basic essential maintenance habits take us far toward disease and injury prevention, social acceptance, higher self-esteem, and many other health benefits. Many lives have been cut short or made dismal due to incessant pain and misery because basic personal maintenance routines were ignored and not practiced.

You remember my baseball hero from Chapter 2 who, after his playing days were done, let himself go and gained all of that weight so quickly? I can still recall my appalled emotion upon seeing just how poorly he had maintained his physical condition, and that brief visual cemented into my mind just how important the preservation of my organic structure would be. I vowed to always remain firmly entrenched in Healthyville for as long as I could by maintaining my body and my healthy habits.

But trust me here, I completely comprehend how difficult the maintenance process is. I told you above about gaining those 30 pounds even with eating a healthy diet, lifting weights, running those 20 miles a week, and playing in hundreds of softball games. But please don't ask, "Then why bother with this fitness stuff?"

First of all, maintaining your health and well-being is so important in order to avoid as many of those bad health outcomes we discussed in Chapter 3. Habitual maintenance is preferable to major repair and restoration projects every few years, and in the long run will save you a significant sum of money.

Now, just so you know, I was not bestowed with the strongest set of teeth upon conception. So as my life has progressed, I have had to regularly visit the dentist starting in early childhood, mostly for general maintenance (cleaning) but sometimes for more extensive work (a filling). However, despite my poor dental genes, I do, if you count a couple of crowns, still have all of my teeth (not counting my wisdom teeth or the one I lost because of the dentist-who-must-be named) because I have steadfastly maintained my dental hygiene routines including going to see the dentist at least twice a year since I was a kid.

However, at one point, I did not go to a dentist for any professional maintenance for almost three years. Although I kept brushing my teeth, flossing, and rinsing my mouth with a fluoride rinse, the condition of my teeth, to use a highly scientific term, started looking really gross, and I knew there was more than likely clandestine deterioration transpiring that I could not see.

When I finally did return to the dentist's office, I walked out of my initial visit (I knew it was going to be wicked) with six or seven scheduled follow-up visits to stabilize and improve the condition and appearance of my teeth. Yes, I was looking at a major restoration project. Again, I cannot overemphasize the importance of routine general and professional maintenance to limit the deterioration of your well-being mansion.

Back at the turn of the millennium, I asked myself how those 30 pounds so clandestinely besieged my body since my marathoning days despite continuously practicing all of my healthy habits. My best guess was that I failed to monitor my bulk. I rarely stepped upon a scale to monitor my weight and my body sneakily became heavier and heavier with the passage of the years.

This was about the time the Mothership people sent the Rocky Mountain guru of continuous improvement to our widget factory, and one of the first things he did was set up a system of scorecards for everyone, or as the professionals say, metrics. We created and maintained those scorecards to make sure we did not backslide back into those Wild West days of fabrication folly. More on using scorecards and apps in a moment but knowing where you are is vitally important to assess the required level of maintenance you require.

And here is another tip. At the widget factory, I knew all the people in the facilities' maintenance department. They didn't actually manufacture any of the widgets; their only job was to make sure the buildings we all worked in and the major equipment that we all used were properly maintained. And like my dad's fun and offbeat stock crew, they were all an entertaining bunch of people to work with. Thus, while maintaining your physical (and mental) mansion of glory, recruit several friends or family members to perform together those important maintenance assignments, such as exercising and eating well. A good time is normally had by all.

GAME PLAN PRINCIPLE 6: CONFLICTING GOALS

Ben Franklin said the two certain things in life were death and taxes. I kept trying to tell him that the third certainty in life was conflicting goals, but he didn't think that was cool enough to put into his *Poor Richard's Almanac*, so that certainty never became famous. I never found out who that poor Richard guy was, either.

Anyway, whether you are in college, raising a family, providing care for your elders, or your grandkids, or all of the above, I am certain you have conflicting goals. Taking care of your own life, health, and well-being often gets pushed back behind the stage somewhere. Sailing toward one goal often means watching another fade below the horizon. However, it is vitally important that you spend some time on your own health's behalf despite all of your other desires and commitments in life.

Your journey through those turbulent waters of conflicting goals must include spending time with each of your teammates out there on the floor. Learning to play my guitar conflicted with too many other goals in my life, including staying healthy, so it had to sit in my closet for 40 years. Fortunately, because I made my health a priority during my working years, I am still healthy enough now in spite of recent broken bones to finally begin to seriously learn how to play the instrument. Thus, despite all of your other priorities, do not let your health sit in the closet for 40 years. My guitar was fine, but you may not make it out of there.

GAME PLAN PRINCIPLE 7: CHOOSE TOOLS THAT WORK FOR YOU

I made my living adding and subtracting numbers, and then putting them into little boxes. Sometimes I even multiplied, but that division thing was really hard. Thank goodness, I had a computer to help me out with all of those mathematical manipulations.

Most of you are further along in the modern world than I am (I'm actually one of the 14 people in the civilized world that has never had a Facebook account and count me out of the metaverse for now), so you probably know about phone and computer applications to help you in your quest to eat healthier, enjoy life more, and become fitter.

I am sure countless apps are available out there that will help motivate you, encourage you, and make it fun for you on your journey to Healthyville. Even Uncle Sam has many free apps, as we will discover in the next few chapters. But just remember what I said about all of Ponce's people out there who want to sell you magic elixirs, rejuvenators, and nothing for something.

As for me, I will continue to track my cycling mileage on old-fashioned school notebook paper when and if I get back on the bike. That's how I kept track of those 30,000 miles I ran and my 200-plus races. No one knew what an app was that far back in prehistoric times. And, although I tried once, I never seriously tracked my calorie consumption either. That always seemed too involved and way too far down into the weeds and electrons for me, but I'm sure there is an app out there for that if you want to. Just stepping on the scale at regular intervals tells me everything I need to know.

I think you millennials and zoomers would be proud of me the other day, however, because I discovered an app on my phone that tracked my steps when on my walks through the woods. I know, I know, it's a small step into the modern world for me, but it was fun to see how many steps I had taken. I'm sure you will be far better than me at finding motivating tools, so go for it! Experiment and find the tools that work best for you on your journey to Healthyville.

GAME PLAN PRINCIPLE 8: DON'T BE DISTRACTED BY YOUTH

Youth can cover up a lot of lifestyle transgressions, but eventually, if you are lucky, the body and mind ages, and depending on your state of health, life can become rapidly miserable. Somewhere in your fourth decade of life, you will theoretically reach the summit of your potential peak performance as the chart of my 5k racing times illustrated back in Chapter 2.

I ran my fastest 5k race when I was 33 years old, and despite continuing to train at the same level, my performances began to erode. I came close to equaling that time during the rest of my thirties, but despite my efforts, I never matched my personal record. However, because I kept training and eating well, my performance decline was only marginal over time rather than resembling falling off a cliff.

Younger millennials and zoomers, please don't be distracted by your youth and wait to pursue a healthy lifestyle until the penalties of your poor well-being routines start rolling in. You can only ignore your health for so long until those consequences come back to haunt you. Don't let your healthspan part from your lifespan well before it should. If you are still young, it's easier to avoid problems now than trying to fix major transgressions once they occur in the future. Your eventual decline will occur much more gradually.

GAME PLAN PRINCIPLE 9: DON'T BE DISTRACTED BY TALENT

I described the wealth of talent I found myself competing against back when I first started running and racing, and not being the brightest person on the planet, I nearly killed myself running those hundred-mile weeks trying to keep up with them. But for many people, worshipping talented athletes often gives them an excuse not to exercise because they know they will never be as good as Ms. Serena or the Olympic marathon guy. Do not go there.

Don't conclude that since you are not a natural athlete, you do not need to be out there exercising or eating healthily because that cannot be much further than the truth. Despite not being a star athlete, you are still a human being, and we all need the same general building blocks and endeavors to keep us healthy, athlete or not.

And oh, by the way, if you are one of those natural, talented athletes, do not get lazy like my boyhood baseball hero and ignore your nutrition and cease exercising after your glory days. Twenty-plus years later, I handily beat a couple of those runners that would trounce me when I was doing all of that mega-milage because I had taken care of myself and apparently they were not as vigilant in maintaining what they had possessed. So stay in the game.

GAME PLAN PRINCIPLE 10: DON'T BE DISTRACTED BY SELF-DOUBT

Trust me, I'm all over this one. I have gotten to this point in attempting to write this book and I am now earnestly having harsh doubts I can actually achieve this endeavor. The words have not been exactly flowing from my head through my fingers onto the computer screen for the last several days. I think they call that writer's block. I have no idea, I'm not a writer. So, when all else fails, I will resort to telling another of my stories about why I have such imposing doubt about completing this book.

As I rolled into my fifties, I began to think about what I was going to do in retirement. I knew I didn't want to plop on the couch and watch television all day. No, I wanted to help people live healthier lives. I don't remember exactly how, but I came up with the idea of becoming a personal trainer. Several of my friends at the widget factory thought I would succeed in that undertaking, because you know, I was that runner guy, so I pursued it. I chose one of the certification programs, purchased the study materials, took CPR and first aid classes, studied hard, and passed the accreditation test.

One of my widget factory friends was a petite lady in terms of height but not width. Yes, she had struggled with her weight for a long time, and one January as many often do, she set a goal to become heathier and volunteered to work with her newly minted personal trainer friend, me. I had no idea what I was doing, and I got everything all wrong. I introduced her to the weight machines at the gym and the step machines, but after a few weeks like so many, she gave up her gym experiment and I gave up on my personal trainer foray. We both tried, but in the end, she continued to be petite, wide, and delightful at work, and I let my personal training certificate slip into oblivion, never to be used again.

So yes, I have severe doubts about accomplishing my mission of completing this tome, in the hope of helping you become healthier. And, I am sure you probably have earnest doubts about actually transforming into that fitter, healthier, happier person this time around. But since those short-lived personal trainer days, I have continued to have a strong desire to help people trim down, strengthen up, and be able to enjoy life more.

And apparently, that vision is needed now more than ever. When I got up this morning and logged onto my computer to read my digital "newspaper" while having my coffee, a picture popped up on the screen of one of our beaches, apparently close to one of our retirement communities.

Every person in the picture looked as old as I am but possessed a BMI ratio well into the overweight range, and they did not have muscles like Mr. Rock. It just breaks my heart to see a picture like that not because of the way they look, but because of the extra issues they more than likely have to deal with due to their unhealthy state. I can only imagine how many doctor visits they attend and how many medications they consume for aches, pains, and other health issues.

And just so you know, I am not trying to body-shame anyone here. Heck, I am so bow legged I cannot even hold a baseball between my knees when I have my feet together. I can hold a beach ball, though. And I have never been mistaken for Tom, the *Top Gun* guy, when I stroll down the beach. I just know what people who are carrying too much weight will face when they get older, and I don't want you to go there. When you get to be my age, you will have enough pain in your body even if you are not overweight.

Thus, despite my self-doubt, I will finish writing this book for you. And you will not be without doubts when you begin your mission, but you can become healthier and, dare I say, happier when you do. Again, you are not trying to be a world-class athlete. Praise yourself more for your effort instead of your results, and just keep getting out there on the floor with your teammates. They don't care if you can't shoot the sky hook like Kareem. They will work with you. Just be like E-bike Mike and his spouse and get out there. So let us both push through this self-doubt thing (assuming you have some) and do this.

GAME PLAN PRINCIPLE 11: FOCUS ON WHAT YOU CAN CONTROL

My cycling buddy that was with me when we met E-bike Mike a while back has a favorite adage. He likes to say all we can do is just take care of our own little bubble and hope everything else works out. He's right. To keep from sinking into entrenched despair, try to focus on what you can control and manage (and yes, it's difficult to do) given your current situation, means, and skills the best you can.

Back when I was playing shortstop, before every pitch, I would tell myself "Do what you gotta do." Granted, it wasn't the most Shakespearean of phrases, and it had some grammatical issues, but the internal pronouncement kept me focused on the play at hand and to do what I had to do if the ball was hit to me. I couldn't worry about the ball being hit to right field because that was our right fielder's responsibility and outside my bubble of control. All I knew was that I had to cover second base and just hope the ball was caught.

Now I'm not saying to go around all day saying to yourself, "Do what you gotta do," but yes, focus on taking care of what you *can* take care of. If your new wholesome recipe you found above calls for garden-fresh green beans, carrots, and corn over rice which a bunch of expensive spices, but you don't have the money to buy all of those extravagant ingredients, go over to aisle two and buy a can of green beans, a can of carrots, and a can of corn. And instead of buying the expensive box of rice with the fancy spices, buy the economical bag of plain rice and cook it the old-fashioned way, with perhaps a little salt. The dish may not taste quite as delectable as the expensive gourmet version, but your adaptation of the recipe is good, inexpensive, and wholesome food. That's what genuinely counts.

Life has a knack of getting in the way of your journey to health and welfare. I promise you, Father Time and his band of bummers will throw everything, including that proverbial kitchen sink (and potholes) in your path to improvement and maintenance of your health and well-being. But again, stay on your journey and do what you have to do to take care of your own little bubble to improve your health.

This is an appropriate day to mention this because I went to see my orthopedic doctor this morning for the first time since my bike crash and apparently my clavicle (collar bone) is not healing quite like it should. So now I am looking at a couple weeks of physical therapy and then the decision whether or not surgery will be required to reposition my clavicle to its proper place.

Yes, today has been a depressing day, and I know you will face days like this as well. I want to be back on the bike already, but that is out of my control, for now. I don't have my release any longer, but all I can do now is focus on the physical therapy and go from there.

We will talk more about how to deal with these depressing days (and I have experienced my fair share) when we get to Chapter 9, but for now, you and I just need to do what we "gotta" do and focus only on what we can control right now during our expeditions toward making our lives better, healthier, and happier. And if you want to go around all day saying, "do what you gotta do," be my guest. I don't have that phrase copyrighted.

GAME PLAN PRINCIPLE 12: DON'T BE AFRAID TO CHANGE COURSE

Back in Chapter 2, I spoke of our first decade in life when we were rapidly growing, exploring, learning, making mistakes, and how it was in that process of starting, stopping, moving forward, backward, experimenting, making sometimes gross mistakes and sometimes meaningful accomplishments. And, in that process of trial and error, we matured, moved forward, and improved ourselves and our lives.

When you are out there on the floor with your teammates (given your age), you will discover through trial and error what works best for you in your interactions with them. Perhaps you are just not into running, so try brisk walking, cycling, or an aerobics class. If you find a great nutritional dish but it's too laborious to prepare or too expensive, or your body cannot tolerate a certain food choice any longer, find another recipe. If you are becoming less fond of a social group you are involved in, try another more aligned with your changing interest. Experiment and find out what works best for you, and don't be afraid to change your itinerary when necessary.

And as your game of life goes on, you will have to modify your go-to routines and habits. Improvision of your preferences will increasingly be required the longer your journey here on Mother Earth continues. I had to give up running, but I found cycling. Now, with my crash and the fact that I'm not getting any younger, I may have to someday acquire an e-bike like Mike, or one of those three-wheeled bikes I have seen beginning to proliferate. I started out on a tricycle at age three and will probably end my cycling career on another one.

So again, whether it be because of illness, accident, or just age, continue to improvise your means and methods as circumstances dictate by using the method of trial and error (again with sound guidance when required) to improve your current situation, and do not be afraid to adapt new pathways in your life as my marigold had to do this past summer. I promised I would tell you my flower's story of improving and lengthening its life, despite what happened.

This past spring, I planted several marigold seeds in a pot filled with good soil and nutritious food for them. Once they sprouted, I continued to water them, feed them, and provide them with lots of Florida sunshine. By summer, one had grown to over five feet tall. One day, during one of our regularly scheduled summer thunderstorms, a powerful gust of wind came across the porch and broke the marigold's stem about halfway up. The top half of the marigold landed on top of the porch rail so that the stem was bent at a 90-degree angle.

As I have learned over the years, things happen, and because I had other priorities, I left the plant as it landed. To my vast surprise, not only did the plant survive, but new growth began spouting from the section of the stem that was bent over, and over the course of a few weeks, new blooms appeared. Granted, the flowers weren't as huge as before the accident, but my marigold had adapted and overcome its compromised body limitations. Somehow, it rerouted water and nutrients through the broken stem to the new flowers.

My marigold story is even more meaningful in my mind now since I crashed a few weeks ago, broke my body in several places, and because some of those bones are not mending quite the way they should. Both you and I need to persevere to always improvise as life (thankfully) goes on and not be afraid to adapt course changes from time to time as required toward continuously improving and maintaining our health, well-being, and love of life whether it's a voluntary course change or not.

ARE YOU READY FOR THIS?

One more story before we go meet our distinguished teammates. Just so you know, writing is an excruciating process for me, not unlike my guitar playing endeavors. As I said earlier, I'm starting to struggle here. I genuinely must earn, through ample effort, every sentence I am putting into this book. And Mel didn't pen any books on how to write, so I can't rely on him to help me out here.

However, when I got to college, I had to take a business writing class, and when I got my first assignment back, I had earned a D-minus. I don't remember what the letter was about, but it was so defective, the professor read it out loud to the entire class so they would know how not to write a business letter that dumb. Talk about a two by four between the eyes.

However, back in my eleventh grade English class, I got an A+ on a writing assignment that I had worked hard and long on, so I knew I had a little talent. I just needed to put in the effort and exertion. And even way back in high school when my brain was young and supple, putting words that made sense and understandable onto paper (that was way, way back before laptops) was so demanding for me. It wasn't easy, like being the starting third baseman that year on the high school baseball team. That D- got my attention, though, and I put the required effort into that college class for the remainder of the semester.

I'm telling you this story because I sincerely do not want you to receive a D- concerning your health such as a cardiac arrest, stroke, or other debilitating disease caused by inactivity, not eating the proper food, and weighting much more than you should. I know how hard it is to learn and do something that does not come easily to you. Mel reminds me of that almost every day. But receiving a D- is difficult to overcome.

Again, I understand how challenging losing weight is going to be if that is one of your tasks. Dang, it was hard enough for me, you know, the athlete guy to lose those 20 pounds. And I understand how hard it is going to be to improve your diet if you are pulled in 85 different directions every day and you just want to throw some [insert four-letter word] into the microwave.

And I know how difficult getting enough exercise will be if that is not your passion. But please, put forth the effort to get to know your well-being teammates over the next few chapters, begin working with them, and start taking small steps to improve your teamwork. Hopefully, your first health grade will be at least a C+ (or better) and not that D-.

My final grade in that business writing class, by the way, was an A, after considerable effort during the balance of the semester. However, it would have been far easier if I had taken that first assignment more seriously and earned higher than a D- out of the gate. Are you young zoomers (and all the rest of you) paying attention here?

The effort in overcoming the effects of a cardiac arrest or stroke would probably be far greater and probably far scarier than overcoming that D- in my writing class. Putting forth the effort now toward improving your health will be much easier than dealing with your first serious health D-minus in the future. Again, habitual maintenance is always preferable to major repair and restoration missions.

Okay, so now it is time for that pop quiz I told you to be prepared for. How healthy are you right now? Have you already received your first D-minus? Have you had that stroke? Do you already have type 2 diabetes? Okay, if that is your case, just stay calm and let me talk you back from the edge of the cliff. I have stared down into the abyss, not because of my health, but for other reasons. I thankfully chose not to jump, and I do not want you to, either.

I still have too many responsibilities to take care of in my life, and goals I want to achieve, places I want to see, and things I want to do. You know, that bucket list thing we all have. I am sure you have one too, so if you have received your first D-, please stay in the game and channel my marigold. Find a way to continue to live and bloom again.

If you need to, go back, and get real with our reality checks. Study, and study again, our game plan principles (particularly the first five). You will then have an idea of what to do when you get out there on the floor in your new game of living a healthy life with your new beneficial and enthusiastic teammates. The more you get to know and participate with them, the more your skills and healthy habits will become seamlessly integrated into your improving well-being. Eventually, you will feel the flow of a healthy life.

That's how I am approaching my guitar education (not to mention this writing endeavor), so I'm struggling right there along with you. However, my six-string adeptness is slowly growing, one note at a time, and so will your health, one step at a time. I still haven't perfected "Sor's Waltz" after executing hundreds of renditions, but with each new performance of the melody, the slightest granules of improvement are appearing, though as we learned, my learning curve trajectory is a bit wobbly, but at least headed in the right direction.

And you too will find that walking those 50 yards will slowly grow to walking 500 yards and still feeling like you can do even more if you stay in the game (though some days you can only manage 400 yards). And who knows, if you steadfastly continue getting out there, perhaps someday day you can participate in that 5k without blowing a gasket.

Yes, it's going to take a while to learn to play my guitar with any semblance of skill, but I am enjoying experiencing the finest little nuances of progress and occasionally experiencing a bit of the flow. You too may be on your quest for a while (hopefully for the rest of your life) on your journey to Healthyville as our first check of reality reminds us. And, some practice sessions just don't go well, and I have to tell myself, tomorrow will be better, and they usually are. Again, Sir Paul warned us long ago of that long and winding reality, but just keep getting out there on the floor participating with your teammates.

And just a reminder in your endeavor toward becoming healthier, George and Voltaire would be elated if you just earned a solid B grade. I'm fairly certain your homeostasis partner would be okay with that stable B average, too. Again, we are not trying to become world-class athletes here, or go for an Olympic gold medal, or win a Super Bowl. We are just trying to be reasonably sound and healthy enough to hug our great grandchildren someday.

So, rather you are a rising zoomer, a mid-court millennial, gen-Xer, or retired boomer (or beyond), stay in the game of that wonderful gift we call life for as long as you can. Learn, practice, continuously improve incrementally, maintain your health the best you can with the assistance of your teammates, and always know where you are along your long and winding journey. Life is worth it, even in less-than-ideal conditions.

At my age, given the fact the slope I am now skiing down is getting steeper and steeper, simply maintaining the health I have is my goal. I'm just trying the best I can to ski parallel to the mountain and prolong my inevitable arrival at the bottom where you know who is waiting.

So, take a deep breath here, and exhale slowly. We have now stared straight into the eye of reality and have thoroughly gone over the game plan. And it is now time to go meet our well-being teammates. I hear tell they are extremely eager to work with you. Are you ready for this? I think you are. Whisper to your homeostasis partner, we can do this. Yes, we can do this.

CHAPTER 6: WE ARE WHAT WE EAT

Some guy back in the 1800s said we are what we eat. I think his name was Ludwig van Beethoven. Oh wait, he was the music guy who wrote the "Moonlight Sonata" that Mel didn't want me to play just yet. The guy that said we are what we eat was a fellow by the name of Ludwig Feuerbach. I'm always getting my Ludwigs mixed up, sorry. Anyway, this particular Ludwig (who, by the way, stole the phrase from some French guy, so Jeanne told me) was using this famous phrase in some kind of high-level philosophical dissertation. But as you know by now, I'm an athlete and not a philosopher, therefore I am going to use the phrase literally.

So, this has to be some kind of a record. We're going to take a short timeout here eight seconds into the chapter. Has that ever been done? And there I go again, using another sports analogy. I promised a sports-neutral analogy for my readers who are not fond of athletic competitions, but I do apologize. This new analogy is a bit lame.

Are you ready for this? We are going to build a new you from the foundation up! I warned you it was rather unimaginative and how arduous this writing thing is for me. But let's go with it because again, I genuinely want to help you build yourself into a healthy and happier person. Please stay tuned for the revealing of the breath-taking blueprints for constructing your well-being foundation of the new you. Now, back to Ludwig.

———

RATHER, it was Ludwig, the French guy (or Jeanne), or someone back in antiquity who first said it: what we eat is extremely important in building and maintaining our bodies and the foundation of our health. Our bodies are always replacing our cells and the building blocks of these new cells come from the nutrients in the food we consume. And I have to tell you, it doesn't take a rocket scientist, nutritionist, or athlete for that matter, to see most Americans are replacing those cells at warp speed, or hyper-drive for you Jedi folks. People are simply eating too much of the wrong food. America, including Houston, we have a problem.

In the old days, when cars still had carburetors, bad fuel would gunk it up and the vehicle wouldn't run very well. I'm not sure how all of that worked, but I know consuming too much of today's empty-calorie, ultra-processed food and virtually no vegetables along with too many sugary drinks will gunk up a lot of things inside your body, even if you don't have a carburetor. I don't want to get too gross here, but that's why there are so many, you know, laxatives on the grocery store shelves these days. Products to help move things along, if you will.

As I said back in Chapter 3, eating and drinking this gunky junk leads to health issues, including obesity, type 2 diabetes, cardiovas-cular disease, stroke, and many other severe diseases, all of which are usually avoidable. And this is not breaking news. The fiber book I purchased way back before the Carter administration told me that.

As you will recall, that's why I started adding those steamed vegetables to my diet.

Fifty years later, I have never been overweight (except during that brief foray there at the turn of the millennium I spoke of in the last chapter). I don't have type 2 diabetes or any other chronic disease. And at this point nearly seven decades into my life, I do not take any prescription medication, and yes, as I type this passage, I am knocking on that proverbial wood. More on knocking on wood and hoping for the best in Chapter 10.

Back when we briefly met with your team, I said your teammate Fuel is what you eat, and if you consume a garbage diet, garbage will be produced inside your body, that is, gunky junk. As the 2020–2025 *Dietary Guidelines for Americans* states exceedingly more eloquently than I just did, "the foods and beverages that people consume have a profound impact on their health." The quality of your nutrition is the foundation of the new you we will construct here shortly.

The Guidelines were first published back in 1980 and the report is now required by the 1990 National Nutrition Monitoring and Related Research Act. The US Department of Agriculture (USDA) and the Health and Human Services (HHS) are tasked to jointly publish the Guidelines every five years, which contain nutritional and dietary information for the public based on the latest scientific and medical knowledge.

Each new iteration of the Guidelines builds upon previous editions and evolves as scientific knowledge grows. We will briefly review the Guidelines and other concepts they contain, but I highly recommend going to www.dietaryguidelines.gov to review them for yourself. You have already paid for this wealth of knowledge, so use it. If Ponce had only possessed this wealth of knowledge back in his conquistador days, perhaps he could have spent his retirement years here on the peninsula at his freshwater spring watching the mermaids swimming around.

The scientific evidence is becoming increasingly robust that diet-related chronic diseases pose major health issues for most Americans.

Our eating patterns have persisted far beneath the recommendations of the *Guidelines* for many years. And, as you know by now, 60% of Americans suffer from one or more of those diet-related chronic diseases.

Thus, the *Dietary Guidelines* relying on the science, has now been geared not only toward healthy individuals but also those with an overweight condition who have developed a chronic disease. That is, no matter what your current health status, you can benefit by shifting your food and beverage choices toward healthier dietary patterns. And following the Guidelines can benefit zoomers to boomers and all others, no matter your race, ethnicity, economic position, gender, political ideology, or marital status. But here is a spoiler alert: remember the food pyramids? The current edition doesn't have them anymore. I think they buried them somewhere outside of Des Moines.

The fundamental mission of the *Dietary Guidelines* is health promotion and disease prevention. And even though some people with chronic disease were included in the Guideline studies, they are not intended to treat chronic disease, but to avoid them. So, if you already have a chronic illness, always check with your medical professional before altering your dietary patterns. However, your health provider more than likely can show you how to adapt the Guidelines to meet your specific needs as part of your overall treatment plan.

The current Guidelines include four principal strategies that talk about consuming healthy eating patterns throughout your entire life. To put it in their words, "the Guidelines are a customizable framework of core elements within which individuals make tailored and affordable choices that meet their personal, cultural, and traditional preferences." Yes, their words are considerably more cultured than mine. I suppose telling you to make "tailored and affordable choices" sounds much more sophisticated than me telling you to just use trial and error.

I'm certainly not as smart as all of those scientists and medical doctor people, but I can make this nutrition thing very simple. Just eat real food (that's safe). The closer you get to eating food the way it came off the farm or out of your garden, the better your health will be. And the least processed that food is (but properly prepared), the better. Think garden tomatoes, green beans, cucumbers, broccoli, cauliflower, apples, lean chicken, and fish, etc.

Now mind you, sugar comes from sugar cane, which is a plant and is grown on vast farms down on the lower end of the peninsula, and some people grow it in their garden in these parts, but to get to granulated sugar (or old-fashion cane syrup as my ancestors once brewed), a great deal of processing has to be done. And well, sugar is sugar, and while it doesn't have to be totally avoided, it should be limited, as we will learn later.

And, you don't have to become a vegetarian, vegan, go organic, or non-GMO, or whatever (unless you have specific requirements you have discussed with your healthcare provider). You can choose one of those dietary patterns, but those hunter-gatherer people back in the day ate nothing but organic food, and I'm fairly certain their life expectancy wasn't nearly as long as ours. Of course, they had those saber-toothed tigers, woolly mammoths, and such chasing after them, so that may have had something to do with their shorter lifespan. I'm not sure how much cardiovascular disease they had, but I'm also fairly certain that if I came around a corner and saw a saber-toothed tiger growling at me and ready to pounce, I probably would have some kind of coronary heart event no matter how good of an athlete I am.

Also, I have told you about my carrots, salads, and steamed vegetables, but I have been known to eat a slice of pepperoni pizza, or two, with a fizzy drink. We used to have periodic staff meetings at the widget factory, and inevitably, a couple of those gargantuan containers of doughnuts would show up. Most of the time, the sight of those deep-fried sugar-laden lard rings, some with sprinkles on top, turned my stomach. I'm reasonably sure those doughnuts didn't come off the farm that way. But on the rare occasion I consumed one of my favorite blueberry cake doughnuts, it was front page news at the staff meeting.

My point is, your diet doesn't have to be exactly perfect. Granted, perfect is better, but pretty good is better than pretty bad. So again, just channel George and Voltaire and at least be reasonably good. But just so you know, they would be good with you being perfect, too. And good luck with that. I'm certainly not perfect, but I am healthier than most.

———

OKAY, before we review the Guidelines, let's take another timeout. Oh, if you are one of my readers building the foundation of the new you, take a break for a few minutes. Keeping these two analogies straight is going to be hard. By the way, doing hard things is beneficial, particularly for someone my age and everyone else for that matter. More on that in Chapter 8.

But let me give you an update on my bike crash. Fifty days after that ill-fated incident, I tentatively climbed back on my beloved bicycle to access how my body was proceeding with its recovery and reconstruction project. Like they always said, you have to get back up on the horse. The plan was to ride out for five miles and then turn around and ride back for a total of ten miles. I told you I was good at that adding thing. The weather was nice, and it felt so wonderful to be back in the saddle, literally.

Fortunately, a couple of my friends were starting down the track as I departed on my post-crash maiden voyage, so I followed them to make it easier (you remember that drafting thing from our virtual ride). I could barely keep up with them, particularly when pedaling uphill, but again, it felt so groovy (I used to be a hippie) to be riding again. As I began accessing my condition (my shoulder felt decent, the hip still had something going on down there, the ribs were fine), everything seemed to work not perfectly, but fairly decently. George would have been happy. I wound up riding out seven miles with my friends instead of five before I turned around.

I rode back to the parking lot with high anticipation. The plan was to finish my come back ride and surprise my other friends who would gather for their regularly scheduled ride that evening. It was so good to see them again. My friend who takes care of his bubble informed me of what was going on in my hip (he knows about such things).

Another one of my friends in the group, who was literally born on the same day, in the same small city, and probably the same hospital as me, saw me and the first thing he said to me was that I had not gotten any prettier since my crash. I'm so loved. I told him I didn't land on my face, so they didn't have to do any plastic surgery. Sorry, dude.

Now, a month later, I am riding with them again, sort of. Nearly two months off the bike took its toll on my fitness level and endurance. I have stayed with them a couple of times when they were riding conservatively, but more often than not, they ride faster than I can manage and slowly fade out of sight into the distance as I am left gasping for air. Yesterday, I got dropped off the back of the group barely a quarter of the way into the ride.

I could get mad. I could get sad, but I am not going to choose either of those options. Remember when we were going over the game plan, we looked reality straight in the eye, and I told you Sir Paul said our journey will be a long and winding affair with ample ebbs and flows? Flowing out of my last epic ebb is not going to be undemanding for me. It's going to be hard, and I have a lot of work to do, but I am embracing the comeback effort.

And here is another issue with my regeneration project toward getting back riding with the gang. My diminished conditioning is only part of my challenge. Remember, I told you that four weeks after my crash, I was down to 158 or so pounds because apparently one's body burns a significant sum of calories when healing bones? Well, almost eight weeks later, I weighed in at 166! Yes, my homeostasis partner evidently in desperate panic to get back to our normal 160-162 weight range dramatically overshot that level. That's what they do.

For you see, we don't get to choose our homeostasis partner. Our constant companion was passed down to us from our long lineage of cavepeople ancestors, many who actually had to deal with those saber-toothed tiger creatures. Back before humans developed agriculture and those big, scary beasts were still running around, food was hard to come by, particularly when our ancestors were part of the food chain. It wasn't as if they had restaurants with golden arches three caves down on the right. Back then, given that hamburgers and fries were so hard to come by, their homeostasis partners always erred on the side of preventing starvation, thus packing on extra pounds when possible. Hence, the 166 pounds I am now carrying around.

Back when I could run with the wind, I knew that every extra pound I weighed was costing me two seconds or so per each mile. People would come up to me and ask how they could run faster. I would compassionately tell them to lose ten pounds and they could lower their 5k time by one minute. Usually, they just scrunched up their forehead and walked away, but that is reality.

I don't know how much each pound cost me on the bike. I am sure it's less than two seconds per mile, but we ride a significantly greater distance than I used to run in those races. And those extra four or five pounds alongside my diminished (but now steadily increasing) stamina is the reason my friends have literally been riding off into the sunset without me (of course, my age could have something to do with it also). And your additional pounds will slow your life down too, and depending on your overage, will cause significant structural damage inside your body. Your knees, ankles, and hips may already be telling you that.

However, I'm not a physiology major, but I know gaining back twice as much weight as I had lost was not totally my homeostasis partner's fault. I was the one who let the reins of the partnership go and watched the scale increase every week. Accordingly, with that green light, my homeostasis partner decided to pack on a few extra pounds in case I hit another pothole while riding my bike. That's what they do.

That is why I am reminding you of the importance of maintaining (and regularly monitoring) your hopefully healthy relationship with your cherished homeostasis companion. Don't let the collaboration reins with your partner go for long periods of time or you will end up putting on 30 pounds (or more) like I did after my marathoning days despite still running 20 miles a week.

So out of respect for my homeostasis partner, I have only gradually increased my weekly cycling milage back to normal levels. I definitely don't want to blow anymore gaskets. Also, I have downsized my daily salads a bit and decreased my evening main course proportions a tad. Nothing drastic, and my weight is beginning to slowly return to its normal range.

———

It's time to get back to our regularly scheduled program and start reviewing the *Dietary Guidelines*. But before we do, let me say this. When I finally sat down to write this book for you (it was in the conceptualization stage, seemingly for a century), I certainly did not plan on having a major bicycle accident, resulting in many broken bones. Although it wasn't voluntary (trust me on that), hopefully it's giving you a window into how all of this works.

You have now seen in real time how Sir Paul's reflection that life is a long and winding affair can manifest itself and how I am dealing with the potholes along the way. You, too, will encounter ruts in the road on your own journey. Straight-line progress toward a goal of improvement or simply maintaining a status quo plane is not reality. You know what they say about [insert four-letter word] happening. But do not get discouraged and don't beat yourself up or give up. Just stay the course and keep the gyros spinning.

Okay, back to the Guidelines.

GUIDELINE ONE: FOLLOW A HEALTHY DIETARY PATTERN

The first dietary guideline tells us what we already know: that we should follow "a healthy dietary pattern at every life stage." Okay, that sounds simple enough. I understand what a life stage is, but what is a "healthy dietary pattern"? Well, in their words, a healthy dietary pattern "consist(s) of nutrient-dense forms of foods and beverages across all food groups in recommended amounts, and within calorie limits."

This is starting to remind me of when I look up one word in the dictionary and then have to go look up another word to find out what the definition of the first word meant. I think my record is looking up four words before finally understanding the definition of the first one. I told you I am not exactly gifted.

Dietary patterns. First of all, the foods and beverages that we regularly consume from day to day make up our dietary pattern, and if you are anything like me, your pattern is fairly consistent over time for better or worse. Food groups, of course, are fruits, vegetables, grains, protein foods, dairy, and oils such as olive oil, vegetable oil, etc. (but not motor oil). Nutrient-dense foods from these food groups contain generous measures of vitamins, minerals, complex carbohydrates, protein, etc. That is, the essential building materials utilized by our bodies to keep us healthy.

The science has become compellingly stout according to the Guidelines that consuming a dietary pattern comprising nutrient-dense foods across all the food groups leads to numerous health benefits and reduces your risk of developing diet-related chronic diseases. Conversely, if you regularly consume high quantities of red and processed meats (juicy steaks, sausage, and pepperoni), foods and beverages loaded with sugar (candy bars and soda), and refined grains (white bread and doughnuts) detrimental health outcomes are likely to occur. Just eat mostly real food as close to the way it came off the farm. Your body will thank you.

Calorie levels. In general, maintaining a healthy dietary pattern will keep you within your appropriate calorie levels to support a healthy weight. Your specific daily calorie level varies depending on many factors, such as your age, height, gender, physical activity level, etc., and will vary over time. Your calorie requirements should also be guided by your need to lose, maintain, or actually gain weight. Back in Chapter 3, we discussed the Body Mass Index (BMI) calculator on the CDC website, which will give you a general idea which one of those categories you fall into.

In Appendix 2 of the Guidelines, you can find your daily calorie needs depending on your age, sex, and physical activity level, given that you are in the normal BMI range. Obviously, if you are above your healthy BMI range, you will need to consume less than your recommended daily calorie level or increase your activity level (more on physical activity levels in the next chapter). But I know from experience how exceedingly difficult, not to mention time consuming, it is to count the calories you consume.

So, as in Chapter 5, the best way to know if your calorie intake is above what your body requires to maintain a stable weight is to simply step on the scale periodically, as one of our game plan principles suggests. When I discovered I was 30 pounds heavier than I was during my marathoning days, I definitely made stepping on the scale a regular habit.

The Guidelines recommend that most, if not all, of your nutritional requirements (protein, carbohydrates, fat, vitamins, minerals, etc.) be met by consuming nutrient-dense foods and beverages. And I can attest, eating mainly a variety of real food across the food groups has worked for me. Only in infrequent cases will dietary supplements or consumption of fortified food be required, although Ponce may disagree. I'm sure he has some pills to sell you. Always check with your trusted medical provider for your specific situation, not Ponce.

Food preparation. Nutrient density in food and beverages is often determined by the way it is prepared. Adding sugar, salt, refined grains, and fat during the cooking procedure decreases nutrient density levels in food (and beverages). I grew up in a family that cooked collard greens at family gatherings (or were they mustard greens?). It's a staple down here in the south.

Generally, they are prepared by placing them in a pot along with bacon or a ham hock and lots of salt and boiling them for an hour (or more) until they are a mushy mess depleted of a very high percentage of their nutrients and loaded with a lot of stuff not particularly kind to your figure or heart. But that's just me. People down here love them doused with enough hot pepper vinegar to buckle my knees. Feel free to call me a wimp.

However, I cooked some collard greens a few years ago using my own recipe. I simply put them in a pot and boiled them until they were still slightly crisp. I took them out of the pot, sprinkled them with a bit of garlic salt, and the difference in taste was amazing, although they are still not my favorite food.

I'm not a food scientist, but I would wager my version was much more nutrient dense and contained far less saturated fat and sodium than the traditional method of preparing them. Another example of food preparation affecting its nutrient count would be fried green tomatoes (they are so delicious) versus the fresh tomatoes in my salad. I'm fairly certain you can guess which version of those tomatoes are more nutrient-dense. Thus, how you prepare your meals makes a difference how nutrient-dense and beneficial your food will be when you sit down to eat.

Meal portions. Okay, let's now talk about your meal portions. A while ago, when Eisenhower was president (okay, a long time ago), my hometown got its very first McDonald's restaurant complete with the golden arches on either side of the white, red-striped building. The sign out front told how many hamburgers the company had sold. I think they were up to 132 when I first went there as a kid. It may have been 132,000. I can't remember that far back.

Anyway, our brand-new McDonald's came with no drive-through windows back then. You actually had to park your vehicle and walk up to the counter, which was under the roof overhang. You couldn't even go inside the building unless you worked there. The bathrooms were out behind the restaurant. Life was so hard back then. By the way, our current McDonald's today near that original site has two drive-through lanes. Life is so much better.

The menu back then consisted of nine items: a hamburger, a cheeseburger, fries, a milkshake, three types of soft drinks, coffee, and milk. That was it, and none of those items were supersized, either. The original burger (that I think you can still get today) was on a regular bun and came with a few dabs of ketchup and mustard along with pickles and some chopped onion pieces. No lettuce or tomato to be found. The entire ensemble weighed about three and a half ounces and contained about 250 calories. About two and a half ounces of fries came in a little paper envelope and registered a bit more than 200 on the calorie counter. Sodas and shakes came in seven-ounce cups, and oh, by the way, there were no refill machines back then.

So, a burger, fries, and a soda totaled less than 600 calories and cost about two-quarters. Full grown people considered that a complete meal back then. Fast forward to today, when ordering a hamburger with two quarter pound patties with cheese, large fries, and a large chocolate shake, and eating and drinking it all, you would be consuming more than 2,000 calories in one sitting which is a full day's allotment for most people who are not active. And I'm not just picking on the golden arches people. Most all the fast-food burger, fried chicken, fried fish, and most other restaurants all have meals that contain a day's worth of calories. So please pay attention to your meal portions and don't overload the boat.

So, summarizing this first Guideline, try to regularly eat and imbibe a variety of mostly nutrient-dense (real) food as close to the way it came off the farm as possible and tolerable to your taste. I'll pass on the collard greens regardless of the way they are cooked, but I eat my share of spinach, broccoli, green beans, and cauliflower. Pay attention to the way you prepare your food, the portions you consume, and monitor your total calorie intake by visiting your scale at least once a week. And give or take a tweak here or there from time to time, consuming a healthy dietary pattern should hopefully remain remarkably consistent throughout your entire life.

GUIDELINE TWO: CUSTOMIZE YOUR HEALTHY DIETARY PATTERN

America is a richly diverse nation made up of people, from newborns to centenarians, from many racial and ethnic backgrounds, and from a wide range of socioeconomic levels. Thus, the Guidelines were specifically designed so you can "customize and enjoy food and beverage choices to reflect personal preferences, cultural traditions, and budgetary considerations" as the second Guideline tells us. Thank goodness I can choose spinach instead of collard greens and broccoli over Brussels sprouts.

The Guidelines do not tell you specifically what foods to eat but give you recommendations by food groups and subgroups. Let's take the food group of vegetables, for example. This vast food group is broken down into five subgroups: dark green vegetables (broccoli, kale, spinach, etc.), red and orange vegetables (tomatoes, carrots, etc.), beans, peas, and lentils (but not green beans) as one subgroup, starchy vegetables (corn, white potatoes, etc.), and all other vegetables (avocado, celery, mushrooms, etc.) that do not fit nicely into one of the first four subgroups like those green beans.

If you venture back to Appendix 3 in the Guidelines, you will find the recommended amounts of these subgroups that you should consume on a daily or weekly basis given your calorie needs listed in Appendix 2. I know, I know, this is beginning to sound a lot like rocket science. It would make my head hurt if I had to figure all of those tables out and I used to make my living putting numbers into those little boxes. For you more techy people, you can go to MyPlate.gov for some help. These government people are trying hard to help you and me out with their knowledge, tools, and apps. I appreciate them.

If you don't want to rely on high-tech apps (my hand is raised), just pick some different colored vegetables, some carrots and spinach, some kidney and fava beans, a potato or two, and maybe some cauliflower and onions to consume regularly and you're basically there. If your taste or culture likes garbanzo beans, great. If you prefer water chestnuts, go for it. My daily salad with its carrots, cucumbers, tomatoes, and spinach (even if I add a little less nutrient-dense iceberg lettuce) significantly gets me launched toward my daily vegetable requirement before I even get to my steamed broccoli, cauliflower, zucchini, and green beans in the evening.

The same strategy goes for the other food groups to include in your hopefully improving nutrient-dense dietary pattern. Pick a few fresh, canned, dried, or frozen fruits like pears, persimmons, pomegranates, or whatever your favorites are (and watch out for added sugar). Pick a few (hopefully mostly whole rather than refined) grains like brown rice, quinoa, and whole-grain cereal that you prefer. And choose a few proteins foods (the leaner the better), and some dairy (or fortified soy products).

I struggle with consuming enough fruits. Most every day that I was working at the widget factory, I would eat an apple, a pear, a nectarine, or a peach. But if I would have had Appendix 3 back then, it probably would have told me I still was not ingesting enough fruit. Hopefully, I was making up for it with my overconsumption of vegetables. Today, I even struggle with those apples, pears, and such. I purchase a package or two of strawberries, blueberries, or blackberries depending on which one is on sale when I visit the grocery store every week. And I have some raisins in the pantry. But still, I struggle with my fruit consumption.

I also have a difficult time with the dairy group. I just don't like to drink milk. The dairy cows I've seen grazing around have often thanked me for that. I have been trying to have some yogurt (watch out for the added sugar) with those strawberries for breakfast a few days a week and eating a piece of cheese most days. Sadly, I am not alone in falling short of the recommended levels for these food groups. We will talk more about this when we review the next Guideline.

So, let's talk about using herbs and spices to flavor your food to reflect your personal and cultural preferences while possibly (hopefully) reducing added sodium, sugar, and saturated fat to your meals. Way back when I was in college, I went to the home of one of my Indian friends for a dinner party. He and several of his friends also from India prepared some of their traditional dishes from back home.

I'm not sure how much salt, sugar, or saturated fat they used, but they certainly used a plethora of zesty spices. Cumin, curry powder, cayenne pepper, turmeric, they were all there. I'm not sure how my American friends attending liked the food, but I think my hair was on fire when I finally left the party. I know my taste buds were. But a good time was had by all, and it was a new culinary experience for me. I actually have some cumin and turmeric in my spice cabinet. So again, strive to employ herbs and spices to limit relying on salt, saturated fat, and sugar to flavor your food and beverages. And keep a fire extinguisher around in case something catches on fire.

When we were going over the game plan in the last chapter, one of the principles we studied was to focus on what you can control. I have been fortunate in my life because I have always been able to afford those fresh vegetables that I would later steam or put into my salad. I never have had the fanciest automobile, biggest television, or latest gadgets, but I've always eaten healthy enough to keep George and Voltaire happy.

To me, being healthy is significantly more important than having stuff. And while eating healthfully can be expensive, it can be affordable and fit within your budget. Hopefully, you remember that fancy recipe that we made more affordable by going over to aisle two and buying those cans of vegetables instead of fresh ones from the produce department.

Americans fall into a wide range of socioeconomic levels. If you fall into one of the lower levels, focus on what you can afford and seek knowledge (another game plan principle) from the USDA. They publish a wealth of nutritional information, including the Thrifty Food Plan, which specifies categories and amounts of foods that provide adequate nutrition. And if you are at the lowest of socioeconomic levels, their Supplemental Nutrition Assistance Program (SNAP) can provide you with nutritional benefits to help provide healthy food for you and your family.

Okay, this Guideline has been all about customizing your food and beverage choices. Let's look at a real-life example. A picture was in the paper this morning showing a new restaurant opening in the area featuring down-home southern cooking, also known as "comfort food." No matter where you live in America, I am sure you have your own down-home, comfort food recipes that may not exactly be the healthiest you could prepare and restaurants in your area that serve them. I have visited the New England area many times, and they have a few of their own down-home recipes that are totally different from ours, just as delicious, but not particularly nutrient dense and also loaded with salt, sugar, or saturated fat. By the way, is the big blue bug still hanging out somewhere just outside of Providence?

Anyway, the waitress in the picture was serving a new customer. On the plate were four pieces of fried chicken with a big plop of mashed potatoes smothered in gravy. That was it. Not a piece of broccoli, salad, or even collard greens, for that matter, in sight. The new restaurant also specialized in extremely rich pies for dessert that contained about 14,396 calories per slice. I can only imagine the salt and saturated fat in that chicken, mashed potatoes, and gravy, and let's not even add up the sugar level in those pies.

I would substitute the mashed potatoes for whole-grain rice, hold the gravy, please, add some green beans or black-eyed peas, a salad, and skip dessert. I would eat perhaps two pieces of the fried chicken that I so love (George said two were okay but not four), but if I did ever visit that restaurant, it would have to be a special occasion or only once in a month that featured two full moons particularly if I couldn't make those substitutions.

Guideline Two's summary, as it turns out, is virtually the same as Guideline One's summary. Just try to regularly eat and drink a variety of mostly nutrient-dense (real) food from all of the food groups as closely as possible to the way it came off the farm and tolerable to your taste by using the trial-and-error method. I'm sorry, I meant to say by making "tailored and affordable choices" to reflect your personal preferences. As with Guideline One, not much rocket science required here.

———

OKAY, before we review Guideline Three, let's take another timeout here or a short break from your building effort. Let me give you an update on E-bike Mike. He's alive and well! He is still out there riding, and I have even seen him on his standard bicycle a time or two recently. If he rides that bike full time, I'm not sure what we would call him. "Non-E-bike Mike" just doesn't quite have the same ring to it as E-bike Mike.

I'm not smart enough to understand half the stuff he talks about. I always ask how his riding is going, and he starts talking about torque limiters, suppression systems, group sets, bicycle geometry, and stuff way over my head, but he is entertaining.

He was describing one of his rides on one of our many single-track trails we are blessed with, streaking downhill when suddenly, he had to make a 90-degree turn. He allowed that with his girth (although slightly shrinking), Newton was not his friend. I actually got that joke knowing a little something about the laws of motion. Not many people out there can incorporate Sir Isaac in the punch line of a joke, but E-bike Mike certainly can. If you are not exactly the alpha physical specimen of the human race, just be like E-bike Mike and keep getting out there! And then go home and enjoy a tasty, healthy, and nutrient-dense meal.

———

GUIDELINE THREE: CONSUME A NURIENT-DENSE DIET WITHIN CALORIE LIMITS

The third Guideline tells us to "focus on meeting food group needs with nutrient-dense foods and beverages and stay within calorie limits." Isn't that what they just said in the first two guidelines? These guidelines are reminding me of that old song from 1960-something that went second verse (and the third), same as the first. Throw in my refrain concerning eating real food as close to the way it came off the farm, and we may have a hit song here. I'll have to look my rock and roll buddy up.

Sadly though, most Americans have a substantial amount of improving to do toward achieving a healthy dietary pattern and staying within their calorie limits. More than 80% of Americans do not consume enough fruits, vegetables, and dairy. I fall into that category in two out of the three of those food groups. And with all due respect to Meatloaf (may you rest in peace), in this case, two out of three is bad. And three out of three goes a long way toward explaining why most Americans are not in the best of health these days. Just so you know, I did just eat a couple ounces of raisins, and this morning, I ate a piece of that low-fat cheese. I'm trying Meatloaf.

Approximately 60% of Americans consume the Guideline recommendation for the grain food group. After all, we live in a country abundant with amber waves of grain. However, you do not need to use my childhood electron microscope (more on that scope in the next chapter) to peruse the data to clearly see that all is not well concerning our consumption of the grain food group. Over 90% of Americans consume enough refined grains such as white bread, pizza, pretzels, and doughnuts, but only two or three percent of us consume enough whole grains like found in whole-grain bread and cereals.

Why is that an issue? Because refined grains contain little to no fiber like whole wheat bread and, given the fact that 90% of Americans don't eat enough vegetables, explains why there are so many of those products to help move things along. Eating abundant low-fiber food like lots of cookies, doughnuts, and pastries and not enough vegetables leads to gunky pipes inside your body.

This is not breaking news. My fiber book spoke of how to avoid gunky conduits five decades ago. I don't want to get too gross here, but when I was 50-something, I finally forced myself to have a colonoscopy done. That was exciting, as I mentioned a while back, when discussing that liquid dynamite concoction.

By the way, before I get to the results, the American Cancer Society recommends that you get regular colorectal cancer screening starting at age 45, assuming you have an average risk, meaning you do not have a personal or family history of this type of cancer. Incidentally, the recommended age to have your first colonoscopy used to be age 50. That should tell you something about how well Americans are taking care of themselves these days (or not).

Despite being a few years past due for my assessment back then, when it was over, my doctor informed me that my pipelines were in pristine condition and continue doing whatever it was that I was doing. I suspect all those carrots when I was a kid, and all those salads and vegetables as an adult, had something to do with my exemplary colonoscopy results.

Moving on, significantly more than half of Americans consume enough protein, but you have to be careful here. According to our treasured Appendix 3, adults are supposed to only consume about five or six ounces of protein foods per day, not the entire sizzling 14-ounce, slightly trimmed sirloin off the grill, or worse, from the frying pan in one sitting, nor four pieces of fat-laden deep-fried chicken. Moreover, protein foods are also often consumed in casseroles, pasta dishes, and sandwiches that contain higher amounts of saturated fats and sodium.

Replacing high-fat, highly processed meats such as bacon, hot dogs, and salami with a six-ounce piece of baked salmon (since I can't afford it too often, I generally settle for tilapia) could lower your intake of those saturated fats and salt that most Americans consume far in excess of recommended levels. Sautéing a boneless, skinless chicken breast in a little olive oil is another good option. Also, beans, peas, and lentils, which were referred to as legumes in previous Guideline editions, have a similar nutrient profile as protein foods (if you want to go vegan) and can be counted as either vegetable or protein when striving to consume enough of these two food groups.

Once more, summarizing Guideline Three rhymes with Guidelines One and Two. Focus on meeting your food group requirements with mostly nutrient-dense foods and beverages that you enjoy consuming. Many choices populate all of the different food groups, so it should not be too difficult to find choices in each food group. Watch your portions, the way you prepare your food and beverages, and stay regularly in touch with your scale.

And give or take a few tweaks along the way, once you adopt an enjoyable and healthy dietary pattern, hopefully it will remain unfailingly consistent (or at least well enough to please George) throughout the rest of your life. Use the practice principle and the monitor and maintain principle from our game plan (Yoda has a monopoly on that other energy field) to preserve your health. And stay the course to continuously improve your diet incrementally.

GUIDELINE FOUR: LIMIT LOW-NUTRIENT FOODS AND BEVERAGES

The first three Guidelines have been all about what we should eat and drink. The last Guideline tells us what we should not consume, or at least mitigate. Guideline Four tells us to "limit foods and beverages higher in added sugars, saturated fat, and sodium, and alcoholic beverages."

According to this last Guideline, consuming healthy, nutrient-dense food and beverages across the food groups in the recommended amounts, and containing the least amounts of added salt, sugar, and saturated fat, will amount to about 85% of our total daily calorie intake if we stay within our calorie needs in order to nullify weight gain. Let me emphasize that last part: "...if we stay within our calorie needs in order to nullify weight gain." I know that is a big *if* for many of you, but it is so important. By the way, our next teammate that we will meet in the next chapter can certainly help us out here if allowed. So stay tuned.

So, given that information, we only have about 15% of our recommended calorie consumption that can consist of added sugar and saturated fat which amounts to only 300 calories give or take a few, depending on who you are and how much you allow your next teammate to participate in your game of life. They call this the 85/15 guide.

So, you can have one doughnut per day, but that's about it. Also, salt doesn't have any calories, but we all know about too much salt in our diet can lead to higher blood pressure, which can be a major factor causing chronic disease. And if you are more than two years old, you are more than likely consuming (about a 90% chance) far too much sodium, according to the CDC. Skip the potato chips if you had that doughnut.

Wait a minute, I just thought of something (as surprising as that is). You mean George and Voltaire got it wrong? The rule is really 85/15 instead of 80/20. Say it ain't so. Don't worry though, the earth has not reversed its magnetic field, and the sun is still the center of our solar system. You know what George would say? Dude, 80, 85%, same difference. If you are at the 80/20 level, or even the 75/25 level, you are way healthier than most Americans and Voltaire would also give you a thumbs-up.

Anyway, 300 calories (or even 400 if you are hovering in the 75/25 range) is not a lot to work with when considering how much sodium, sugar, and saturated fat to add to flavor your food to your taste. Let me give you an example of how I try to pull that feat off. One of my favorite breakfast cereal contains four ingredients: wholegrain wheat, flaxseed, barley malt (no beer), and a touch of salt (only six percent of my daily allowance) for a total of 220 calories per bowl. And by the way, that bowl of cereal contains more than a third of my daily fiber requirement.

But as we all know, eating dry cereal, particularly one that has no added sugar, is not the way most people enjoy consuming that morning staple, including me. I add less than four ounces of almond milk (about 50 calories) and slightly less than a tablespoon of purely delicious maple syrup (also around 50 calories) to make it taste better. So, dividing those 50 calories of delectable added syrup by the total 320 calories in my cereal bowl equates to about 15% (I had to use my calculator app for that division thing) which meets the 85/15 guide for that meal.

Okay, I will grant you this: that mathematical drill was not the easiest exercise to figure out, and I will also grant you that this last guideline is perhaps the most difficult recommendation to achieve. Most of us love our "comfort" food which normally includes significant quantities of gunky junk that clogs up our carburetors and conduits. However, most of the food and beverage products that we purchase do have those labels to help us with the math, so utilize them when making your food choices.

Let's speak a moment of those "Nutrition Facts" labels we have all seen on food and beverage products at the grocery store. The US Food and Drug Administration (FDA) has recently updated those labels to aid you in making smarter food choices. The serving size information is now in bold print and calories per serving is in even bolder print. Use these tools because they will work for you.

Quoting their more eloquent words, "the Nutrition Facts label helps support healthy dietary patterns by providing information on nutrients of public concern—dietary fiber, vitamin D, calcium, iron, and potassium—and on dietary components to limit, such as added sugars, saturated fat, and sodium." Go to fda.gov for more information. And please read those labels to make smarter food choices for you and your family.

So please, make a genuine effort to limit foods and beverages with high amounts of added sugars, saturated fat, and sodium and alcoholic beverages to only 15% of your total recommended calorie consumption each day. That is only about 300 calories, depending on who you are. George and Voltaire will be taking notes, but they allow a few indulgences as long as you don't go overboard, so keep an eye on your scale to make them happy.

———

To sum up the 2020-2025 *Dietary Guidelines for Americans,* the first three gave us guidance on the food and beverages we should regularly consume, and the last Guideline informed us of the food and beverages we should limit (but not necessarily eliminate) from our dietary patterns in order to give us our best chance of maintaining our weight and avoiding diet-related chronic diseases which pose major health issues for the vast majority of Americans today. Or as I put it, eat real food (that's safe) as close to the way it came off the farm or out of your garden, and as least processed (but properly prepared) as possible.

As I said in the beginning of this chapter, I cannot emphasize enough that the scientific evidence has become increasingly stout that diet-related chronic diseases pose major health issues for the majority of Americans. Please spend some serious time here building your new nutritional foundation from the ground up.

And, speaking of which, let's look at the exceedingly intricate and detailed blueprints for your new nutritional base. Yes, well, like I said, I'm an athlete, not an architect. However, it is simple and to the point, and I cannot overemphasize enough how important your nutritional base is to your health.

Nutrition (Fuel)

Please make a serious effort to genuinely get to know, and how to work more deeply with, your teammate Fuel by using the Guidelines. Both your healthspan and lifespan longevity depend on the depth of your understanding and cooperation with improving your dietary patterns.

And, let me throw in one more little tip that will hopefully help you get across the start line toward improving your nutritional consumption quality, particularly if you already take many medications. Think of the food you ingest as just taking another one of your medications. Many of you probably already spend a considerable amount of time procuring, organizing, and scheduling when you are required to consume all those medications, so just spend a little more additional time procuring quality food and beverages, preparing your meals properly, and enjoying your new "medicine." I will conjecture that your new "medicine" will taste far better than any of your other pills. And chances are, you will be able to eliminate some of those medications that you ingest in pill form.

And if you are not on numerous medications, take our old buddy Ben Franklin's advice that an ounce of prevention is worth a pound of cure, that is, spend time now improving your diet, and you will save a ton of money, time, and hassle in the future. Your healthspan will thank you and continue to grow along with your expanding lifespan.

Old Ben ate decently healthy for his day (he even dabbled in vegetarianism for a while), and he got his share of exercise (mainly swimming and lifting weights) back then between his editorial and governmental duties, and his hobby of flying kites in electrical storms. And the wise old sage lived to be in his mid-eighties, which was more than double the average lifespan back in the 1700s. Today, we would have to live to 150 years old to match that feat.

Yes, we are what we eat, and as a corollary, what we do not eat. Our dietary patterns are extremely important in building and maintaining our bodies and are the foundation of our health. Following the *Dietary Guidelines* can go a long way toward improving your health status. I know I want to keep lengthening my healthspan along with my lifespan (as you more than likely do) for as long as possible, and perhaps I (and you) can break Jeanne's lifespan record, or at least make it to the century mark.

By the way, I just read in the "paper" this morning that a little toy fox terrier named Pebbles (not to be confused with Fred and Wilma's daughter), is now officially the oldest dog in the world at age 22. Using the old-fashion algorithm of one dog year equals seven human years, the little pooch would be more than 150 years old, thus breaking Jeanne's record. However, I did some thorough research and according to the American Kennel Club (AKC), using the latest scientific studies, the little lady is only 104 in human years, so Jeanne is still the longevity record holder in both human and dog years. Incidentally, I'm not sure if Pebbles drinks almond milk or not.

Let me end this chapter with a serious reality check for me, and hopefully for you, too. Two of my friends died this past week, and you know how old I am, not even 70, which in my mind is not that old. I still need to be around another 50 years to break Jeanne's record. And if you are younger than me and think 70 is old, you will eventually know what I mean when and if you are lucky enough to get here.

One of those friends was a former high school classmate who sat ten chairs down from me at our graduation. We knew each other in kindergarten. I did not see her at our 50+1 class reunion a few months ago. Apparently she was very ill and now she is gone like the other one out of six of our former classmates. My other friend was a running buddy from long ago. Sadly, he was actually in a younger age category than me, and he now has already passed, too. Sigh.

Life is just too good, even in the bad times, to leave it so soon. So please, follow the Guidelines' recommendations the best you can and strive to keep learning and improving your dietary pattern. Use our twelve game plan principles and remember to stay grounded in reality employing our four reality checks.

Strive to stay on the well-being path by consuming healthy, nutrient-dense food across all the food groups in proper proportions, and please, continue on the journey with your homeostasis partner (and watch out for potholes) through the rest of this book, and through the rest of your life to improve and maintain your health. You can do this because you are worth it.

We have now met your teammate Fuel. We have built the foundation of the new, healthier you. So again, as that Ludwig guy said (which ever one it was), we are what we eat. And, as the Guidelines say, "make every bite count." And as I say (and George), "at least most of them." Your health is depending on it. But there is much, much more to do here, and more help is on the way. I promise. So, let's continue our journey!

CHAPTER 7: GETTING IN GEAR

I HAVE QUOTED a plethora of famous people, sort of, and here is a quote from another great philosopher of the ages named Bruce. Most people just call him the boss. He's the guy that used to ride through those mansions of glory in a suicide machine back in the day. Anyway, he once said that he was no hero, and the only redemption he could offer was in a pile of sweaty exercise clothes. I think that's what he said. I hear tell he's doing pretty well these days, so I'm going with it. And I know it works for Mr. Brady because he has produced a ton of sweaty clothes, and he has seven Super Bowl rings and a supermodel wife. I'm not sure how many sweaty clothes Mrs. Super-model has produced.

Regardless of whether or not Mr. Bruce actually said that, I'm saying that it is in the process of producing those sweaty clothes where deliverance lies. I don't have any Super Bowls rings, but after a long bike ride, I am emancipated from the stresses and uncertainties in my life, if only fleetingly. It's the afterglow of the flow I spoke of back on our virtual ride. I certainly missed that afterglow after my crash. But as good as it is, that afterglow I keep speaking of is not the major benefit of producing those perspired upon garments. More on this later.

It has been several years now since my dad passed away and once a week, I go visit my mom, who is now 90-something years old, and will soon pass my dad's age. Her mind is still sharp, and she tells me all these stories of events that occurred, and people we knew from the past when I was growing up. Frankly, I had forgotten many of those affairs, but not her. That brain of hers still functions robustly, and sadly, many of these updates she gives me regarding those people from the past are tragic simply because they could, by and large, have been avoided.

She was telling me the other day about someone my same age I knew when I was a kid who had not taken care of himself very well, and now due to poor circulation, his legs have turned blue and purple, and he had to have a couple of his toes cut off. I've already said this too many times here, including the last paragraph, but grotesque stories like this genuinely sadden me because, more than likely, these maladies could have been prevented. Not being a doctor, I do not know the specific and precise cause of purple legs (I think it has something to do with gunky junk), but if I had to guess, a poor diet and lack of sweaty clothes production had something to do with the amputations.

So, let us now get to know your second teammate, Hardware. When we briefly met all of our teammates back in Chapter 4, we learned that Hardware is our physical bodies, those marvelous physical mechanisms that transport us through our life's journey.

As you know by now, I only have scant knowledge of how our bodies actually function on the inside. However, I am like the race car driver who has no idea what is going on beneath the hood, but can drive the wheels off the vehicle, although I am certainly not suggesting you go out and attempt that. What I am suggesting is that you need to regularly take your physical hardware, that is your body, off the couch and out for a spin around the park or down the block, or even run a 5k if you have properly prepared. You want to incinerate as much of that gunky junk inside the engine as you can and keep all the gaskets pliable and sealed in your marvelous machine.

You are only given one glorious vessel to use on your voyage through life. Granted, you can switch out a few parts like knees, hips, hearts, and lungs (those last two usually in a last desperate, often futile attempt to prolong that glorious gift of life), but you only get one body. It can bestow to you immense pleasure or bequeath intense pain. I would suggest, in fact, highly recommend, taking care of that remarkable apparatus by properly fueling and regularly exercising it.

As we spoke of, humans evolved to move back during the cavepeople days (probably before) just to survive, as they were still part of the food chain. They also, like all animals, had that persistent necessity to consume calories just to continue living, so they had to regularly "exercise" just to find enough food.

Today, of course, restaurants, grocery stores, and even food banks are readily available for most people. Not much need any longer to burn numerous calories just to procure them. And last time I checked, we don't have any saber-toothed tigers to run away from, but we still absolutely need to maintain some level of physical fitness to keep all of our cylinders firing and free of gunky junk.

We all now know about leaving that car in the garage for a couple of years while keeping up with those Kardashian people, and upon finally taking it out for a spin, blowing that gasket thing. And, as we discussed back in Chapter 4, I'm also fairly certain that if you went out and tried to run that 5k after that period with no exercise, you would not only blow that gasket, but I can promise you this, your homeostasis partner would be irate with your behavior and repay you with substantial pain and soreness.

However, once again, as they did with our dietary pattern and food consumption, those fine government people at the US Department of Agriculture (USDA) and the Health and Human Services (HHS) are here to enlighten us why physical activity is so important and provide some guidelines concerning how much and how often we should get our bodies stirring.

This information is free (www.health.gov/PAGuidelines) and you don't have to buy any of Ponce's new outlandish (and highly priced) exercise equipment that promises you abs of steel after only five seconds of use per day. I hear his serpentine oil business is doing so well that he is expanding his brand into exercise equipment (and I'm not talking about those dumbbells, weight machines, and stationary bikes you see at the gym, which are a good thing).

———

OKAY, let's take a short break here, or a timeout, whichever you prefer. Let me tell you about my visit to the eye doctor yesterday. I have been visiting this place annually since I was the third baseman for my high school baseball team back in the last century. I will never forget the night I realized I needed a healthy dose of visual rectification, whatever that means (my thesaurus said to use that word).

We were playing in the district tournament down in the big town before Mickey got there and our team was up to bat. I was sitting on the bench next to the other third baseman on the team, and I'm not sure why, but he couldn't play that evening because he had visited the eye doctor during the day. He was sporting a new pair of glasses, and I asked him if I could try them on. He said sure and handed them over. I put them on, and I think I recall my jaw dropping and hitting the bench we were sitting on. It reminded me of when I got my first electron microscope I spoke of in our last chapter.

I remember taking the scope out of the box and plugging it in. A small nightlight-type bulb came on at the base of the instrument so you could better see your slides. That is an electron microscope, correct? Anyway, I put a slide of a bug or something under the scope and peered through the eyepiece. That insect looked immense through the scope, though rather blurry, actually very blurry, but I didn't care. I was so excited I ran to get my mom to come look.

She looked through the scope, then fiddled with a little knob on the side of the gadget and said, "Now, look." Who knew about focus knobs when you were ten? That bug was crystal clear, and when I put my baseball buddy's glasses on, the world suddenly became visually percipient again. I could actually see that, in fact, their center-fielder had two individual legs instead of a bunch of blurry ones. After the game, I told my mom to please get me an appointment with the eye doctor.

My eyesight hasn't gotten any better over the years (I can see the big E), so there I was today, decades later, filling out forms (that I filled out last year) as were several other patients sitting in the lobby. If they weren't pouring over paperwork, they were pouring over their phones. The television was on and there was a cooking show being broadcast, but no one was paying any mind to the silent monitor.

The luminary of the show, who looked to be in her mid-thirties, was preparing gourmet cheeseburgers. Her friend, about the same age, came over to help, and while the literally half-inch thick burgers were baking in the oven, they prepared what looked like strawberry milkshakes (that would make the golden arches people proud) with vast swirls of real whipped cream and served themselves in gargantuan tumblers complete with extra wide straws. As they sipped their shakes, they prepared heavily battered onion rings and fried them in butter.

When the burgers were done, they began construction of their towering sandwiches, complete with not one but two patties, three buns, and some of those butter-fried onion rings. Now, we all know about that famous sandwich shop with six-inch-long subs, but these ladies assembled burger ensembles that stood nearly six inches high. Dagwood would have been happy!

They sat down to enjoy their creations, complete with some kind of pastry dessert that was saturated with and baked (or fried—I couldn't keep up with the scroll at of bottom of the screen) in pure butter. Even if I have some of the details incorrect, the meal more than likely contained a full day's worth of calories, maybe two, and I can't even imagine how much saturated fat and sodium they consumed in one sitting, not to mention the sugar in the pastries and milkshakes.

Life is good for these cooking show people now, assumingly well paid, popular, and admired. And most of the cooking show personalities I saw on the internet after a cursory search, including our two cooking show ladies above, were, well, let's just say, a bit weight-challenged (and not on the thin side).

However, if you have been paying attention, particularly to our game plan principle concerning not being distracted by your youth, you now know where these celebrity cooking ladies consuming their six-inch-high burgers are headed as they approach their fifties and sixties with all that extra freight aboard. I will speculate that it will not be pretty and will probably be painful, and their lives will be labored. I have seen it happen before my eyes too many times.

I'm fairly positive they are not going to last nearly as long as the renowned Little Haven team did against Father Time and his cunning crew of cruelty fabricators. Well before they approach Medicare eligibility, their lives will more than likely become increasingly more agonizing (that arthritis thing for one), their schedules will probably be populated with more doctor visits than guest appearances, and I cannot imagine how many medications they will need to consume to stay alive. The progression of their healthspan will swiftly decelerate (or terminate) as the length of their lifespan continues to drag on into an ever-deepening mire of misery.

Anyway, about the time the ladies sat down to enjoy their culinary creations, I was called back to see my doctor, who knows my eyes well. As he examined my eyes (not my head), I told him about my bike crash and how much I exercise. Although I can't see because of astigmatism, he confirmed my eyes are actually very healthy for someone my age and that he didn't find any gunky junk in either. He began telling me how great exercise was for my eyes. I told him he was writing this chapter for me, and he said so many studies have been done, it's now widely accepted. Thanks, Doc!

———

BEFORE WE GET BACK to the sweaty clothes of Monsieurs Bruce and Brady, and the USDA/HHS Physical Activity Guidelines, let's further develop our sports-neutral analogy for all of you non-sports fans by examining our emerging, and oh so intricate, blueprints. Again, I'm not an architect, as you have figured out by now.

In the last chapter, we began building the foundation of the new and improved you by learning how to upgrade your dietary patterns by consuming more nutrient-dense (real) foods and beverages, and limiting your intake of the bad stuff like saturated fat, sodium, sugar, etc. I think those cooking show ladies used up their annual allotment in one sitting. Anyway, we are now going to build the first pillar of the new you on top of your freshly poured nutritional footing. And, you guessed it, this first pillar will be all about producing sweaty garments.

Now, I get it. A significant number of you do not even like to think about producing clammy clothes. Down here on the peninsula, all you have to do in July is go outside and you will start perspiring upon your clothes even if you are sitting in the shade. But just sitting in the shade (or in an air-conditioned room), whether secreting perspiration or not, will not help you get fit as a feline in the forest. You actually have to chase (or escape from like in the old days) that feline a bit to benefit your physical body.

Like that car in the shed, you have to regularly utilize your body, or you will lose many functional capabilities it once could perform when you were a youngster, and your quality of life will begin to wane rather dramatically the longer you remain physically inactive particularly after passing your prime as we have spoken of.

So, instead of dreading departing out into the great wide open and breaking a sweat as you take your cat for a walk, assuming said feline would actually allow you to do that, mentally tell yourself to embrace the serenity of the sweat you will generate as you depart outside as an ode to your health. That mental visualization assignment not working for you, huh? I never was good at that either. And I can assure you, I never saw George sitting at his desk by his campfire, mentally envisioning how to produce sweaty clothes.

However, as an ancient athlete, I know how important regularly exercising your vessel for life is whether yours is a dingy or a yacht like Mr. Brady's, and after sailing past your mid-thirties, I know how rapidly your physical abilities can deteriorate. After being off the bike for just 50 days, it took me over two months and many miles to again be able to keep up with my riding friends.

And just to update you, now that the last spring breaker just left the peninsula, I'm back down to my normal 162 pounds, which helps with keeping pace with my peers. Full disclosure here, I actually weighed in at 162 and four ounces at the grocery store last week, but I know George would say close enough, you're good, dude.

Again, please do not give up and conclude that you just can't get out there and get your heart pumping a little faster. I'm not a heart surgeon, of course, but I know it has a few valves (and maybe some gaskets) and keeping that amazing apparatus, that literally pumps your life's blood, running on all cylinders is so vitally important to your health, your quality of life, and being around to see your grandkids.

Forget the mental visualization thing, just employ our game plan principle to not be distracted by self-doubt. Be like E-bike Mike and get out there and go walk those 50 yards with your homeostasis spouse. Go seek some of that afterglow of the flow. E-bike Mike tells some of his best jokes after his ride. The enjoyment of life is too delightful to let it slip into the abyss between your healthspan and your lifespan. You can do this. You need to do this.

However, the afterglow of the flow following a bout of exercise, as wonderful as it can be, is not the main reason to tear yourself away from the *Kardashians* episodes and engage in an episode or two of physical activity. As the second edition of the Physical Activity for Americans states much more articulately than I have, "being physically active is one of the most important actions that people of all ages can take to improve their health." But no matter how you say it, the level of your physical activity will determine the strength and durability of the first pillar of the new, healthier you.

If you work with them, your teammates, Fuel and Hardware, can be magicians on the court against Father Time and his cohorts to give you a chance to head into overtime in your game of life. And just so you know, I haven't read every word of the 118-page Physical Activity Guidelines, but I don't think they used the term sweaty one time, so you won't have to employ any mental visualization drills.

In addition to disease prevention, scientific evidence is now strongly compelling that regular moderate-to-vigorous exercise improves your physical function, which enables you to embrace your day with more energy and less fatigue. Yes, that magical physical fitness dream, everyone's dream. And trust me on this one, the older you get, the more important physical fitness becomes in reducing injuries from falls, maintaining your mental capacities (and my friends say I need all the mental help I can get), and retaining your independence as you age.

Speaking of falling (spoiler alert: I didn't wind up in the hospital this time), I was ascending the three steps to the porch this morning and my right foot didn't quite clear the top one, and I came tumbling down on the same shoulder I landed on in the pothole debacle. However, I popped right back up. No harm, no foul. The point here is, my body is still agile enough that I didn't face-plant and need plastic surgery, though my buddy who said I didn't get any prettier after my pothole confrontation might be disappointed.

I still have the strength and balance to maneuver my body to minimize the force of most falls, the pothole incident aside. I learned how to tumble while diminishing bodily damage early in my childhood, and thankfully, because I have taken care of myself, I am still able to do that for the most part after nearly seven decades of water flowing beneath the bridge I used to cross going to Grandma's house. More on Grandma's river below.

And for you younger folks, improved physical function gives you more energy to take care of the nine million endeavors you have to execute every day to raise the kids, perform on the job, and take care of all the chores, errands, and household responsibilities you are tasked with. And at the end of the day, the quality of your sleep will be improved, and your dreams will be more vivid. Okay, I made that last one up about your dreams being more vivid. I just wanted to see if you were paying attention, but the Guidelines tell us that moderate-to-vigorous physical activity increases the time we are in deep sleep which that internet thing tells me we need to feel refreshed when we wake up and eager to go the next day.

Additional research is revealing that regular moderate-to-vigorous physical activity delivers many more health benefits including increases in cardiorespiratory fitness, stronger bones and muscles, decreases in anxiety and depression symptoms, the slowing or avoidance of many chronic diseases, improved weight status, and many, many more health and well-being benefits.

Apparently, your teammates Fuel and Hardware are in a fierce competition for your team's Most Valuable Player award, which benefits you all the more. But they do work so splendidly together. So again, work with them both to strengthen your new foundation of nutrition and the first pillar of physical activity toward building a healthy and happier life for you to savor. It can be done one meal and one step at the time, over and over and over again.

Before we look further into what we mean by moderate-to-vigorous physical activity and what kind of physical exercise to involve ourselves in, let's discuss, unfortunately, most everyone's favorite pastime: "sedentary behavior" which the Guidelines defines as "any waking behavior characterized by a low level of energy expenditure while sitting, reclining, or lying."

According to the Guidelines, most people spend over eight hours each day being sedentary, and truth be told, if I did the math, I probably fall into that category, also spending more than of half my waking hours in a sedentary mode. That's kind of what a person writing a book does, and no, I'm not going to stand up while I attempt to complete this manuscript. And here is the bad news. The 2018 Physical Activity Guidelines Advisory Committee (those science people who conducted the research for the USDA/HHS) found that sedentary behavior is strongly related to "all-cause adult mortality" and death due to cardiovascular disease.

But here is the good news. The risk of high volumes of sedentary behavior can be offset by generous amounts of moderate-to-vigorous exercise. I suppose that's why I'm still so healthy after spending nearly 40 years in front of that computer at the widget factory, putting all those numbers into little boxes. Sadly though, the Guidelines go on to say that a dreadfully small percentage of Americans achieve their recommended volume of physical activity; hence, our pandemic of obesity and chronic disease in the United States.

PHYSICAL ACTIVITY INTENSITY

I have mentioned moderate-to-vigorous exercise several times now, and what I am referring to is the intensity level of our activity endeavors. Okay, we are going to have to do some math here, so stay with me. I promise it's not hard, although I have my calculator app open on my computer just in case I need it.

To assess the intensity of our exercise, we need a unit of measure. All of those scientist people use something called a metabolic equivalent of task, or MET, and not to be confused with that baseball team up in New York known as the Mets.

One MET is equivalent to the energy you are expending while

sitting in your favorite chair watching another thrilling episode of *The Kardashians*. Now, when the next episode comes on, you recognize that you have already seen that particular installment, so since you haven't managed any exercise in forever, you decide to go out for a walk until the next electrifying edition comes on. By the way, I am assuming those *Kardashians* episodes last an hour, I have no idea.

Let's say you walked at a rate of three miles per hour (hopefully all the gaskets held up) and got back just in time for another captivating Kardashian edition an hour later. First of all, your homeostasis partner is going to be seriously irate with you, and again, you are going to hear about it for the next several days.

However, during your excursion into the great outdoors, you spent three and one-half times more energy during your hike than sitting there watching that last episode of those famous people being famous. Those scientist people would say that you participated in a moderate-intensity activity requiring 3.5 METs during that hour-long walk.

That is how to keep score of your exercise activity. If you are participating in a physical action requiring less than three METs, you are performing a light-intensity activity. Some examples include leisurely walking along at less than two miles per hour while listening to the songbirds, cooking, or washing clothes using a washing machine instead of a scrub board, etc.

If you are out in the yard mowing with a push mower, raking leaves, or playing a set or two of doubles tennis, you are expending somewhere between three and six METs which the Guidelines define as moderate-intensity exercise as you did on your three-mile walk above. If you are bowling, you are at the lower level of the moderate zone and if you are mowing with that non-self-propelled push mower, you are near the top of that range.

I have never done this down here on the peninsula, but if you are outside shoveling snow, you are burning energy at the rate of more than six METs, which is classified as a vigorous-intensity activity. Other vigorous level exercise includes running a mile in ten minutes or fewer, cycling four-minute miles, playing soccer, swimming laps, etc.

So, if you are performing a light-intensity exercise, you are expending less than three METs of energy, but at least you would be getting some exercise (that is what counts) and is vital toward progressing to being able to perform higher levels of exercise intensity. If you are executing a moderate-intensity activity, you are expending between three and six METs of energy, and more than six METs if engaged in a vigorous-intensity activity, or more than six times the amount of energy you would be expending when reclining in your chair watching those Kardashian people. Understanding the intensity level of your physical activities will help you assess your current physical activity level, which we will discuss now.

PHYSICAL ACTIVITY LEVELS

Okay, let's take inventory here. Let's pretend for a moment and say you spend all day sitting on the couch watching *The Kardashians*, sports, soap operas, news, or whatever else can be found deep down inside the bowels of cable television or your streaming service, I would sadly have to tell you that you are considered inactive because you are not getting any moderate- or vigorous-intensity exercise. Even if you went out and walked those 50 yards that your homeostasis partner allowed you to do, you would still be sorted into the inactive crowd, although walking those 50 yards is a good start toward advancement to the next level of physical activity.

Let's assume that you, like I did all those years, sit at your desk, bench, or workstation all day engaged in whatever your boss person requires you to do; not much physical activity going on there. However, once a week after work, you decide to bowl for 90 minutes, which we learned above is a moderate level activity.

Great, you are now getting some exercise and have moved into a higher level of physical activity! But if that is all the moderate level physical activity you otherwise get during the rest of the week, you still fall into the category of being insufficiently active, which means you are getting some moderate-intensity exercise, but less than 150 minutes a week.

But then one day, remembering that those 50 yards you ambled a while back felt decent, you decide to walk twice a week after dinner. You walk 100 yards that first evening, which your homeostasis partner reluctantly allowed. Over the course of the next several weeks, you work your way up to the point where you are trekking a mile and a half through the neighborhood in 30 minutes (the same speed you walked between those *Kardashians* episodes above). Congratulations!

So, when your new exercise routine becomes your norm, your physical activity level will be considered active by the Guidelines because each week you are now getting at least 150 minutes of moderate level exercise (90 minutes of bowling plus your two 30-minute sessions of brisk walking). I think I did that math right.

By now, you are feeling great, and by the way, so is your homeostasis partner. So instead of walking after dinner, you decide to run a couple of times a week. In close cooperation with your beloved collaborator, you jog for five minutes that first afternoon (before dinner). Just so you know, I do not recommend running (or jogging) right after dinner, though walking is fine. Just take my word for it. It is not fun.

Though a bit sore, you complete six minutes a couple of days later. The next week, you two head out for a seven-minute run, but you struggle, so your homeostasis associate fervently suggests to only run for five minutes the next time out. You willingly comply, and lo and behold, you complete this five-minute jaunt with gusto. You build up, consolidate, perhaps even take a step or two less, and build up again, incrementally, of course. That's the way we used to do it in the last century until we got to the running level where we wanted to reside.

Eventually, after many weeks, possibly months, you get to the point where a 30-minute run covering three miles is fairly routine.

Nice! And, as we learned above, running 10-minute miles is considered a vigorous exercise, so you get to count that effort twice because the Guidelines tell us that one minute of vigorous exercise equals two minutes of moderate exercise. So now, you are getting the equivalent of 210 minutes of physical exercise because your 60 minutes of running now counts as 120 minutes of activity plus your 90 minutes of bowling.

After several months of that routine, you get serious about your exercise program. First of all, you patiently add another 30-minute run to your week, and you have improved your bowling game so much that you've been asked to join a bowling league that bowls two nights a week for an hour and a half.

If you do the math and add all that up (calculator apps are allowed), you are now getting the equivalent of six hours of physical activity each week which includes the 180 minutes of running (three vigorous runs for 30 minutes times two) plus those 180 minutes of bowling for a total of 360 minutes. The Physical Activity Guidelines would crown you as a highly active person because you are getting more than 300 minutes of exercise each week. Good for you!

———

OKAY, let's take a timeout here to catch our breath and look at your new theoretical exercise program through the lens of some of our reality checks and game plan principles. First of all, you didn't part with any of your money for any of Ponce's products because you knew quick fixes are fantasy and fraught with failure.

You also knew, from the constant reminders of your homeostasis coach, that your long and winding journey from sitting all day at your workstation, then coming home to plop into your favorite chair to watch your big screen for the rest of the evening, that is, being an inactive creature, to transforming into a highly active, healthier person should happen slowly and incrementally, step by step, because you did not want to blow any of your gaskets.

Mel, who is incrementally teaching me to play the guitar, as you recall, would be proud of you, too. Incidentally, I can almost get through Mel's dumbed-down version of "Sor's Waltz" now without too many mistakes, and my playing is getting a bit smoother, but it has taken a while as your real journey from being inactive to active should to avoid blowing any gaskets, pulling muscles, and keeping your homeostasis partner happy.

Adding up all of those exercise minutes was a lot of math even using my computer's calculator app, so channeling another one of our game plan principles, choose a tool, app, or website (or just a pencil and piece of notebook paper like I did way back when and still do) that helps you with that accounting endeavor.

Many of you, probably most, are much more adept at using apps than I am, so I do recommend using one of these tools to motivate you and help you become more knowledgeable. Every cyclist I ride with now has a computer on their bikes calculating their effort and easily uploaded to track their progress. They are all shocked that I don't have one on my bike, but that's just me.

With all these wonderful new activities you are now participating in, your reservoir of free time is probably evaporating rapidly, particularly if you are juggling work, kids, chores, errands, etc., all of which are extremely worthy. You remember those pesky conflicting goals that Mr. Franklin didn't think were as cool as death and taxes when we were going over the game plan.

How many of you millennials have six hours to run around and bowl? Zoomers? Gen X (even if your millennial/zoomer kids are out from under your roof by now)? But don't leave your health in the closet for 40 years like I had to with my guitar. The guitar was fine, but you probably won't be after 40 years of being physically inactive. Find a way to spend some time on your own healthy behalf along with all of your other goals and commitments in life, even if it's not six hours every week.

Any amount of moderate-intensity exercise counts toward your weekly activity goal in pursuit of your improved health, so improvise the best you can throughout the day. Instead of parking at the front door, park as far away as reasonably and safely possible to get some extra steps in while you are shopping. Sneak in a five or ten-minute trek at lunch if you possibly can. A few people did that at the widget factory most every day, including me. All of these "bouts" of exercise, as the Guidelines call them, contribute toward the improvement and maintenance of our physical health.

And combine activities if possible. For years, I pushed my children around in one of those running strollers for hundreds, if not thousands, of miles, when they were little interacting with them and getting some exercise at the same time. They loved it and we all have fond memories of those days.

Okay, timeout's over. Let's get back to our physical activity discussion.

———

To summarize where our current physical activity level lies, if you are participating in no physical activity other than the basic movements of daily life, you would be assessed as an inactive individual. You are considered insufficiently active if you are getting some amount of moderate-intensity exercise each week (and remember to count your vigorous exercise twice, even if it's only for five minutes), but not more than 150 minutes. Active people get more than 150 minutes of moderate-intensity exercise each week, and highly active people surpass 300 minutes.

Progressing toward higher physical activity levels provides substantial health gains, particularly if you reside in one of the first two echelons. But remember to listen to your homeostasis companion as you move from one level of activity to the next because the risk of injuring your bones, muscles, and other bodily infrastructure (including your gaskets) increases the faster you try to scurry from one activity level to the next. We will be discussing how to safely engage and increase your exercise program while mitigating the risk of injuries in a moment.

PHYSICAL ACTIVITY TYPES

Let's look more closely at the different types of physical activity and exercise we have been discussing. Although those scientist people who wrote the Guidelines categorize physical activity types a bit differently than me, it's all the same. However, the most important point to remember is that it is vital to engage in all of these different types of physical activity which I define as exercises to strengthen your heart and lungs (otherwise known as aerobic or cardio exercise), bone and muscle-strengthening activity, and endeavors to improve and maintain your balance and your flexibility.

For the most part, all the activity we have been discussing so far, brisk walking, running, swimming, cycling, etc., is classified as aerobic exercise because our body's large muscles move in a rhythmic fashion and causes our hearts to beat faster and our lungs to breathe with more intensity.

We all know lifting weights and performing push-ups are muscle-strengthening exercises. Nothing difficult to understand there. However, only the muscles lifting the weight benefit from the activity. That's why there are all of those different weight machines in your typical gym. Each one is designed to work a different muscle group in your body.

If you don't want to use those boring weight machines, you can go climb those fancy rock walls in some gyms now. And you can trust me on this, you will work out just about every muscle in your body all the way down to the muscles in your little fingers after scaling several of those multicolored "rock" walls. By the way, the view is only a little scary from 20 feet off the floor.

The Guidelines separate bone-strengthening from muscle-strengthening activities, and I presume technically they are correct (they are smarter than me), but you just about can't do one without doing the other. That's why I lump them together. And many of these activities, such as push-ups, running, and weightlifting, strengthen both your bones and your muscles, not to mention your heart and lungs. I can promise you, if you can do 20 push-ups in 38.3 seconds, your heart and lungs will be working harder than they normally do, thus strengthening them.

You may recall my fortuitous luck when in my fifties, the gym I was frequenting began offering that yoga class. I cannot tell you how beneficial learning those stretching poses have been over the last 15 years or so in keeping my body flexible. I can still touch my toes with my fist when bending over. Being flexible means your joints can move through their full range of motion, keeping your body working closer to the way it did when you were twelve and reduces your chances of injury and pain as you proceed through the years.

While I don't do a full hour in class twice a week anymore like I used to, I do spend a couple of ten-minute sessions each week performing those key stretches. Maintaining your flexibility is far simpler than gaining it back once you start to feel like the Tin Man after he was caught in the rain and rusted up. And a squirt of oil here and there won't help you out, as Ponce proclaims. So, if you're feeling a bit like Dorothy's oxidized buddy, include flexibility endeavors into your physical activity program.

Pursue a class at the gym (as I did) or online, or assuming you know what you are doing, do your own stretching movements. But just remember, if you feel more like the Tin Man than the feline you took for a walk a while ago, the road to suppleness may take a while to traverse as it did for me, so seek knowledge from a reputable entity and be patient. It's worth it. Your body will thank you.

A segment of that yoga class I participated in back then included a few balancing poses. The Guidelines tell us that balancing activities "improve the ability to resist forces within or outside of the body that cause falls while a person is stationary or moving." Those scientist people have a way with words, don't they? I'm not entirely sure what all of that means except the falling part. I'm getting legitimately accomplished at that lately.

But all kidding aside, according to a study by the CDC released in 2016, every second of every day in the United States an older adult falls rendering the act of falling the leading cause of injury and death among older Americans. And sadly, these falls often lead to the end of independence for these senior citizens. Every day, ten thousand additional Americans are becoming Medicare eligible. And if you are not 65 yet, with any luck, you will be someday, so participating in balancing activities (and muscle- and bone-strengthening) exercises becomes more important as you age.

Although it is a superb balance activity, I would not recommend tightrope walking without a net even if the rope is only six inches or so above the ground. However, walking along a four by four piece of lumber laid upon and secured to the ground is much safer. The Guidelines suggest walking backward, but I am not keen on that suggestion, given I don't have eyes in the back of my head, nor the ability to turn my head 270 degrees like owls can. They suggest standing on one leg, which was involved in those yoga poses I engaged in during those classes. For safety reasons, if you feel a bit wobbly, perform your one-legged exercises next to a chair or table to catch yourself if necessary.

In summation, slowly work your way up to achieving at least 150 minutes of aerobic activity each week along with a couple of weekly sessions of bone and muscle-strengthening exercises that include all of your major muscle groups. And in addition, be sure to include balance and flexibility activities into your routine.

Even if you are suffering from one or more chronic diseases, increased physical activity can be beneficial to you, but always listen to your homeostasis partner, and most definitely to your medical provider before beginning any new physical activity or exercise regimen if you are indeed suffering from one or more of those disorders.

PHYSICAL ACTIVITY SAFETY

As promised above, let us now discuss what the Guidelines have to say about participating in safe physical activity. They tell us that physical activity has many health benefits, but "injuries and other adverse events sometimes happen." They definitely got that part right! Falling into a stealthy pothole did produce an adverse event for me while cycling. They go on to say that "the most common injuries affect the musculoskeletal system." Apparently, these scientist people have some sort of covert drone following me around. It's starting to get a little eerie.

Besides musculoskeletal injuries and bike crashes, they also warn other adverse events can occur, such as overheating and dehydration. Down here on the peninsula, the number one safely concern when performing physical activity outdoors is hydration, particularly in the warmer months of the year which, by the way, is most of them. That's why I carry two bottles filled with electrolyte fluid when I go ride no matter what month it is.

One morning, my friend who takes care of his bubble and I were riding on the trail, and we came across a lady lying in the grass pink as a freshly steamed lobster. As my friend began checking her pulse and pupils for dilation, her friend fortunately arrived about that time with a cold bottle of water. Tragedy averted. No matter if you're down here on the peninsula or Portland, Oregon (or Maine), or even in Anchorage, assure you are properly hydrated before and while exercising.

You're probably starting to think there's no way you are going to get out there and chance injury after hearing all of my stories, but trust me, physical activity can be very safe. Just understand the risk, which for most activities is exceptionally minimal. And choose exercises appropriate for your current fitness status. Also, as I have been preaching to you, listen to (but gently nudge) your homeostasis partner and only increase your physical activity gradually.

Additionally, whatever activities you choose, protect yourself by wearing the appropriate safety equipment. I absolutely always wear my helmet without exception when I climb aboard my bicycle. And that helmet has saved my life.

One morning years ago, I dropped off my car for my hippie mechanic to perform some major surgery on my vehicle. I had brought my old, cheap fat tire bike that a neighbor had given me so that I could ride the six or eight miles back home to avoid waiting all day at the garage. I was just puttering along down the sidewalk no more than eight or ten miles per hour when I saw a huge garbage can up ahead on the edge of the sidewalk. No problem, plenty of room.

Suddenly, as I approached the trash receptacle, I spied a Spanish bayonet on the other side of the sidewalk across from the can. If you don't know what a Spanish bayonet is (code name: *Yucca aloifolia*), it has leaves like daggers and can cause serious puncture wounds to your body when colliding into it. It was too late to brake, so I tried to squeeze through the gap between the two objects. I didn't make it.

I was paying closer attention to the treacherous plant, and though I thought I had the garbage can cleared, the bike's handlebar clipped it, spinning it out of my hands, and sending me overboard. Using the instinct I learned as a kid, I spun my body and landed on my back. However, my head violently whiplashed back and crashed into the pavement. I was a bit dazed, and may even have been knocked out briefly, but I was okay, no broken bones. However, the force of the blow had broken the helmet. If I hadn't had that piece of safety gear on, it could have been game over. My helmet gave its life up for me.

Also, assure that your applicable safety equipment for your chosen activity fits you properly and is adequately maintained. I most definitely had to give my helmet a proper burial and purchase a new one after the *Yucca aloifolia* incident above. And through all those years of running, I learned properly fitted, quality footwear is a must for avoiding unnecessary injury when embarking upon regular walking, hiking, or running expeditions.

But most importantly, high-quality, well-maintained safety gear is not going to help or protect you a bit, unless you use it consistently and correctly while enjoying your chosen activity. Back in high school (and Little League), I wasn't even allowed in the batter's box unless I was sporting a batting helmet.

And be mindful of the environment where you participate in your physical activity effort. Choose a well-lit and maintained park, for instance, when walking after work. I live in the lightning capital of the United States down here on the peninsula, and we have to be attentive to that phenomenon, especially in the summer months. I have run in a tropical storm before, but I wouldn't recommend that endeavor, particularly when power lines are lying on the ground all over the place. I told you, I'm not the brightest bulb in the stadium lights.

In summary, the Guidelines tell us to "make sensible choices about when and how to be active." Exercise in the cool of the morning or later in the evening instead of the mid-day. Swimming laps instead of running may be wise on an exceptionally sweltering day. Consider the air quality when being active outside as excessive air pollution, smoke, etc., in the air can lead to several adverse health outcomes.

And as I've already mentioned, stay in consultation with your health care provider concerning your activity level, intensity, and which type of activities are best for you if you have an underlying medical condition or chronic disease. I have seen people walking and riding who are suffering from poor circulation (purple legs) on the trail, apparently at the urging of their health care provider. As we have seen, even with a chronic disease, you can benefit from exercising.

So, now you know the basics. As we have learned, you know what types of physical activity you should perform, how much exercise you should achieve, and at what intensity level, given your current health and physical status. You have many activity options to meet the recommendations in the Physical Guidelines and any little morsel of movement will benefit your one and only lifetime vehicle.

But the most important mission you need to execute is to just get out there and start exerting some energy if you haven't already. Of course, it is best to start when you were eight months old like I did (according to Mom), but no matter how old you are when you begin, you will benefit from increasing your physical activity toward recommended levels.

Start increasing your exertion one step at a time the same way I have been approaching my guitar playing one note at a time. I still haven't perfected Mel's version of "Sor's Waltz" as I have mentioned, but again, with each new rendition I perform, and there have now been hundreds, the slightest granules of improvement are appearing. Yes, it's going to take a while, just as your journey to Healthyville will take depending on where you have to start. But just keep getting out there. Your improving health will be worth it.

And if you still have children at home, start them young. Feed them well, get them engaged in outdoor activities, and on their way to a healthy lifestyle. Take them to the park regularly, and let them be kids, the running around is good for them. And just maybe, they will continue their beneficial lifestyle for their duration of their lives. I hope so, and I know you do too.

So again, life is too precious to let it pass you by. I will communicate the same advice to you I did when we were discussing our nutrition, follow these Physical Guidelines recommendations the best you can, and strive to keep improving your physical fitness. Employ our twelve game plan principles on your continuous mission and journey down the road toward Healthyville. Remember our four reality checks and be on the lookout for Ponce.

So, to close this chapter, I want to leave you with one more story about that river I spoke of above. I used to go over the river on my way to visit Grandma, and yes, we did actually go through the woods to see her. It was truly a gorgeous river, free-flowing and crystal clear. The family of my boyhood friend that lived across the road (the one who was the natural musician and looked a lot like Mel) had a place out in the forest very near that gorgeous river.

One summer when I was about 15, his family spent a week out

there and I got to come along. Talk about a kid's dream. My friend was a year older than me, so he could legally drive. Every morning we would head down to the river, launch the boat, and off we would go fishing on that beautiful waterway. Despite not having any clue what we were doing, I think we did actually catch a fish or two.

One morning, we were drifting down the swift current of the river, casting our purple plastic worms into the clear water and somehow, I temporarily lost my balance and dropped my dad's nice rod and reel overboard. I told my friend that we seriously needed to go back and find that rod because I did not want to go home and have to tell my dad that I lost it overboard. So, we cranked up the motor, journeyed back upstream to where we thought I had dropped it, and lo and behold, there it was lying on the bottom under ten feet of crystal-clear water speedily flowing by.

To this day, I don't know how we did it, but using his fishing gear, we angled my dad's rod off the bottom, up through the current, and safely into the boat. Phew. It was a miracle. However, if that happened today, I would have had to face my father and told him what happened. While that would not have been a pleasant experience, my father would have been okay with the fact that I had owned up to the mistake and if I replaced the rod, which I would have definitely done. Of course, that was the summer before I started working at his grocery store, so at $1.60 an hour and only working on Saturdays, my first 43 paychecks would have gone to purchasing that new rod and reel.

Fortunately, the water was still crystal clear back then, but the next year, they built a dam across the river not too far downstream from where we were fishing that day. Today, that once beautiful river is a dark, sluggish flow of water with practically no visibility more than a few inches below the surface. The river has gone dark because the tea-colored tannic acid from the oak trees lining its shores does not get flushed regularly out to the sea because of the obstruction. Actually, the reservoir behind the dam covers the spot where we fished that day.

As beautiful as the river was back then, it did, however, have some minor issues. Truth be told, if I had dropped my dad's rod and reel overboard in the afternoon, we probably wouldn't have been able to retrieve it unless we had meticulously marked the location and come back the next morning to that exact spot on the river. I'm not sure if we could have pulled that feat off.

The gorgeous waterway could easily handle the osprey, turtles, otters, and alligators periodically doing their business in the water, if you know what I mean, and let's not even think about what the fish and mermaids were doing below the surface. But by noon, after many boats had gone up and down the river, stirring up the muck from the bottom and its shores, it resembled the muddy Mississippi. However, the river still free and swiftly flowing back then, could easily flush out overnight all the daily distresses inflicted upon it, and by the next morning, its water sparkled clear again. But not these days.

I don't want to get into the political aspects or whether or not the dam should be removed or not. The reservoir that was created by the dam, so they say, is home today of some of the best largemouth bass fishing in the world. However, due to the dam, mullet, striped bass, and manatees (mermaids according to Ponce) cannot migrate up the river from the Atlantic Ocean as easily (they now need human assistance) as they used to be able to when it was free-flowing.

I am telling you this seemingly unrelated story because I want to leave a stark, unadulterated image in your mind of what is very likely going on inside your body if you have not been eating a high-fiber, healthy diet (assuming you have no dietary restrictions suggested by your health care provider), and not getting adequate exercise. You are more than likely building tiny dams (or Hooveresque ones) all over your body clogging up your arteries, and shall we say your main waste removal system down in your intestines, not to mention hardening your valves, arteries, and gaskets. In other words, you are gunking things up inside, and it's the only body you are ever going to have. You need to take care of it.

Notice that I did not mention how big that river is. Its magnitude is somewhere between the mighty Mississippi and the literary brook running through the meadow. My point? Moving helps prevent clogs in the viaducts inside your body, no matter how large you are. Many studies have confirmed those who are overweight but participate in adequate exercise (like E-bike Mike) have better health outcomes in life than those who are thin and sedentary. Getting in gear and moving is important regardless of how much you weight. But exercise is not a get-out-of-jail-free card. You remember our running guy who died while running.

If your diet still consists mainly of consuming gunky junk and nutritionally barren ready-to-eat food with its added salt, sugar, saturated fat, artificial flavors, etc., no matter how much exercise you participate in, your chances of dying before your time are elevated. Therefore, please spend some serious time building your new nutritional foundation from the ground up if required, like Jolly-man Stan is now doing, and please stick with it.

And make a serious effort to get to know, and work more deeply with, your teammate Hardware, that pillar of physical activity, like E-bike Mike and his wife are doing (though they need to spend some more time building their nutritional base). Both your healthspan and lifespan longevity depend on the depth of your participation and teamwork toward improving your dietary pattern and prudently exercising. But just so you know, it's not astrophysics. Just eat real food (within your calorie requirements) and keep moving.

So again, as I mentioned numerous times now, the joys of life are just too delightful to squander away by perpetually eating gunky junk and sitting on your couch all day, every day, and missing out on the joy of attending your fiftieth (plus one) high school reunion (or your thirtieth for that matter) and seeing your grandchildren. Those easy chair, junk food consuming acts may be satisfying to you, but you are most definitely not gratifying your ship's hardware, not to mention your vessel's software that we will review in the next chapter.

But before moving on, let us briefly discuss your software and that other vital organ inside your magnificent organic assemblage besides your heart and lungs. It's the one inside your cranium, that is, your brain. You most definitely want to mitigate any gunky junk from accumulating up there the best you can, and here is a spoiler alert, that resplendent processor sequences code much more efficiently and effectively when you consume wholesome food and habitually exercise.

Starting to see a theme here? Great! Let's move on and continue learning how to preserve our awe-inspiring animated being, and in particular, our software.

CHAPTER 8: E=MC^2

I WOULD WAGER THAT 99% of people in the world have no idea what Einstein's most famous equation actually means. I am fairly certain that it does not mean that Elvis was twice as famous as Mariah Carey. But Albert was quite a character and exceedingly brilliant, so I wouldn't put it past his capabilities, even though Ms. Carey wasn't even born when he died. However, really smart scientist people have proven many suppositions that he long ago postulated, so who knows, that equation may actually have something to do with Elvis and Ms. Carey.

As you know, I'm not a theoretical physicist, but I think Einstein's theory has something to do with the faster, and faster, and faster, and faster you go, time slows down. I am not sure about Albert, but for me, time seems to just keep speeding up the more I try to slow it down. The other day I was getting my first real job at the widget factory and now I have a Medicare card; how did that happen? I guess it's too late to ask Albert. I undoubtedly wouldn't understand what he said, anyway. E-bike Mike probably could, though.

Speaking of theoretical physicist, I was watching one of those PBS science shows awhile back, and they were talking about how our universe has eleven dimensions. I'm not sure how all of that works, but they had an extremely brilliant academic person named Dr. Randall, who is a leading expert in particle physics and cosmetology —I mean, cosmology. Sorry, Dr. Randall.

Anyway, she was talking about the sixth dimension. I didn't understand a word she said, but I do know about the Fifth Dimension. They were a very famous R&B band in the late sixties and celebrated for theorizing about Jupiter aligning with Mars, love steering the stars, and the age of Aquarius dawning, which would then lead to peace, harmony, and understanding. I theorize those planets haven't actually aligned just yet, but more on that in Chapter 10.

When we briefly met your teammates back in Chapter 4, we learned that Software was that magnificent functioning organ located between your ears, that is, your brain. And you may not know this, but your brain is the most complex entity found so far in the entire universe. You didn't know you were that impressive, did you?

Your brain contains billions of neurons, which are little communication messengers that use electrical impulses and chemical indicators to transmit information via trillions of connections throughout different parts of your brain and entire nervous system. Talk about the information superhighway (sorry, that's such an antiquated term), that's what you have going on inside your cranium.

Like your heart and lungs, your brain is always on and taking care of affairs that you probably have no idea it has to undertake. That three-pound mass of gray matter is working much harder than any other organ in your body and consumes roughly 20% of your overall energy. Paraphrasing now from a National Geographic article for kids (I told you I wasn't that smart), your awe-inspiring brain (don't ask me how) produces more than enough electricity to power my electron microscope (assuming I still had it) with its 10-watt light bulb.

Your brain is not your heart, but it is at the heart of who you are. You don't want any gunky junk residing up there short circuiting any of your communication messengers and transmission corridors. Thus, like the rest of your body, your brain needs to be regularly nourished, exercised, and cleansed in many ways.

More on how to keep your cognition device clean and robust later, but I am sure you are aware of the many ill outcomes that gunky rubbish can inflict upon your brain. We will only talk about two of these hideous diseases, but hopefully that will motivate you enough to take care of your most valuable body part that cannot be replaced or done without like your appendix.

————

Before we discuss those software malfunctions, let's call our first timeout of the chapter, or take your first break from your building activities. By the way, we will discuss the next phase of your reconstruction mission shortly.

I wasn't going to tell you this, but 21 days ago, I had yet another wreck on my bicycle and re-injured my shoulder that was so brutally violated during the pothole incident. Apparently, things happen in waves. I hadn't had a cycling accident in five years, and now, I have had two in five months. My new friend Jolly-man Stan has now started calling me "Crash." By the way, he has now lost 51 pounds. He is becoming less and less rotund every week. Anyway, I suppose I need to expeditiously complete this book before anything else detrimental to my body transpires. Thankfully, I didn't wind up in the hospital this time.

I had already completed a spirited 30 miles with the group, and was attempting to achieve another chilled 20 miles, riding alone, and enjoying the delightful morning. I came down a hill and around a corner when a group of riders coming my way appeared. However, another cyclist, all of a sudden, came blowing past them, heading straight toward me.

It all happened in an instant. When the passing rider and I looked directly at each other, we were like two deer in the headlights. Neither of us could decide which way to maneuver. Fortunately, we didn't hit head-on, but rather viciously sideswiped each other. Unfortunately, we struck left side to left side, which, as you will recall, was the scene of the crime in the pothole debacle. If we had hit on our right sides, I would have been fine.

The force of the blow didn't actually knock me down, but I voluntarily collapsed in the grass along the trail, and just howled out of frustration, because I knew what I was going to have to deal with over the next few weeks. As it turned out, it was one of my best riding buddies that I had "brushed" against, and he is sturdily put together.

He was so distraught, but I assured him that I was okay. Thankfully, he lived close by and hastily pedaled home to get his car while I slowly trudged my way a half mile down the track to a picnic area where he picked me up. Thoughtfully, he brought me an ice-cold bottle of water and an ice pack for my shoulder. He loaded my bike into his vehicle, and we drove back to the main parking lot ten miles away where my automobile was parked.

After he reloaded my bike into my vehicle, I assured him again that everything was going to be fine and not to worry. After my initial scream of exasperation, nothing was to be gained by being upset. I just needed to focus on what was to be done, initially to figure out if I could drive my standard transmission automobile back home. Fortunately, I managed that challenge.

So today, three weeks later, I climbed back aboard my bicycle to access how my body would respond. The ride went very well, and thankfully, I had lost only a minimal amount of conditioning for several reasons.

First of all, I resided on a much higher fitness plane when this last accident occurred than I inhabited when the pothole incident transpired. Also, I wasn't quite as beat up this time, so I could immediately continue exercising. Over the past three weeks, I have averaged more than five hours per week briskly walking through the forest, and yes, I had some interesting encounters with several furry forest creatures during those hikes, and I'll tell you about one in particular in a moment.

I also managed to execute a couple hours of bone and muscle-strengthening exercises along with some flexibility activities over the past three weeks. During my last session yesterday, I could not quite do my push-ups, but I could do my sit-ups, planks, and back exercises. I can gently curl my ten-pound weight with my sore shoulder, but I can't press the weight over my head just yet. So, I am almost back to performing my regular, twice weekly, half-hour stints of those various activities.

Finally, during those three weeks, I actually lost twelve ounces. Remember George said it was okay if I weighed four ounces more than the high end of my normal 160-162 range? Well, when I weighed in at my usual time a couple of days ago on the iconic weight scale at my grocery store, I tipped the dial over to 161.5 pounds. As we have discussed, less mass equals more power on the bike. I think Sir Isaac said that. I'll have to ask E-bike Mike someday. Anyway, those hiking excursions did their job incinerating calories, and just so you know, I didn't change my diet.

In the last chapter, we spoke of safely participating in physical exercise, and it is that time of the year here on the peninsula when it begins to markedly heat up but with little rain until our regularly scheduled afternoon thunder squalls, tropical storms, and hurricanes commence. I think it has only rained once during these past three weeks, and the forest is extremely dry.

On one of my excursions, after having sufficiently hydrated, I was well into my hike and headed back to my starting point, walking along a clay road the Forestry Service had built to do some logging. I came around a corner and up ahead, a black bear was lying in the road where a puddle normally exists, but now contained no water, just moist clay.

The bear looked at me and lethargically stood up. So as that discretion versus valor decision was racing through those trillions of transmission lines in my brain, I took a small step backward while trying to decide my next move. Apparently seeing I wasn't an imminent threat, the bear listlessly plopped back to the ground. I think the poor beast was just exhausted from the heat and dehydration.

Just so you know, again in the name of safely participating in physical activity, I did have a bear protection device with me, otherwise known as a three-wood. My three-wood is actually made out of wood, having purchased it 50-something years ago. For non-sports fan readers, a three-wood is one of those stick things golfers use to hit their golf balls.

Fortunately, I didn't need my safety "stick" this time. Black bears around these parts have charged people, but must of the time, they use that discretion thing over valor and head back into the woods. However, since he was evidently exhausted, I chose the valor path for him, used discretion by rerouting my course, and let him lie. Fortunately, the rest of my journey was uneventful, even though I kept looking over my shoulder. So just as a reminder, stay safe while exercising, assure you are well hydrated, and watch out for black bears, potholes, and my buddy's shoulder.

———

OKAY, back to the action. For you non-sports fans, now is time to continue fabrication of the new healthier you according to our sports-neutral analogy building plans. The next component of our construction will be a second pillar placed in the center of your nutritional foundation and next to your first column of physical activity.

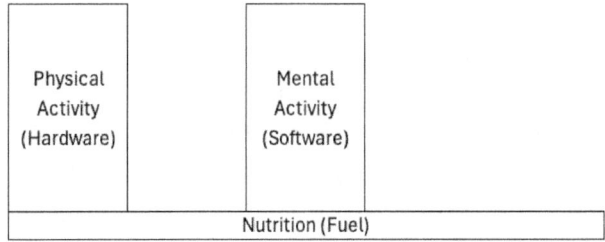

Your brain is most definitely the load-bearing center post of who you are, and as we shall see, the pillar by far the most protected. That most complex entity is your only body part that has its own built-in helmet; that is, your skull. So, I guess Mr. Brady (of course, assuming he is in fact human) actually wears two helmets when he goes off with his buccaneers to battle Ponce and his conquistadors.

As we briefly spoke of above, many ill outcomes can manifest themselves inside our most valuable and supremely complex organ as we age. Just by the sheer number of neurons, neurotransmitters, and communication pathways in our brains, malfunctions will occur as we continue our journey down our long and winding path through life. Everyone knows about all those potholes that occur on our millions of miles of roads in American (I know about one in particular), and the same thing occurs in that crown jewel between our ears. Let's briefly look at only a couple of the most common brain illnesses that can ravage and pillage who we are and the ones we love.

Today, millions of Americans suffer from some type of dementia, which is a general term for those with an impaired ability to think, remember, and make decisions concerning their everyday activities. The severest stage of dementia leads to total dependence on others for basic daily living activities.

Alzheimer's disease, which makes up somewhere between 60 and 80% of dementia cases and affects mostly those over 65, is currently ranked as the sixth leading cause of death among adults in the United States. And sadly, that number is increasing. Approximately six million Americans now suffer from Alzheimer's, which is more people than live in Los Angeles.

When I was growing up and struggling with the concept of death, I thought humans should grow to a certain point mentally, and then go backward so they wouldn't know they were about to die. Little did I know when I was eight or nine that diseases of this nature already existed. Dementia, in all of its forms, is such an insidious, cruel disease.

I have a friend I knew at the widget factory, and I still occasionally see him on the bike trail. His mother is slipping ever deeper into the clutches of Alzheimer's. Coincidently, I worked with her before I got the job at the widget factory, and every time I saw my friend, I would ask him to tell her hello for me. She was such a sweet lady. The last time I saw him a couple months ago, I asked if she would remember me. He said no, she barely recognizes him. It breaks my heart. I also watched my intelligent grandmother slip into the bowels of the dark abyss. Sigh.

Moving on from dementia, according to the CDC, every 40 seconds someone in America suffers from a stroke which equates to about 800,000 people annually, and sadly, 135,000 or so die. Approximately three-quarters of those folks are having a stroke for the first time while the rest are suffering through another one, usually within five years of their first. Almost 90% of these strokes are caused by a blockage of blood flow to the brain. Also, strokes are a leading cause of serious long-term disability and reduces mobility for more than half the folks over 65 who are stricken. Horrible stuff.

And by the way, if you or someone with you starts showing the signs of having a stroke, immediate action is imperative. Do not hesitate to call 9-1-1. According to the CDC, the chances of survival are highest when emergency treatment begins promptly, and if patients suffering from a stroke arrive at the emergency room within three hours of the first symptoms, the chances of disabilities are lessened. Know the warning signs and symptoms of stroke and act immediately.

Many other afflictions can harm or impair our brain, some of which we cannot prevent, such as those because of our family history, but many that we can, or at least mitigate. So, what can we do to avoid as many of these cerebral disorders as possible?

EAT WELL AND EXERCISE

According to those way-smarter-than-me scientist people from the National Institute of Health (NIH), many protective factors that reduce cardiovascular risk, namely participating in regular exercise and consuming a healthy diet that we have spoken of in the last two chapters, seems to also support the health of our brains as we all inevitably age. Increasing our cognitive effort and training also seems to be beneficial, as we shall review a bit later. In summary, leading a healthy lifestyle the best we can, both physically and mentally, may be our best protection in preserving our aging brains.

Swinging back to dementia for just a moment, the people from the www.alzheimers.gov website warn us to watch out for false Alzheimer's cures. To quote, "Although you might see commercials or online advertisements for products promising to improve brain health and prevent dementia, be cautious about such products." They didn't specifically name Ponce, but apparently, he is on their radar. So, it's not just me warning you about the misadventures of our conniving conquistador!

Thus, while no product currently exists to effectively avert or treat Alzheimer's and other related dementias (although the former richest computer guy in the world, Mr. Gates, is on a crusade to find a cure along with many other scientist people), if you are diagnosed with one of these diseases, medications can help manage your symptoms. Working closely with your medical and healthcare team provides your best chance for early and accurate diagnosis, optimal treatment plans, and to anticipate future care needs for you and your family.

Those smart scientist people from the NIH tell us that besides participating in regular exercise and consuming a healthy diet to support the health of our brains as we grow older (searching my thesaurus for a more interesting word than older, it told me to use hoarier, but I rejected that suggestion), increasing our cognitive effort and training also seems to be beneficial in our quest to keep our cranial computer and software healthy.

So how can we increase our cognitive effort and training, and what else can we do to increase and maintain our cerebral computer's function and well-being? Please continue with me on our journey.

DOING A HARD THING

I was reading an article published by some seriously intelligent people from the Harvard Medical School, and they said our brains have the ability to learn and grow as we get older because our gray matter is capable of neuroplasticity which is basically the brain's ability to transform its trillions of transmission passageways and rewire itself in response to our experiences in life.

Think of the brain of a toddler. Neuroplasticity is most rapid and prolific in the first five years of a child's life as they enthusiastically absorb the new biosphere they have been immersed into. Their little brains are relentlessly, seemingly at light speed (ask Albert or E-bike Mike what that is, not me), changing as you watch them transfigure right before your very eyes on a day-to-day basis.

Their young cranial software systems are rapidly being coded and recoded at hyper-drive speed (warp speed for my generation) as they form, cast out, and reform habits, behaviors, and routines. By the time they are three or four years old, they have practically mastered a foreign language, as crying is their native language the day they were born.

And here is the good news. Our brains never lose this extraordinary capacity to transform itself, no matter how long we are fortunate enough to live. However, just as we need to routinely exercise our physical ship as we sail through life, we also have to consistently engage our cognitive functions with new and reasonably challenging endeavors. Jeanne told me when she was 115, she was thinking about learning to speak Spanish since France was so close to Spain.

Those Harvard people suggested selecting a demanding activity that you are interested in learning and practicing as a great way to increase (and keep) your cognitive skills and capabilities. One example of a demanding activity they suggested was to embrace "learning an instrument."

I'm not sure if they were talking about learning to use their

Magnetic Resonance Imaging instrument, or their Dual Energy X-ray Absorptiometry contraption, but I think I will just keep learning to play my guitar. Mel said he would keep teaching me, although I have seen him close his eyes at times and just shake his head.

That grit lady, Dr. Angela Duckworth, made her kids do a hard thing when they were growing up. And she's significantly smarter than I am; in fact, she is a certified genius, so doing a hard thing must be a valuable undertaking. She let her children pick their own pursuit that involved daily practice, and they had to stick with their chosen challenging activity for an entire year or until they came to a natural stopping point in their extracurricular expedition.

Getting back to those Harvard people, like Dr. Duckworth, they suggest pursuing an endeavor that requires thought, continuous learning, and committed practice can be one of the best approaches in keeping our brains healthy. Sound familiar? As always, channel our reality checks and game plan principles when initializing your effort to learn your chosen hard thing.

If you don't want to learn how to use their Dual Energy X-ray Absorptiometry apparatus, you can choose to learn the piano, or violin, or ukulele for that matter. If you don't like music, you can learn a new language, take up painting pictures, learn to cook beyond heat until bubbly (or just microwaving you know what), or restore old hot rods.

I don't know if this writing thing is making my neurons any healthier, but truth be told, even though it's hard, I have enjoyed writing again now that I finally have some time to pursue it. However, Mel is now killing me with some harmonized scales even though I still haven't mastered "Sor's Waltz." After struggling with certain passages, I sometimes involuntarily blurt out, Mel, you're hurting my head. He again just closes his eyes and shakes his head. I think I heard him audibly sigh this morning.

But just remember our game plan principle concerning conflicting goals. Don't pick 18 different extracurricular pursuits and expect to master any of them. Depending on your available time, chose only one or two. I have some time now, so I picked two pursuits, writing, and learning to play the guitar, but learning Spanish (since several of my riding friends are Hispanic), painting pictures in oils, and improving my chess game are waiting in the wings.

And if you are at that stage in your life where you barely have time to breathe, even five minutes a day pursuing your personal hard thing can benefit your well-being, not to mention your sanity. Write a paragraph in your diary or sketch a couple of pictures in your sketch book during a moment of downtime, even if it's only for five minutes. I keep one of my two guitars by my bed and try to get an extra five or ten minutes of practice in before retiring for the evening.

FIND YOUR FOCUS KNOB

Okay, here is a test. How many of you have not touched your phone in the last 14.343 seconds (assuming, of course, that you are not reading this book on your cell phone)? Is your television or computer screen on? How many times have you switched your attention back and forth to each device? A while back, some Boston College scientists performed a study that had people in a room with both a television on and their computer. They found their test subjects switched their eyes back and forth between screens every 14 seconds.

Back when I was working at the widget factory, a young millennial colleague (who, by the way, I got along with very well) sitting next to me was analyzing some numbers on his computer screen, checking his text messages, listening to a podcast, and eating a snack. I chuckled at the scene and told him he was a multitasking fiend. He said of course, that's what we do. That resulted in a good-natured debate about whether or not our brains could actually multitask or not.

From the research I have done, those cavepeople back before I was even born (and Jeanne, for that matter) had to multitask at times. On hunting and gathering expeditions through the forest, when one of those saber-toothed tigers suddenly appeared on the scene with menacing teeth exposed (after all, that is what they were famous for), not only did those cavepeople have to flee for their lives, but they had to hold on to the berries they had collected, be sure they didn't run into a tree or step in a pothole, and make sure they were running faster than the cave person behind them so that they wouldn't become a tasty feline hors d'oeuvres. That was multitasking at its best right there in order to just stay alive. I would like to see my millennial colleague top that!

Anyway, the NIH published an article a while back by two PhD people, and they said that our brains lack the architecture to perform two or more tasks simultaneously, and that we inflate our ability to multitask. Take that, my millennial colleague! The boomer strikes back! Truth be told, I do miss seeing that dude everyday now that I have retired from the widget factory.

In addition, those two PhD people from the NIH also said that we barely notice we are multitasking. I usually "watch" either a news program or bicycle racing (like the Tour de France) when I am preparing my meals. Have you ever been updating your Facebook page while talking to a friend on the phone? I can truthfully say I have never done that since I am one of the 14 people (or is it only 13 now) in the world that doesn't have a social media account.

Our PhD professors went on to say that frequently switching between two (or more) tasks almost always takes longer to complete them than if we worked on them individually, and normally the completed tasks done simultaneously include more errors. And truth be told, it takes me longer to prepare my meals when multitasking between that endeavor and watching the bike race.

And here is the scariest multitasking example for me as a cyclist. Have you ever read and sent text messages while driving? When I acquired my beloved bike several years ago, our beautiful, paved 15-mile closed track had not been built, so I had to either ride on the roads or through neighborhoods. I was petrified the first time I rode out amid traffic with a group of other cyclists, but I always thought that if I did get hit by a vehicle, it would be from behind. But the two closest times I have nearly been struck by speeding vehicles, it has been head-on.

Back during the initial COVID-19 lockdown, I was out riding solo on my side of the road and entering a gentle left-hand turn. A dude driving a semi-guided missile, otherwise known as a speeding pickup truck, was entering the turn from the other direction and apparently had been watching too many NASCAR races as he was coming out of the turn using all the road including my side. I immediately ditched the bike, and just before sailing through the grass trying to stay upright, I noticed he was looking at his phone. I'm not sure if he was texting or not. It was a good thing another vehicle wasn't coming behind me or I could have witnessed a pile up in turn three between those two vehicles.

But the scariest incident I have been involved in on the bike was on a group ride down a busy, two-lane country road that fortunately had a wide shoulder. I was the ninth rider of ten and well right of the white line (of course, we were riding with traffic) when someone up front yelled. When that happens, normally an accordion effect (like I mentioned on our virtual ride) makes its way back through the Peloton. And when the lady in front of me hit her brakes authoritatively, I also braked, turned slightly to the left, and barely crossed the white line into the traffic lane in an effort to avoid hammering her.

After narrowly evading my friend, I found out what the yelling up front was about. When I looked up, a huge, heavy-duty pickup truck hauling a swaying trailer at 60-something miles per hour was passing another vehicle just feet in front of me. My brain somehow, within a split second, processed that the truck would not annihilate me, but I knew it was going to be close. I literally came within six inches of being totally obliterated, and no, my life did not flash before my eyes.

I felt the surging wind, provoked by the passing truck, gush by me seemingly with hurricane force, which, yes, living on the peninsula, I have experienced. The big guy riding behind me told me he could see the truck would not hit me, but he wasn't so sure about the vacillating trailer. But enough about my near life-ending calamities.

However, just to wrap that subject up, no, you do not feel most alive when you are closest to death. I've been there. Yes, adrenaline surges through your veins, triggering your fight-or-flight response. But staring into the headlights of a four-ton truck barreling down upon you, despite the release of the happy hormones, endorphin and dopamine, along with the adrenaline (the underpinning substances of the afterglow of the flow), does not construct a most peaceful, easy, and animated disposition. At least it didn't for me, nor my two riding friends. The three of us rode in silence for a mile or so just trying to gather ourselves together and wrap our heads around what had just happened. As the peloton faded off into the distance, instead of feeling most alive, we were just relieved we were still living.

I would argue that experiencing our hearts and lungs dynamically pumping our life enhancing blood and oxygen throughout our bodies during aerobic exercise along with the abundant release of those happy hormones, but with a sparing of the intense adrenaline surge that peril evokes, experiencing the joy of the effort and the afterglow of the flow without the eminent danger of sudden termination, makes you feel most alive. It's as close as you are going to come to feeling like a kid again.

I would also argue that you feel most alive when sharing space and experience with a loved one, workmates, or with friends. Or helping someone less fortunate than yourself. I would wager those experiences are some of your fondest memories. But full disclosure here, these last few paragraphs are based on my personal experience and not from research by any of those scientist people.

Anyway, back to my screen-switching, media-multitasking colleague. As you know, televisions, tablets, media displays, and video screens are everywhere, with that phone sitting by you or in your hand being the most ubiquitous and all those digital agents are vying for your fragmented attention. They even have media screens on gas pumps today. Seriously? Do I really need to be entertained or enlightened while refueling my automobile?

Our two PhD professors found that today's youth spend an average of seven or eight hours absorbing various forms of digital media and about a third of that time is spent switching back and forth, multitasking between screens. And America's youth, including my millennial colleague, are not alone.

According to those scientist people from the American Psychological Association (APA), almost 90% of all American adults constantly or often check their smartphones, social media accounts, and other media devices, which is linked to significantly higher levels of stress in their lives. And the continual switching may actually alter how your brain functions and deteriorating your ability to focus and learn due to an ever-shrinking attention span and intolerance of boredom.

According to Cal Newport, the PhD who has written extensively on working deeply, fragmented attention leads to exhaustion and anxiety. It makes me want to just scream, "Stop! You're killing yourself!" But that's not my place in your life. However, those APA experts have found that two out of three of you actually agree with me that you should mitigate your multimedia intoxication, but less than a third of you actually attempt to do anything about your elevated stress level, fragmented attention, and inability to concentrate and stay focused.

As my theory postulates, all this stress, anxiety, and exhaustion probably goes a long way in explaining why Mars and Jupiter haven't quite aligned just yet and the age of Aquarius hasn't dawned. According to the CDC, stress can lead to a litany of mental health issues from fear, anger, and sadness to difficulties in concentrating, sleeping, and singing. Okay, scratch singing (it's actually beneficial to your psyche). As you know, I like to make sure you are paying attention because of the consequences of these matters we are discussing. And if you are already suffering from any chronic diseases or mental conditions which most Americans are, stress can worsen your condition.

You will remember the first time I looked at that bug through my electron microscope. Even though I thought it was genuinely neat-o (as kids used to say back then) to see a bug that big even if it was out of focus, when my mom adjusted that little knob, the clarity of the specimen under the scope was amazing, and I didn't settle for fuzzy specimens any longer when peering through my electron magnifying instrument. I would suggest adjusting your focus knob in your life if continual screen-switching, multitasking, and your social media accounts have you harried.

Do you know where your focus knob is? I'm not going to suggest that you should go absolutely digitally dark, as they say. However, a diminutive bit (for starters) of digital detoxification might be in order to regain your focus and concentration capacity. Find your balance between your metaverse and your actual physical and mental realm.

Working on your hard thing, that is, your new demanding activity, whether it be gardening, learning a language, volunteering, or learning to use that Computerized Tomography device thing, will help to strengthen your ability to focus. But you need to put your phone, tablet, social media, or all of the above away. Just focus on your hard thing for a while with no interruptions or screen-switching.

And here's a secret. If you inaugurate an oil painting pastime and can't quite match the quality and beauty of a famous Vermeer painting like the *Girl with a Pearl Earring* (that's *Meisje met de parel* in Dutch, so they tell me) as my long-lost middle school buddy did, it would be perfectly satisfactory to color in one of those adult coloring books. Those NIH people say, even though they express further studies are warranted, participating in this engaging activity for 20 minutes can meaningfully ease your anxiety. And, you have my permission to color outside the lines and use any color your brain advocates. That undertaking is what they call creativity.

Somewhere along the line in high school, I think, I acquired (can't remember how) one of those paint-by-number sets. The rather intricate kit was a recreation of Gainsborough's *The Blue Boy* painting and included probably a couple dozen assorted colors. And yes, I painted outside the lines and blended adjacent colors to render the painting more realistic. It turned out incredibly well (for me), but I have no idea what happened to that painting. I'm fairly certain it's not hanging by Leonardo's *Mona Lisa* in the Louvre over there in France. Jeanne said she didn't see it the last time she was there.

———

Okay, let's take another timeout here, and relax for a few moments from erecting that significantly important second pillar of your mental health and soundness. Fortunately, this break is not for another bike crash. Phew! However, two days after that initial ride I spoke of in our first break above, I was out riding in the morning due to forecasted afternoon showers. I knew something wasn't right. Yes, it was warm, however, the heat index was not 114 like it is today (I'm not kidding about that), but I knew something wasn't quite right.

I went through my normal two bottles of electrolyte drink, and I still felt dehydrated. As it turned out, I had an ear infection of some sort that kept me off the bike for yet another two weeks, but I'm back riding as of last Saturday. However, that illness took something out of me, as I could not keep up with my friends for more than a few miles before I started falling behind.

But I digress. No, this timeout is not about my latest pothole happenstance or temporary illness in my thankfully long (and getting longer) and still winding excursion through life. By the way, Sir Paul just turned 80 years old several days ago and apparently is rocking with the boss. Anyway, in this break, let's review what we've learned so far in this chapter concerning how to keep the most complex entity ever found in our universe, that is, your brain, growing stronger, healthier, and free of as much gunky junk as possible.

According to those smart scientist people at the NIH, consuming a healthy diet supports the health of our brains as we grow older. You will remember from Chapter 6 that eating real food (that's safe) as close to the way it came off the farm or out of your garden, and as least processed (but properly prepared) as possible, goes far in not only keeping our bodies healthy and clicking on most of our remaining cylinders, but also helps keep our brain's billions of neurons, cognitive circuits, and transmission lines up and running.

And you should remember in Chapter 7, my optical specialist telling me how my exercise is keeping my eyes healthy along with the rest of my body, and those NIH scientists above telling us that exercise seems to support the health of our brains as we continue to meander down our lives' highway. Thus, according to all of these smart people, sitting in your chair all day, eating gunky junk, and watching the Kardashians do whatever the Kardashians do, is not the preferred docket to prolong the longevity of your life's journey.

We have also learned that along with eating healthily and exercising, immersing ourselves into learning a hard thing aids in increasing our mental capacities and assists in keeping those capabilities nimble and open for the business of keeping us alive and well. Learning and habitually practicing a demanding skill you are interested in acquiring is an excellent approach to increasing and maintaining your cognitive proficiencies and competencies. And again, my friends tell me I need all the cognitive skills improvement I can procure, so that's why I keep petitioning Mel to help me learn to play the guitar.

We also just looked at the importance of finding our focus knob and mitigating our multitasking, incessant screen-switching, and non-stop stimuli overload to begin alleviating our stress, anxiety, and exhaustion levels in our cranial computer, not to mention the rest of our body. Participating in a bit of digital detoxification and increasing our focused activity can aid in soothing our brains and body. And oh, by the way, I just checked. They still have those paint-by-number sets out there, and the good news is you can purchase one requiring only kid-level skills all the way to those approaching masterpiece echelons.

Let me talk about those paint-by-number kits (and adult coloring books) for a moment. Subtle differences exist between learning your hard thing and working on your paint-by-number undertaking. I'm certainly no expert here, like Dr. Duckworth, but let's say you buy your first paint-by-number project.

When you sit down and open your new kit for the first time, assuming you have never picked up an artist paint brush in your life, completing the painting in this new endeavor will probably fall into the category of doing a hard thing, particularly if you chose to do a rendition of van Gogh's *The Starry Night* first time around a canvas.

You will learn about the new colors, then about which paint brush to use when, etc. I assume these sets have some kind of secret decoder ring to tell you what color to put where on the canvas, so you will have to learn all of that, too. When engaging in this process, particularly for the first time, your cranial circuits are being reconfigured via that neuroplasticity process, helping to keep your trillions of transmission passageways up-to-date, supple, and healthy. Yay!

However, by the time you complete your 14th masterpiece, and the paint seemingly flows effortlessly upon the canvas without you hardly thinking about it, you have moved from the learning stage to the flow state of this undertaking, and out of the realm of doing a hard thing. Your brain has got this now and is no longer being rewired, but that is not necessarily a bad thing.

Your absorbing new passion is moving you into a meditative state, focusing your attention only on the present and not past or future worries, if only temporarily. Your stress level is moderating, and your mood is improving. You remember the afterglow of the flow on our virtual bike ride? It's the same difference. And your new passion is improving your motor skills, relieving your anxiety, and improving your brain functions. You may even be able to fall asleep more easily and sleep more soundly.

Some experts say coloring by adults also activates their logic. I don't know about all of that, but can you imagine an old Star Trek episode where Captain Kirk runs onto the bridge of the *Enterprise* and sees Mr. Spock sitting there coloring? Rather alarmed, particularly with Klingon ships in the vicinity, Captain Kirk grabs his communicator and calls Bones, who along with Scotty and his junior engineer (guess who's not going to be beamed back up to the *Enterprise*) are down on planet Pluto (which used to be our planet until the Klingons pilfered it from us) in a phaser fight with a band of those Klingon marauders who are pestering the natives. Bones, what's going on with Spock? He's just improving his logic, Sir.

Anyway, after acquiring and initiating your 15th paint-by-number masterwork, you become a bit bored, so you decide to try to paint a self-portrait of yourself wearing a straw hat like Elisabeth Le Brun did back just before I was born in 1782. You purchase your paints, brushes, a straw hat, etc., and now you are staring at a blank, white canvas with no lines or numbers sitting there on your easel. Just a bit intimidating? Maybe?

Yes, you are switching back to doing a hard thing, and your brain will be back in the re-engineering mood and your stress levels may rise a bit. But again, that is not a bad tack. You are learning to navigate between learning and habitually practicing a demanding skill, but immersing yourself back into an absorbing activity depending on whether you are recoding your cranial circuits or aiming to relax them.

Sometimes I wish Mel had some kind of play-by-numbers gizmo for those harmonized scales, so my brain would stop hurting for a while. However, I am gradually getting to the point in my countless renditions of "Sor's Waltz" where I am feeling ethereal moments of the flow transpiring, thus relaxing my brain more than stressing it, like when attempting to perform those scales.

I have long since memorized the waltz, so I don't have to look at the music while playing. I still miss plenty of notes when playing yet another iteration of the score, but my fingers now know their way around the fretboard without me thinking where to place them during each interpretation. I'm slowly getting to the point where I can listen to (and sometimes enjoy) the sound emerging from the guitar while performing that piece. Of course, anytime I want to get back to re-engineering my neuroplasticity competences, Mel has those harmonized scales waiting for me.

This timeout has been rather extended, but to quickly summarize, to maintain and improve the health of our mental capacities, eat healthy food as we discussed in Chapter 6, participate in sufficient physical activity as we covered in the last chapter, and strive to tax your brain a bit by continuously learning a demanding pursuit while also habitually adjusting your focus knob and giving your brain time to relax sufficiently with an appealing activity. No rocket science going on here, or the use of Ponce's products.

———

OKAY, let's get back out on the floor, or back to building your well-being structure, and look now at a few more activities we can do to keep our brains healthy.

SOCIAL ENGAGEMENT

Let us close our eyes for a moment (oh, well yes, keep them open so you can continue reading) and time travel back to the days of our legendary cavepeople that we are so fortunate survived somehow through the eons of time and saber-toothed tigers, not to mention herds of stampeding woolly mammoths roaming around.

As I mentioned in the last chapter, our cavepeople forebearers were social creatures because their survival depended on being social creatures back in those days. For most of us (I'm certainly not going to speak for everyone), being an integrated member of your society still matters today, having had our DNA encoded by those social creature cavepeople.

A while back, a UCLA genomics researcher named Steve Cole peered through his molecular microscope (I'm guessing his instrument was a bit more powerful that my electron microscope and he had figured out where the focus knob was) at some white blood cells from various people of both sexes who reported themselves as being very lonely. Every one of those samples of their disease-fighting cells looked as if they were under siege and responding to a bacterial infection just because they were lonely. Yikes!

Many scientists today are researching and finding that being lonely can attack our bodies and diminish our lifespans, not to mention our healthspans. The lack of social connections increases our susceptibility to many of those chronic illnesses we discussed in Chapter 3, including dementia and strokes we spoke of above. But just so you know, simply living alone does not necessarily lead to heightened destinies toward disease. Many people who live alone are not lonely. Nevertheless, we all have a deep need in our genes to be socially connected with a clan who has shared values and experiences, whether they are our vocation companions, family members, friends, neighbors, or all of the above.

I am most definitely not the social butterfly with hundreds of friends and family members in my orbit, as I don't regularly see my former workmates at the widget factory or grocery story anymore. But I make it a point to be in regular contact with members of my family and a few of my former work colleagues. And of course, I consistently ride with my cycling friends several times a week, weather permitting, as my friend who takes care of his bubble always says. Maintaining our social networks frees our white blood cells from fighting loneliness to being in an improved position to fend off many infectious agents intent on assaulting our body and brain, thus helping to keep us in the game of life.

Having grown up as a rather shy lad, I understand how many people can suffer from loneliness. People will always be out there that you cannot get along with, but if you look bravely enough, and passionately enough, you should be able to find a friend or two. For instance, if you are more comfortable with animals than people, you could volunteer at the humane society for animals in your area, which would give you a chance to become friends with kindred spirits (pets and people who also like pets). However, as you know,

I'm an athlete, not a psychologist, but I will tell you this as always: if all else fails, seek help by consulting a professional. Your health and well-being are worth it.

Some scientists out there are working on medications to end loneliness, but I'm fairly certain Ponce is already all over it and has his "labs" running night and day, producing fountain of youth products to eliminate loneliness. Just be aware.

We all evolved as social creatures. We don't have to run away with the clan from saber-toothed tigers anymore, but we still need to be coupled to society. The consequences of not having friends, family, or a social network to interact with can be dismal. And as I have said, Father Time and his unsavory platoon of plunderers are insidious and eventually ruinous, so fostering social interactions is imperative in fending them off for as long as possible. Staying socially engaged is crucial and vitally important to your mental and physical health. Your cranial supercomputer will thank you.

A LITTLE LEVITY

When I began writing this chapter a while back, I had no idea it would grow to contain so many words. Perhaps I could have edited out a story or two, but how could your life possibly have continued if you hadn't heard about my black bear encounters, my legendary three-wood, my multitasking millennial workmate, and Spock's coloring capers? Probably quite nicely, however, you have undoubtedly heard that old saying that a little levity goes a long way, not to mention that laughter is the best medicine. I think Aristotle said that (remember, he was the dude in that rock band with Plato and Socrates way back when).

According to some scholarly medical professionals from the Mayo Clinic, data is mounting that laughter can be a great form of stress relief along with bestowing many other positive benefits. Laughter can't cure cancer, but in addition to relieving stress, high comedy can ease your pain by triggering your body's natural painkilling substances, lighten your mood (I'm not sure about putting you in the mood), improve your immune system, and aid you in dealing with difficult situations. Humor is also a great way to connect with other people.

Notice, I said high comedy above. Those Mayo Clinic medical people say we should not laugh at the expense of others. And everyone that worked at the widget factory sat through many human resource presentations warning us about the consequences of telling the wrong joke in front of the wrong person. Most all of us are guilty of laughing at the expense of others from time to time, but if this is your rule rather than your exception, your cranial computer may have issues worth checking out.

And don't be afraid to laugh at yourself. My riding buddy, who was born on the same day in the same town as me, knew when he told me I had not gotten any prettier after my pothole debacle that his comment would initiate laughter. It did. He knew I could take a joke and he can too. Finding a way to laugh at yourself relieves the pressure and stress you may be feeling.

A while back, I was out riding with the group, and we were flying through a particularly fast section of the track. Complete concentration was at a premium lest dire carnage. The rider in front of me is a medical doctor in town, a good friend, and way smarter than me. As we were winding downhill, back and forth through the arcing curves at just under Mach 1, my physician friend nonchalantly reached up and batted at an overhanging vine swaying overhead as we screamed by. I chuckled and commented, ah, a bit of levity. He smiled back and said absolutely, as our stress levels mitigated a tad.

Also, the NIH cites many studies concerning the therapeutic benefits of laughter. In one study, they state that while the evidence could be more robust, negative consequences and undesirable ramifications are virtually non-existent concerning laughter therapies. Thus, like that unwritten no harm, no foul rule in basketball: keep laughing in your game of life. And plentiful chuckling is a non-invasive, complimentary intervention that has been shown as effective in providing positive outcomes. By the way, did you hear the one about the crazy writer cycling guy? Never mind, let's move on.

NOVELTY

Several months ago, I began riding my bicycle down the trail one sunny afternoon, and barely into the ride, I saw another cyclist approaching up ahead. As he neared, we recognized each other, and he reversed course. We continued down the trail casually chatting as we often have. I don't remember specifically what we talked about that day, but upon turning around at the end of the line and heading back to the parking lot, I remember our growing concern about the approaching inclement weather on the horizon.

He had parked his vehicle at one of the intermediate parking lots since he lived nearby, so with nine miles to go, he pulled off and didn't get rained upon. I wasn't as fortunate. As I continued down the trail, I can still take you to the place on the route back to the trailhead where the rain fell the heaviest (it was near the spot my doctor friend swatted at the overhanging vine). I then remember the weather clearing, and by the time I got back to the parking lot, the rain had completely stopped, although I made the decision to go rinse my bike off with the water hose.

I have literally been on hundreds, if not thousands, of bike rides, many of them with this particular friend. Why do I remember this one so vividly? Because that was the day that I was so unceremoniously slam dunked to the tarmac by the immaculately camouflaged pothole on my way to the bike wash area. Those NIH scientists tell us that we remember events shrouded with novelty, and I can promise you this: hitting rock-hard asphalt with such stern authority was novel to me.

I'm not recommending going out and crashing into potholes as a brilliant way to procure some novelty to enhance your memory, nor staring into the headlights of oncoming vehicles for that matter, but when we experience something new, that feel-good dopamine hormone is released into a region of our brain called the hippocampus (should I use the joke, I had no idea they had a campus for hippos? Nah). That is why new impressions and experiences normally make us delighted, enhance our memory formation capability, and motivate us to explore even more. This evolutionary adaptation goes a long way in explaining why our cavepeople ancestors eventually exited their caves and spread to all corners of our planet, and more than likely, somewhere beyond in the future.

Those NIH researchers go on to tell us in another publication that being exposed to surroundings bursting with fresh stimuli can benefit our cognition capabilities. They based their findings after studying the behaviors of their pet mice, but since many of my friends say I have the mind of a mouse, I'm all in with their pronouncements.

And how can anyone possibly argue with such prestigious people wearing white coats that recommend playing video games, especially for older characters like me? However, those scientists said that while participating in video games could be an additional (and enjoyable) method of improving cognitive well-being, they concluded that the virtual world was no substitute for real-world experiences. Agreed! You can't smell a virtual rose, no matter how pretty it is on the screen. Nevertheless, playing video games can benefit your brain as long as you don't get carried away.

However, playing video games is akin to working out on those weight machines at the gym. Each piece of equipment is designed to work one specific muscle group, hence the multitude of those muscle machines at the fitness center. And playing video games also generally exercise only a limited set of skills according to those smart people from the AARP. Playing the latest car racer game works a different set of physical and cognitive skills than those games where you create new civilizations.

Another finding of the NIH rodent researchers you need to pay attention to is the fact that their pet mice who were fearful of novelty, by and large, didn't live as long as their more adventurous rodent darlings who loved to explore fun new environments (I'm not sure if their rats played video games or not). As they state, "Individuals who are fearful of novelty have a larger hypothalamic-pituitary-adrenal-axis response than do non-fearful individuals." Yes, well, I think what those scientist people are trying to say is that those of us who do regularly seek out new experiences have been shown to live longer, happier lives.

You don't have to go out and scale Mont Ventoux on your bicycle like those Tour de France riders, or explore the rain forest of Madagascar, but you could benefit from checking out that new restaurant downtown or going to the antique car and art show on the square this weekend.

But as we all know, there is a downside to too much novelty seeking, and the dark side is becoming more prevalent. I would suggest that the addiction to novelty is why people can't seem to put their phone or tablet down, ever. Something new is always just a click, tap, or swipe away. That's why I don't ride my bike on open roads anymore because people cannot seem to be able to put their device away even while driving. And, playing video games can also become extremely addictive and has been known to cause a job to be lost, or a close relationship to be compromised. Please find help if you are being dragged into the black hole of addiction for any reason.

When I was working at the grocery store, one of my absolute favorite customers was the Boogie Woogie Reverend. He was indeed a novel dude! An article appeared in the local paper one morning about his musical flairs, and within a week or two, I saw him in the store. I didn't hesitate to strike up a conversation with him, and we soon became good friends. He showed me some clips of him playing the keyboard in a couple of his concerts, and that chap could torch those keys. You couldn't even see his fingers, as they were just a blur moving across the black and white keyboard.

Over the course of time, he found out that I was a cyclist, and he told me one evening that I do it the right way. I asked, "What are you talking about, Rev?" He said you get naturally high on the dopamine when riding and come down naturally. He then told me of his heavy-duty drug use in his earlier rock and roll years and said coming down tranquilly from those novelty-seeking transgressions is not a thing. I don't know, I've never been there. But I could see in his eyes that night, he meant it.

So again, go out and seek some novelty in your life. Find something new to do or place to explore to help your brain stay in the game. However, all of those rodent experiments were unnecessary to tell us how much fun it is to play like a kid again. We all love to get new toys, treats, and play games, and it's helping our brains stay fit and firmer. Well, I'm not sure about firmer, but healthier anyway (again, just trying to make sure you are paying attention). Just remember, though, keep your novelty seeking within reasonable provinces, and again, find your balance between your metaverse and the actual physical (and cerebral) real world.

CLEANSING OUR BRAINS

I remember one evening once upon a time, I was working late into the night at the widget factory. All of the main lights had been turned off, and I was working by the light of my desk lamp. Suddenly, all the lights in the area came back on all at once. I was temporarily blinded. I instinctively pressed the button on my desk to activate the laser shields. *The Return of the Jedi* had just come out, or maybe it was *The Wrath of Khan*. I can't remember, so I didn't know whether to grab my light saber or my phaser. It turned out it was the cleaning person who had activated the photon force fields of electromagnetic illumination.

I continued working industriously, putting those numbers into little boxes, and when the cleaning person, not expecting me, walked into my work area, I said "Hello." I think I recall having to submit a Facilities Request form the next morning to replace a ceiling tile. After recovering for a few seconds, the cleaning person collected all of the day's rubbish from the trash receptacles in the communal workspace. As the warden of the day's waste removal exited the area, I communicated my appreciation for taking care of such an important daily duty at the widget factory. I think the cleaning person was in a hurry to get out of there. I'm not sure why.

As we spoke of above, your diligently functioning brain is toiling harder than any other organ in your body and consuming 20% or more of your daily energy expenditures. Any time fuel is transformed into energy, by-products of waste, that is, gunky junk, is created. Fortunately, like at the widget factory, your brain has its own cleaning crew, and most of the gunky junk scouring goes on after hours, while you are asleep.

The purging of all that gunky debris in your cranial processer is only one of the many talents of your fourth teammate, the Repair Shop, we will discuss in the next chapter. But for now, to the best of your ability, try to prioritize your slumber. Though Mr. Petty said the waiting was the hardest part, for me (and I know many of you out there in the middle of life can relate) the hardest part working all those years at the widget factory was getting enough sleep. Working all day, coming home, going for a run, being dad, helping with the meal preparation and cleanup, bedtime reading, sometimes softball late into the night, and then returning to the widget factory before the sun came up the next morning; yes, getting enough sleep was the hardest part for me during all those years.

So again, to keep your gray matter polished as best you can, try to get at least eight hours of sleep each day, including midday siestas, as sleep scientists recommend, allowing your cleaning crew to perform their duties. But as always, and you know the refrain by now, Ponce has all kinds of fountain of youth magical sleep-aid merchandise for you to avoid, and if you are truly having issues acquiring enough sleep for other reasons than being too busy with life, get with your medical provider, not Ponce.

———

Before we move on to the next chapter where we properly meet our last teammate, the Repair Shop, and build that final pillar of your well-being structure, let's again visit Grandma's once nearly pristine river. I traverse that formally free-flowing and once gorgeous waterway often now, and yes, it is still gunky because of the obstruction of the river's current downstream.

Even its once world-famous tributary is now showing serious signs of stress from the river's gunky backflow (and for many other reasons) into the once pristine freshwater spring where the catfish and bass used to play football among vast fields of undulating, fungus-free eel grass which is now struggling to survive. I'm not sure if the catfish are still there, but I know exceedingly few mermaids can now feast on the grass because of the river's blockage. Just a reminder here to improve your diet and increase your exercise to prevent too many dams forming in your cardiovascular systems and neural networks.

In other news, Grandma had a brother that was a genuine character just as that spunky lady was. She had to be growing up with four brothers who were, shall we say, quite alive with boisterous merriment despite the hard times they all grew up in. I guess that explains a lot about the highly serious academic nature of this book. I am blood-kin to these people. But speaking of academics, I remember when I was about to graduate with my employable degree from the university, Grandma's brother told me one day, and I may be slightly paraphrasing here, they could pilfer my money, they could break my body, but they could never embezzle my education.

That profound proverb is most definitely true to a point. Your scholarly edification can be thieved by prolific gunky junk clogging up your critical cranial circuits, obstructing your neuro-communication messengers, and creating colossal potholes in your computer's transmission corridors. Yes, my (long since passed) treasured great-uncle, with all due respect, our minds and education can be stolen away. Stay on your journey toward better health.

By the way, I saw Jolly-man Stan yesterday, and he told me he has now lost 65 pounds, and his medical provider is ecstatic. He still has a significant way to go, but he's diligently marching toward his goal weight. However, I warned him that his journey to his sought-after weight level is going to become more difficult with each pound he loses. As you will recall, years went by before I finally lost that 20 pounds.

I also forewarned him that even if he gets to his aspired objective, he cannot stop performing those new healthy habits that have gotten him there, as we have discussed several times. Keeping those 20 pounds off has not been a leisurely boat ride down Grandma's river for me, and it won't be for him (or you) either. Just some additional reminders to keep in mind on your continuing expedition to becoming healthy.

Our brains, despite being the hearts of who we are, are still only parts of our physical body, so it makes logical sense that eating well and exercising benefits your brain as it does the rest of your organic structure. Perhaps Mr. Spock is done with his coloring exercises now, and he can verify this line of logic for us. Or maybe not. Let's not bother him when he's coloring so diligently. After all, Captain Kirk didn't interrupt him, even with Klingons about, so we better not either, else we find ourselves in the line of phaser fire.

In addition to keeping your brain physically healthy by eating soundly and exercising, continue to challenge your cognitive circuits by regularly doing your hard thing. But balance your head hurting endeavors with regularly adjusting your focus knob by indulging yourself in your calming and absorbing activity. Feel free to color along with Mr. Spock. Who knows, it may increase your logical powers, but please, don't interrupt him or you may find yourself a victim of the Vulcan nerve pinch!

The Jolly-man also told me today about his absorbing/hard thing fascination. He said he has been collecting antique clocks, which is his absorbing activity, for decades. None of his treasures are electric. Can you imagine how long it takes to wind up 43 vintage clocks? He said he just loves watching all the hands, gears, levers, and springs do their thing and keep those clocks all ticking. His hard thing is that he can actually fix them when they take a turn for the worse and expire. For me, trying to repair one of those intricate works of craftsmanship would be akin to performing brain surgery. Avoid being my patient at all costs!

And of course, a little levity does indeed go a long way in maintaining your cognitive vigor, especially when laughing with members of your clan, or complete strangers, for that matter. Humor is one of the best avenues to maintain long-standing friendships and acquire new friends in your social network. Like that guy with his fancy molecular microscope told us, avoiding loneliness frees our white blood cells to combat microscopic bacterial marauders instead of the stress of being home alone all the time. But just so you know, I'm still jealous of his swanky molecular gadget. I'm just going to take my little electron microscope and go home.

And don't forget about those science people whose pet mice that were fearful of novelty didn't live as long as their more adventurous furry pets. Get out of the cave every so often and find something new and fun to do, and hopefully with someone, to help your brain stay in the game. However, don't go overboard on chasing novelty as we spoke of above. Put your phone down now and then, and go color with Mr. Spock, or go to the park and listen to the songbirds.

Though it was the hardest part for me and perhaps you, too, strive to get enough sleep to allow that cleaning crew of yours to clear your cranial circuits and remove all the gunky by-products of your brain's daily energy transformations. Don't scare them though, you may have to replace a ceiling tile.

We have now met your extraordinarily hardworking teammate, Software. And hopefully, crafting your most protected, load-bearing center post of the new healthier you is coming along splendidly. Life is too wonderful to let a bunch of gunky junk accumulate up there and pollute your critical cranial circuits. You don't want your education or your memories to fade. Continue to improve your diet, regularly exercise your glorious physical machine, and continue to increase your cognitive effort and training. You are worth it.

Okay, does your brain hurt from trying to understand all of this hard stuff? I know my brain still hurts from all those harmonized scales Mel has me relentlessly trying to perform, and now he wants me to learn the B-flat scale. And he just keeps shaking his head. Help is waiting just on the other side of the page. Let's head on over to the famed Repair Shop for a bit of respite, buoyancy, equilibrium, and a word of cautioning.

CHAPTER 9: THE THREE R'S & B

MY BRAIN IS BOGGING down now, and it's not just because of Mel's harmonized scales. This writing a book endeavor is hard, in fact, seriously hard (at least for me). Didn't I say something about doing a hard thing was good for our brain in the last chapter? According to Dr. Duckworth, it is, but I'm struggling with putting the finishing touches on Chapter 8 (and Chapter 7 for that matter, and 5, and 2), and now I'm staring at an empty chapter waiting to be written. I need to spend some time here with our Repair Shop teammate for a while (yes, I took a few days off from writing) before I carry forward with completing my mission of writing this book for you.

The last three chapters have been difficult enough for me to pen (or I guess, type), but these next two are going to get even more challenging. As I have mentioned, I have always been an athlete, not a book writer person. And, thanks to discovering that fiber book and eating all of those carrots, my dietary patterns have always been basically nutritionally wholesome (I did say I love pepperoni pizza especially with mushrooms and black olives, didn't I? No? Well, now you know). And despite the jokes (or because of them), my brain, aided by my love of exercise and real food, has served me well. But I am not a subject matter expert on the material to be covered in the next two chapters.

However, I have had experience, for better or worse, with these subjects in my lifetime, just like you. So, let us explore these topics together. And as I kept putting one foot in front of the other back in my marathoning days, I will keep putting one word after another to complete this manuscript that will improve your life in some small (or big) way.

Okay, let me go back and finish up Chapter 8 (I'll worry about Chapters 2, 5, and 7 in the final edit). And by the way, it might be a worthwhile endeavor for you to go back and review the last three chapters. Hopefully, you have absorbed a good deal of useful information, begun implementing that knowledge into improving your health, and perhaps laughed a time or two. But like our game plan principles expound, implementing and maintaining that improvement in your well-being requires practice during your journey toward continuously improving your health and vigor. However, if you are ready to move on down this page, go for it!

It's me again, I'm back now. As I mentioned in Chapter 4, our indispensable Repair Shop teammate is a team and fan favorite, and for good reason. Every single day, we all need to spend time in Restorationville (my spellcheck said that wasn't a real word, but I'm going to employ it anyway). Our world eases and stress levels abate when we pass the ball to this beloved teammate. As I said back then, curling up in bed after a long, stressful day, and drifting off to dreamland is a Repair Shop specialty among many others.

We all need to pass the ball often and consistently to our Repair Shop partner. I just passed the ball there while I took a fifteen-minute break from doing this hard thing of putting one word in front of the last. The sun just came back out after one of our regularly scheduled afternoon showers down here on the peninsula. I consumed a few cashews, lightly salted of course, while I enjoyed a bit of fresh air that smelled pleasantly aromatic after the rain. I certainly needed that short break, which again, is one of our Repair Shop's many talents.

Like those NASCAR people warned us way back when: we can't go full gas all of the time, or we will blow one of our body's gaskets or perhaps our entire engine. And of course, The Who (not the WHO) told us long ago that too much of anything is, well, just too much.

Yes, we all need to slow down and smell the orange blossoms now and then, in fact, quite often. Thirty-something years ago, at the gym I was frequenting, I would see a young, 20-something gentleman there who would literally make your head spin if you tried to visually follow him flitting around the facility. He would practically sprint to each weight machine that suddenly came open because he couldn't stand to wait for more than three seconds on anyone using one of those muscle-strengthening devices. He appeared to be definitely distracted by his youth as one of our game plan principles states not to do.

One day, someone asked him if he ever slowed down. He replied he would rest when they buried him as he raced to the next open machine. If I had to guess, he is resting now. But, if he is still on this side of the grass, I would speculate that his healthspan has expired, and he is residing in that space between there and the end of his lifespan, otherwise known as Miseryville (my spellcheck guru didn't like that word either). His quality of life has more than likely eroded to Grand Canyon proportions.

No, our bodies, both our hardware and software, were not meant to go full gas all the time, non-stop. We need to breathe the engine and cool the tires down every lap or so. And I know this is going to be agonizing for some of you, but sometimes you need to leave the racetrack of your life for a while and go hit the beach (not literally, you don't want to hurt your fist), and not just to take dazzling selfies there to post on your social media platforms as our young lady friend did back in Chapter 3. You actually have to relax your brain, watch the waves roll in, and behold the pelican flyby (all of which she totally missed), or whatever flies (or swims) around on your beach or lake or river. I have seen a mermaid or two at the beach I normally visit.

Back when I was a young lad, you could actually relax on the beach and watch a race at the same time as those NASCAR people used to race there. I never got to witness any of those competitions, but I'm not sure how relaxing that would have been given that often more than 100 cars participated in those races stirring up a ton of sand into the air. And over the course of the race, many of the cars would develop gunky carburetors and spew clouds of smoke into the air, as pollution control devices were not a thing back then. One year, they had to shorten the race due to the rapidly rising high tide which nearly claimed me as a victim once upon a time.

Enough about race cars, pounding sand, and gunky carburetors. I know you non-sports fan readers are just dying to see the continuing development of our breathtaking blueprints for our sports-neutral well-being citadel. So, without further ado, here they are. Take a moment to catch your breath. I know they are that stunning.

Physical Activity (Hardware)	Mental Activity (Software)	Three R's & B (Repair shop)
Nutrition (Fuel)		

Yes, we now need to build that last pillar of the new you. As you can see, that final column will be located opposite your strengthening pillar of physical activity, and aid in the protection of your key center post of mental activity, otherwise known as the heart of who you are. As with your other two pillars of health, your final column stands firmly upon your improving (yes?) nutritional foundation.

———

THOUGH IT IS time for us now to look at what all of those letters represent in this chapter's title, we need to first take a serious timeout here. No, I didn't crash my bike again. One of our regularly scheduled hurricanes is on the way and this storm is brawny! I think I will be all right because I live about 70-something miles from each coast and the storm is coming onto shore a bit further south than originally forecasted. I probably will not experience any hurricane-force winds this time around (perhaps some wind gust approaching hurricane force), but the lower western coast is now getting hammered with catastrophic winds and storm surge. That weather channel person could not even stand up in the pummeling wind and rain. And the beast hasn't even come ashore yet.

I first saw this storm on the weather charts almost two weeks ago when it was still something those weather forecasting people call an invest, which is an area of disturbed weather worthy of keeping an eye on because it could turn into a tropical storm or worse. Generally, about 30 of these invests form each year in the Atlantic with approximately half of those turning into tropical storms. About half of those tropical storms then turn into hurricanes.

Now I am definitely not any sort of weather sage, but when I saw this particular disturbance, for whatever reason, a feeling came over me that this was the big one. My doctor riding friend who likes to bat at low hanging vines while riding said that's called a premonition. When I told Jolly-man Stan about my feeling, I mean my premonition, concerning the approaching storm, he said, "Don't say that."

As the disturbance came through the warm waters of the Caribbean south of Cuba, it picked up wind, strength, and fury. I started preparing for the worst due to its projected path. By the time the storm upper cut western Cuba, it had turned into a Category 3 hurricane, causing massive destruction. Crossing Cuba, it is now headed straight north toward the peninsula and has grown into a massive Category 4 hurricane with sustained winds of over 150 miles per hour.

Refreshingly, as the potential cataclysmic storm is approaching, all levels of government, from the president down to local city offi-cials, are all working in a coordinated effort to help the most people they can here on the peninsula to prepare for the storm. Many resi-dents have been notified to evacuate. I hope they do. I have seen what can happen. Shelters have already been opened. Recovery logistics have been planned. All politics have temporarily been set aside to all work for the common purpose of assisting those in harm's way.

Three days later...

Catastrophic damage abounds. Houses ripped apart by the fierce winds and carried off by the historic storm surge of 12 to 18 feet. This hurricane literally sucked the water out of Tampa Bay and pushed it on shore further south as hurricane winds always rotate counterclock-wise in this hemisphere. In some areas, 90% of the structures are gone. Vehicles, boats, house trailers, smashed trees, and other assorted wreckage are scattered everywhere, rendering the landscape to resemble a war zone. Seafaring shrimp boats are now resting inland on top of the vast piles of debris. Several of the barrier islands are now only accessible by boat because the bridges to the peninsula have been destroyed. More than 100 people have died, and it is still early in the search and rescue process.

Assuredly, this storm will be one of the costliest to date in our country, with estimates of destruction now in the billions. Even far inland in the hometown of Mickey and his Magic Kingdom, historic flooding occurred. A picture of a first responder walking through the streets in chest deep water searching for residents in need appeared in the newspaper.

This massive hurricane took a full 24 hours to amble across the peninsula, and now it's on its way to South Carolina as a Category 1 hurricane. The entire eastern seaboard will more than likely experi-ence destructive tidal surges. I was blessed with no major damage, although I did lose power for more than 30 hours. But again, I am blessed because many people down south still do not have power, and those barrier islands are inhabitable possibly for weeks as the bridges connecting those islands as mentioned above were taken out by the ferocity of the wind and waves.

The evening of the storm's exit from the peninsula just southeast of me, still not having power, I dined by candlelight, eating my cold quinoa and chicken I had prepared several days before along with a salad. I thought of my old friend at the widget factory I used to see often in the breakroom heating up his lunch in the microwave. One day he was telling me a story about how great a cook his wife was, but she could never quite get the meal to the table still hot. She would remind him, "Dear, heat is not a nutrient," so I suppose I was at least eating a nutritional meal despite its lack of temperature.

Anyway, the lesson of this timeout is to prepare yourself both physically and mentally for come what may the best you can. Access your potential risk (more on assessing risk below) given your current standpoint in your life, and I hope you act accordingly to improve your existing health situation even if it is already good enough to please Voltaire. Opportunity is always available for improvement.

Now would be a good time, if you haven't already, to assess your health and well-being. Is there a potential health invest on your well-being charts? Is a tropical storm or major health hurricane coming your way? Please, I urge you, if you are not in the best of health, start now preparing yourself for possible oncoming squalls, or worse.

Many lives were lost here on the peninsula because they ignored preparation protocols and evacuation notices, apparently thinking they could ride the brutal storm out. Major hurricanes have no mercy and neither does Father Time. Act now to improve your health and well-being fortifications instead of reacting to the destruction that could unexpectedly lie ahead. The stronger you are now, the better your chances of survival and the quicker you will recover from your physiological (and psychological) typhoons when they do occur.

————

OKAY, back now to learning what all of those letters represent in this chapter's title. Just so you know, they are not the initials of the Fifth Dimension band members. No, regardless of how my spellcheck guru feels about the village's name, the featured denizens of our beloved Restorationville whom we will discuss below include Recovery, Resilience, Risk, and Balance.

I don't think I left anyone out, but I am fairly certain you know other residents from this refreshing retreat that can help improve your health and mental sanity. As I mentioned earlier, we all absolutely need to spend time in this recuperative hamlet quite regularly, so let us continue our journey.

RECOVERY

My beloved dictionary's fifth definition of recovery expresses the process as the "regaining of health, strength, and control." And those renowned scientist people at the NIH pronounce that recovery is "a process of change through which people improve their health and wellness, live self-directed lives, and strive to reach their full potential." That's certainly a mouth full, but I think those scientist people are saying, in many additional words, what my beloved dictionary stated in six. Regardless of how many words we chose, we all positively need frequent doses of recovery to regain our health and well-being due to the unrelenting insidious assaults from Father Time and his band of troublesome troubadours.

Short Morsels of Respite. I am not sure about single cell amoebas, but during each day most all animals, including us homo sapiens, need frequent moments of relief throughout our day ranging from pausing to take a deep breath to lengthier timeouts, such as a lunch break or siesta, to recover from our mental and physical toils in order to delay total exhaustion until bedtime. Whether you have a strenuous physical job, stressful mental job (or both), or hiking the high ridge, or riding in the Tour de France, breaks in the action are required.

Take your brief pauses, short breaks, and pull out of line every lap or two to let the air flow through your radiator to cool your always-on cranial computer (not to mention your actual heart) and bring a bit of relief to your body. Yes, often pass the ball to your Repair Shop teammate and laugh with your colleagues at appropriate intermissions for a little levity. Lean against your Restorationville pillar often and experience the alleviation and support. And at the end of your workday, settle into your blissful hours of soothing slumber.

Slumber Interludes. As I spoke of in the last chapter, procuring enough sleep was always an issue for me. I can truthfully tell you that at times, I have resembled our friend above, who said he would rest when they buried him. However, I cannot emphasize enough how much our body, and brain in particular as we spoke of in the last chapter, need those slumber hours to recover from our daily fatigue and stresses.

Those CDC scientist people tell us that not getting enough sleep over time is linked to many chronic diseases that threaten our health, not to mention increasing our chances of getting in automobile accidents, making mistakes in our daily activities that could cause serious injury, etc. They go on to say that one-third of Americans normally get less than the recommended amount. If you are having problems procuring enough sleep (due to sleep disorders), consult with your medical provider, and again, not with Ponce. Yes, drifting off to sleep and visiting Dreamville (dang it, my spellcheck authoritarian did not like that word either, although Mr. Petty thought it was cool) is vital to our well-being.

Speaking of Dreamville, many sleep expert science people tell us dreaming is a vital part of our rest during the night, but I am not sure where our dreams come from. I think it has something to do with our brain's cleaning crew sitting around in the breakroom and telling wild tales of adventure, romance, horror, tragedy, and I don't know what all. Last night, my cranial cleaning crew landed an alien spaceship right across the street and let me know that said aliens were after me.

I didn't know if Mr. Vader was on board and Luke was nowhere to be found, so I was a bit stressed with the scenario. Fortunately, the alarm clock went off and I woke up just before the extraterrestrials disembarked.

Earlier in the night, they (my brain's cleaning crew, not the aliens) told me I had to perform a big recital of harmonized scales on my guitar in front of Mel and all of his senior faultfinders. Talk about being seriously stressed out, but again, I was fortunate to wake up right before I walked out on stage. I'm fairly certain that concert would not have gone well despite my plodding, but improving, six-string skills. Incidentally, I'm not making these two dreams up either, so I might need to check on my cranial housekeeping staff. They seem to be stressing me out more than they are surrounding me with fields of flowers. I'm not sure if I can get a new mental sanitization squad. I need to check with those CDC scientist people.

Extended Excursions. Our Recovery Patrol has several other protocols to restore our tired, injured, and restless body and brain. In addition to those brief moments of pause, breaks, lunch hours, naps, and sleep during our day (and night), we all need lengthier periods of recovery sessions; after all, that is why weekends and vacations were invented.

Back in 2013 (as mentioned in Chapter 2), I had a grand total of 14 days off from work, and I have to tell you that was tough. But sometimes, we do what we have to do, and hope we survive. Nevertheless, seize your weekends to recuperate from your long week of trial and toil. My weekends back then consisted of Sunday afternoons, and I normally had to do yard work, but at least I enjoyed that task and finally got to immerse myself in the outdoor biosphere for a while.

And take your vacations if only mini ones. Years ago, employees at the widget factory, instead of taking time off, could work through their allotted vacation hours and receive extra cash at the end of the year. I cannot tell you how many people employed that tact, but they were many.

Finally, the Mothership people changed that policy because they understood the value and importance of extended away time. I took my vacations back then and took my family to many beautiful venues our homeland (and the peninsula) has to offer. And, by the way, recalling those precious moments from such excursions, although not highlighted here, is another specialty of your Repair Shop. Seek them.

Protracted Periods. And then there are those times you may require prolonged periods of recovery due to a significant illness, severe injury, or other acute or chronic incident of infirmity. I used to hate being sick or getting injured, but I eventually learned how to deal with it. Initially, you just have to stop and let your body begin to heal itself. That's what those physiological recovery people call passive recovery, that is, undergoing complete rest. Those six days I spent in the hospital definitely qualified as passive recovery, given the fact that I couldn't walk, and the slightest movement caused excruciating anguish.

As you begin to feel better and, depending on your malady, you can then actively recover. Back when I was running all those miles, some type of injury was practically inevitable. Although I would reluctantly cease running for a period, depending on the severity level of the damaged limb, when the pain begun to subside, I would hop on my old fat tire bike and casually ride through the neighborhood to get the blood flowing through the injured area aiding its healing yet avoiding further injury from the pounding of running too soon. Feather the throttle during your initial active recovery, then steadily increase the pressure to the pedal (incrementally, of course) until you are back to full gas in exercising and living your life.

Hopefully you are not in need of a protracted period of recovery at this point in your life from obesity, chronic disease, substance abuse, depression, getting slammed dunked to the ground by a pothole, etc., but again as they say, [insert that four-letter word] happens. As the doc and I were getting off our bikes yesterday, a gentleman with dirt on his shirt and pain etched in his eyes approached us and asked me if I could help him take his gloves off.

Observing how he was holding his hand across his chest; I knew immediately he had undoubtedly broken his collarbone from an apparently nasty fall from his mountain bike. As I removed his gloves, the doc found the closest emergency care center in the area to access the damage. I assured the poor chap he would probably be fine and told him of breaking my clavicle twice in the last ten months while exhibiting for him how well my shoulder was now functioning.

Again optimistically, you have taken exquisite care of yourself, avoided accidents, and addiction, and all you need to do is keep doing what you have been doing, and procuring your daily timeouts, sleep, leisure, vacations, and other relaxing downtime interludes. However, if you have not taken the best care of yourself (and trust me, you are not alone), or have been inflicted with harm beyond your control, as I said back in Chapter 3, don't beat yourself up or sink into the depths of Mariana's trench of self-pity; just relax, breathe, and recall my marigold story from Chapter 5.

My beautiful marigold was beaten and broken after that storm, but it found a way to recover and create new blooms of life. Perhaps that resilient plant did not recover to its same splendor as before its calamity, but after regrouping, reorganizing its rhythms, and repairing itself the best it could, my charming marigold continued to enjoy its life producing new blooms for me to enjoy, until of course, Father Time eventually rang its time bell sometime late that fall.

And despite the challenges heading into the remainder of your life, you too can recover from most any injury, chronic disease, addiction, or mental illness, to again experience some level of quality you once enjoyed earlier in your life. My broken shoulder is all put back together for the most part, but I realize it will never be the same. However, by applying generous measures of rest, rehabilitation, and strengthening exercises, my damaged shoulder recovered (despite the considerably crunching reverberations going on in there now) to operate well enough to receive a thumbs-up from George. It's not perfect, but highly acceptable.

Yes, effort and recovery protocols were required in my shoulder's reformation. However, the effort was so worth it. Jolly-man Stan has worked hard on his diet and has now lost 93 pounds. He told me today he has certain ladies checking him out now, but he assured me that's not the real reason he lost all his weight. I believe him, of course, but he has added years to both his healthspan and lifespan, which is his true benefit from his diligent effort to recover his health.

I also saw E-bike Mike zooming down the trail on his beefy bike a couple of days ago. He hasn't lost nearly as much weight as the Jolly-man, but he too is adding months, and perhaps years, to his life by exercising. You, too, can do this.

Summarizing, recovery is about regaining your health, strength, and control of your life, as my cherished dictionary stated. By constantly partaking in short morsels of respite to prolonged rehabilitation sessions (if required), you can recover from frantic moments of stress to prolonged illnesses (and broken collarbones and scapulae).

For the most part, you can perform your own recovery protocols, but if you feel like you are not making sufficient (or any) progress toward your physical or mental (or both) reclamation objectives, or you just don't know where to start, please, and I cannot stress this enough, seek qualified physical and mental health professionals as required to aid and assist you (or a loved one) during your efforts toward recovery, particularly if you (or they) are suffering from substance abuse and addiction. And please, do not be ashamed to seek support and assistance.

RESILIENCE

As mentioned in the beginning of this chapter, I am most definitely not an authority nor a subject matter expert on the material covered in this chapter nor the next. But as I mentioned way back in Chapter

2, sometimes you don't know how resilient you are until you are fraught with life's direst confrontations.

During that particularly distressing period in my life, I got so desperate for some hue of relief, I distraughtly typed 'hope' into my search engine. I needed a way to bounce back from what was happening in my life. More on hope in the next chapter and what I discovered along the way, but I have more or less graduated from the reputed institute of harsh realities (granted, not as harsh as some of you have experienced) perhaps not with an A-plus, but at least with a passing grade, barely.

Like the Jolly-man's doctor, life can and often proverbially (or actually) punches us in the face with a variety of traumatic assaults from a light jab of despair to a thunderous right cross of calamity staggering us to our knees or laying us out on the canvass for the count. A sudden job loss, the unexpected death of a loved one, an unexpected medical misfortune such as a severe stroke or heart malfunction, they all take their toll. Menacing adversarial emotions such as grief, pain, despair, anger, or hatred (I could go on), singularly or in battalions, arrive on the scene, and I can tell you from experience, those companions can and will be repulsive and exacting. But we must get back up on our feet.

Resilience is our ability to counter these blows of tribulation, adapt, and carry on in some way despite these difficult affairs transpiring. But looking reality straight in the eye, most of us are not born with an infallible endowment of resilience to aid us in springing back like nothing ever happened after one (or more) of Father Time's stiff jabs or body strikes. I sure wasn't.

One indicator of lacking resilience is low self-esteem. I know from experience that feeling unworthy and useless is not a pleasant place, yet many of us dwell in this densely populated metropolis as one of our reality checks states. Also, incessantly stressing out over your anxieties also treacherously erodes your resilience as does harboring feelings of victimization and resentment. Possessing these behaviors can lead to ruinous coping mechanisms, such as overindulging in food and beverage, engaging in risky behavior, substance abuse, and many more.

Truth be told, I have been guilty of opening a cold one before mid-morning just to sand the edge off my anguish, which I whole-heartedly do not recommend. Thankfully, I barely possessed a suffi-cient degree of fortitude to stop and not head down into the dastardly domain of addiction. Somehow, I found a root growing from the shifty slope to embrace before sliding all the way down into the dark abyss of despair.

But just so you know, even if you possess a reasonable amount of bounce-back proficiency, resilience will not dissipate your problems into the midst of irrelevance. But resilience can help you rebound and overcome (or at least cope with) your setbacks, live to see another day, help you move on, worry less, and again find some semblance of joy.

I mentioned my resilient marigold above as a great example of recovering to a reasonably renovated configuration of health after an unanticipated calamity, but I recently witnessed one of the most profound examples of recovery and resilience by two of the most amazing and inspirational people I have ever observed.

One afternoon recently, I entered the parking lot of our beautiful cycling trail for one of my regularly scheduled rides. As I disem-barked from my vehicle, the most unbelievable scene caught my eye in the handicap-parking area. The couple parked there were about to commence their trip down the trail.

I honestly cannot tell you how they managed to remove their individual machines from their vehicle and climb aboard them. The young lady (she was youthful to me as I am older than some of the mature trees out there) was lying horizontally on her 'bicycle.' She was apparently paralyzed from the waist down and used hand cranks to propel her device down the track. Her male companion was seated in one of those competition wheelchairs because he had no legs.

Despite their (I don't even want to call them handicapped) chal-lenges, they probably covered at least six to eight miles on their various apparatuses. After preparing my bike, my hydration bottles, etc., I started down the track. When I got to the top of the hill (you people on the mainland would probably call it a speed bump in the road) at the two-and-a-half-mile mark, they were ascending Pine Tree Hill as we call it (feel free to laugh at us flatlanders).

She was nearly at the summit, and her mate was propelling himself up the incline with Mr. Rock-like arms in his race chair. They were so incredibility inspiring. I flashed them an enthusiastic thumbs-up as I passed by. She smiled back warmly, but Mr. Rock II was totally focused on his task at hand.

Now some of you may hold that same level of resilience this couple possesses, but most of us do not. If you lack their level of hardiness, the good news is that you can develop your resilience capabilities. Though developing and building your resilience skills more than likely will resemble completing a marathon rather than the 100-yard dash (you remember what Sir Paul said), you can most definitely strengthen your steadfastness over time.

When one of those devastating right hooks of hardship strikes you squarely in the face, do not go into hibernation and dwell on your misfortune. Isolation will eat you up and lead you down paths of unworthiness, and possibly substance abuse and addiction. So, to grow your bounce-back capabilities in times of trauma and heartache, seek support from family, friends, or workmates (or all of the above), and if all else fails, professional guidance.

When I was going through my darkest days, my cubicle mate at the widget factory, who was traversing through his own set of hardships and adversities, and I would spend a few minutes on countless days empathetically listening to and supporting each other. It helped.

Those conversations didn't vaporize our persistent tribulations but did assist us in coping with our distressing circumstances and helped us to somehow press forward through our day with a bit more resolve to accomplish what we had to accomplish. Confiding with trusted friends, family members, or workmates can certainly ameliorate your anxiety to some degree and help you move forward and bolster your resilience.

Also, and I know from experience this is difficult to achieve, do not ignore your significant dilemmas and difficulties or they will undoubtedly manifest into even more egregious complications. Send out a fact-finding team to mine your past successes in difficult situations and again employ those long-lost skills. Perhaps you have forgotten just how strong and resilient you have been in the past. Thus, marshal what resources you have, craft a plan (with trustworthy assistance if required) and face your predicaments in pursuit of a path forward and restored (perhaps even enhanced) life.

And to revisit my mantra back when I was playing shortstop, "do what you gotta do" to improve your health and well-being, as we have discussed over the past three chapters through healthy eating, physical and mental exercise, and social engagement. And, of course, spend the necessary time here in our treasured Restorationville.

The sturdier you are physically and mentally, and the more refreshed and relaxed you are, the better your prospects are in standing up with steadfast resilience to Father Time's insidious associates of mayhem and sudden unforeseen tragedies. Boost your ability and agility to overcome your tribulations by staying healthy as we have discussed and improving your resilience. If you desire your survivability chances to be higher than a tent in a tornado, do not ignore your health and well-being. Please, do not.

Again, as with your road to recovery, use your abilities, attitudes, and employ our game plan principles to strengthen and reinforce your resilience. And of course, keep our reality checks in mind. The road to bolstering your bounce-back capability could be, and probably will be, long and winding with no quick fixes. More than likely, you will be doubtful of your capabilities and seemingly stuck in the homeostatic quagmire for long periods of time, but never give up and strive for continuous progression. And as always, seek professional assistance if making little or no progress.

One final word regarding both of our worthy collaborators,

Recovery and Resilience, coming back from adversity and triumphantly overcoming has its charm, often thrilling, and seemingly more glorifying. I can't tell you how many battles Mr. Brady and his buccaneers have been losing to Ponce and his contentious conquistadors before miraculously rebounding, recovering, and overpowering those dastardly demons late in the clash.

But a significantly better strategy in your ongoing confrontation with Father Time and his treacherous plunderers of your well-being, particularly for you zoomers and millennials, is to not get behind in your game of life with them in the first place. Strive to outflank and stay out front of those perilous pillagers for as long as possible before they finally have their sights set and release their arrows toward your health and well-being. However, they are not the most preeminent archers against agile prey, so strive to improve and strengthen your capabilities, but alas, they are persistent. Just like water over rocks, they eventually win, but stand your ground for as long as possible and don't back down.

Thus, no matter which side of the scoreboard you find yourself on, the prime objective is to start now (or continue) improving yourself and enhancing your health. Be steadfast and patient on your journey, and again, in the spirit of Mr. Petty, don't back down until the final buzzer blares. Who knows, you may be tied with Father Time at the end of regulation and be heading into overtime like Jeanne for so long managed to do.

———

BEFORE WE MOVE ON, let me say a few words about our final two featured dignitaries in Restorationville. Spending time with Risk and Balance may not necessarily lead to the revitalization and invigoration of your downtrodden mind and body but ignoring them can lead to requiring the services of our two previously discussed denizens of Restorationville, Recovery and Resilience.

Thus, I have assigned their talents to the Repair Shop and

embedded those abilities into our third pillar of well-being, because, as George would say, they're close enough. So, as I said earlier, our Repair Shop teammate and our sturdy last pillar can do it all (I didn't say *y'all* that time).

RISK

Citing my beloved dictionary once again, it states that risk is being exposed to a loss or injury. I certainly do know about being exposed to injury lately. And I have lost an object or two in my life (no, not my mind, as some think) whether it be money, artifacts, or acquaintances due to a particular course of action that I (or they) mistakenly undertook or didn't.

Whether it is exposure to loss, or to injury, risk is something that we cannot escape from while living our lives. I'm not sure why Mr. Franklin didn't include risk in his list of certain things in life, such as death and taxes. I'll give him a pass on not including my conflicting goals suggestion.

But regardless of it not making Mr. Franklin's list, risk is a part of our lives. That is reality; however, you have some control over the perils you face in life. You could choose to drive 90 miles per hour down the highway risking life, limb, and speeding tickets (and yes, I have been guilty of this at times in the past). Or you could choose to drive the speed limit as I do now and risk getting run over by those NASCAR wannabe drivers. I may be at risk of getting run over, but at least I'm not at risk of getting a speeding ticket or driving beyond my talent level.

And let's not even talk about the risk of getting hit head-on by distracted drivers who cannot put their phone down while driving. As I said, that's why I don't ride my bike on public roads any longer, as I mentioned in the last chapter. I'll take my chances with oncoming riders (that didn't turn out so well, but at least I survived to tell that story), black bears, deer, and turkeys traversing our trail.

Yes, with everything we do, we face a probability of something bad happening to us. I'm just glad I wasn't born into the Wallenda family and expected to carry on the business. If you don't know, those Wallenda people make their living walking tight ropes high up in the air without safety nets below them. Sounds a bit risky to me, even with my fortunately robust sense of physical balance.

On the other side of the equation, and please don't forget this; when pursuing a given activity, not only do we face the possibility of some type of harm materializing, we also simultaneously face the probability of something good transpiring for us. The hard part, of course, is not the waiting, as Mr. Petty once said, but figuring out which outcome outweighs the other when initiating that given action. Yes, we do risk getting into an accident every time we drive our vehicles on the streets and roads, but driving opens up so many wonderful possibilities to enrich our lives.

I am certainly not an expert at assessing, mitigating, and managing risk. You can look at my investment portfolio and see that. I think it is up to $3.49 now; I haven't checked under the couch cushions for any loose change lately, so I'm not sure. Note to Mr. Gates and the Oracle from Omaha: you have no worries about me overtaking you two as some of the richest people in the world anytime soon. But I do have a basic strategy and several tips to help you assess the risks in your life. Briefly, when undertaking any activity that involves risk (and most every action does), you can choose to avoid the endeavor altogether, mitigate the possibility of an adverse outcome, or commence with the undertaking come what may.

Avoiding Risk. Now, to absolutely avoid all risk in your life, you could craft plans to spend your entire existence inside a padded room, but I must tell you, padded rooms are not the most exciting place to spend one's life. I have never actually lived inside a padded room, but I worked inside one from time to time at the widget factory. It was nice with its soft lighting, soothing music, and black foam walls to entirely bore you, but the risk of bodily harm was virtually nonexistent in there.

Inside that dreary, mind-numbing room, a big dude worked diligently all day by himself at whatever he did in there. He was generally totally happy to see me when I had to come inside. Although he was probably the safest person in the facility, on weekends, he would go risk his proverbial neck (and his real one) putting out fires and performing search and rescue missions with the voluntary firefighting people to try to inject a little excitement into his life. So fair warning, avoiding all risk in your life may be a bit lackluster.

Back before I got the job at the widget factory, I had a very decent job in the big oil town as I mentioned way back in Chapter 2. During that time, I was running 50 or 60 miles each week in preparation to run my first marathon. One Saturday I had to work some overtime, and I remember running eight miles or so to the office, doing my work, then running the eight miles back home. That may not have been the smartest thing to do. Perhaps I was a bit distracted by my youth and talent back then, as our game plan principles suggest not to do.

However, I did the bulk of my marathon training at the huge city park that had a nice three-mile clay path. Every day, hundreds of people would be out there jogging, walking, running, or just relaxing. Part of the clay course ran alongside a heavily traveled thoroughfare, and you could literally see the air because of the smog. Somewhere back in the deep recesses of my brain, I thought vigorously inhaling and expelling that brown air through for my lungs could not be good, and more than likely leaving hazardous debris and other gunky junk spread throughout.

One morning in the deep of winter, I remember looking out from the 31st floor of my office building and seeing all of that pollution compressed downward toward the ground, apparently due to the cold air. I have no idea why. I'm not a meteorologist, but the scene resembled a big dark brown doughnut surrounding the city. I knew I had to get out of there.

Truth be told, I was in my first decade of adult life, and my exit plan was not the most well-executed. My exodus resembled that of a dog scurrying home with its tail between its legs rather than a well-executed mission. But the point is, I chose to avoid the increased risk of developing some type of pulmonary disease over time due to rushing all of that compromised air through my lungs.

Another activity I have mostly avoided all of my life is riding motorcycles despite growing up in the days of those easy rider people and Evel Knievel. As kids riding our bicycles, we did jump over little ramps like Evel did, but never any giant water fountains. Just so you know, Evel did land that jump, but not quite the way he had it planned. As E-bike Mike suggested a while back, gravity sometimes is not your friend, nor was it Evel's that day.

Anyway, having ridden my sleek bicycle for so many thousands of miles, I do get why people ride motorcycles. As I have said, there is something about moving through time and space and feeling the wind in your face. It's like flying on the ground. However, when I was a kid, the father of one of my best friends, who lived just down the road, seriously crashed his motorcycle. I saw what he went through after the accident, and he never was the same due to several severe, permanent disabilities. Thus, with the exception of riding my other best friend's dirt bike a few times back then, I have chosen to never again ride one of those mechanical steeds.

So, when determining to undertake any activity that involves risk, and as I said earlier, most all actions do, you always have the option of avoiding the pursuit for the most part. Sometimes you don't have a choice, but when you do, I would suggest you choose your pursuits involving risk wisely.

Reducing Risk. As I mentioned back in Chapter 3, jumping out of airplanes without a parachute is a bit risky, and thankfully, my dad always wore his chute while jumping out of those flying machines from 1500 feet up in the air thus mitigating his risk of a life-ending landing 80-something years ago. And with all due respect to those Wallenda people, if I were to start a tightrope walking business, I can promise you I would have about three safety nets below me to dampen my fall in case I lost my balance traversing one of those tight ropes. I thought about acquiring a bubble suit to wear when I ride my bicycle, but I don't think they have invented those yet.

Back in Chapter 7, we discussed how to mitigate injury while exercising by wearing properly fitted safety gear and being mindful of your environment. The Physical Guidelines advice of making sensible (and safe) choices regarding when and how to be active can be applied to most any new endeavor you commence and risk you take.

As you know, Mr. Brady always wears his helmet (both of them) when he goes off with his buccaneers to battle Ponce and his conquistadors. And, like Mr. Brady, I never climb aboard my bicycle without having my helmet on, unlike so many people I see out on the bike trail. Also, as I have spoken, I carry my bear protection device when hiking in the forest.

Yes, with practically every choice or action we commence, the possibility of less-than-stellar outcomes is possible. That's part of life. But most of the time, we have ample knowledge and means to reduce our risk of exposure to loss or injury in our daily actions. Ignore these precautions at your own peril, particularly when it comes to choices concerning your overall health.

And let me add a corollary to mitigating risk. Don't be distracted by your talent (or youth) as one of our game plan principles states when engaging in a pursuit. The latest epidemic at the bike park seems to be people (including kids) riding their bikes without holding onto the handlebars, apparently trying to look cool and exhibiting their vast talent (or ego). In my mind, they are showcasing their vast senselessness, which could lead them to becoming the occupant of Room 313, which is just down the hall from where my room was during those six days in the hospital. Please engage your brain when assessing your risk (including in your diet, exercise, and social engagements), and not your ego.

Accepting Risk. I have always said, if you don't want to get bitten by a shark, don't swim in shark-infested waters. But as I have spoken of earlier, I do enjoy visiting the beach and having fun in the surf riding my body board on the waves (my surfing days are long since gone). However, the beach I normally visit can truly be classified as having shark-infested waters; in fact, it is known as the shark bite capital of the world. Excuse me, what did I just write? Let me go back and read that again.

Yikes! Yes, what I just wrote in the preceding paragraph is very much true according to the International Shark Attack File maintained by the Florida Museum at the University of Florida. However, in the ten years before my pothole incident, less than 100 people were bitten by a shark at my beach and none died (the people, not the sharks). Given that millions upon millions of people have visited my famous beach during that decade, apparently our sharks are very picky eaters. Whew!

So, the message here is yes, I have accepted the risk of getting bitten by one of our sharks when playing in the waves, but I have done my research, and I know the odds of getting gnawed upon by one of our picky eaters. I have a far greater chance of dying there from a random lightning strike while sitting under my umbrella than from a shark laceration.

And as I mentioned above, driving your vehicle is another example that you have probably accepted because you know the risk of an injurious consequence is far outweighed by the rewards of that mechanized mobility, particularly if you choose to drive near the speed limit. And I am sure you have taken a driver's education course. I think the Model-T had just come out when I took Driver's Ed as a teen. I can't remember. Anyway, I hope you always wear your seat belt and keep both hands on the wheel (instead of one holding your phone) as those NASCAR racing people always do, although you probably could forgo wearing the fire suit attire they all wear. They do drive a little faster than you, I hope.

And despite spending those six days in the hospital, I still chose to ride my bicycle. Yesterday was such a brilliant day weather-wise, and I got to see so many of my friends. However, my sickbay experience has transformed my outlook on the risk of that particular endeavor. I rarely ride at the speed of sound with that large group I used to ride with namely because I haven't totally regained my conditioning and I can't keep up with them any longer (and at nearly 70 years old, my chances are steadily declining that I will be able to in the future), and additionally, I just don't want to go that fast any longer for safety reasons.

I was riding with my friend who takes care of his bubble a few days ago before their scheduled ride, and I was enlightening him of my transmutation from seeking to break the sound barrier while cycling to now finding joy in riding the bike simply for the sake of riding the bike. He said very good, my son, you have been awakened. I don't know if it's my grand awakening or not, but this morning I saw eight deer, one of which I stopped to watch her nibbling on the foliage ten feet away. The peloton would have simply blasted past her.

Summarizing our discussion concerning risk, when pursuing any new activity, always educate yourself and apply that knowledge to lower your risk of an adverse outcome in your chosen pursuits. And as another of our game plan principles suggests, don't be afraid to alter your course and adapt to your changing abilities, outlook, and levels of risk you are willing to accept.

BALANCE

I know a little something about balance because not keeping my balance while riding my bicycle could result in a close encounter with the unforgiving tarmac, and judging from the pothole incident, normally that is very painful. Nevertheless, as you have probably guessed, that is not the kind of balance we will be discussing here, though it does serve as a good metaphor for living our real lives (not our metaverse lives).

My cherished dictionary's second definition (not sure why it wasn't first) says balance is a state of equilibrium. If we apply that definition to managing and improving our lives, our health, and our well-being, we must endeavor to achieve balance between doing "what we gotta do" with "what we wanna do" to be in equilibrium.

My dictionary's fifth definition states that balance is a state of harmony, which it says is a pleasing arrangement of thoughts, parts, etc. So, if we are seamlessly balancing what we have to do in our lives with what we want to do, particularly concerning our nutrition, physical vigor, and mental soundness and stability, we will be in a perfect harmonious equilibrium like Beethoven's beautiful Moonlight Sonata. And good luck with that!

I have never experienced that level of harmonic bliss and balance in my life, and I doubt you have either, so welcome aboard. Life doesn't always quite turn out the way we have it planned, and, I would add, a fairly significant percentage of the time. Do you feel like you are 16 feet up in the air (without a safety net) on one end of a seesaw with one of E-bike Mike's brown bears on the other end growling at you? I think most of us have been there at one time or another. Or perhaps you feel like that most of the time: up in the air, frizzled, frazzled, and disheveled. Again, welcome aboard.

Know Thyself. Finding perfect harmonious balance in our lives is incredibly complex and constantly in flux. After all, we are not single cell amoebas who just float around and divide all day (talk about a great weight loss plan). And as I said in the beginning of this chapter, I am certainly not a subject matter expert here. I flunked out of the Himalayan guru school of finding peace, balance, and harmony on day one because I could not sit cross-legged due to my bowed legs. I was the first one voted off the mountain.

Nevertheless, after spending considerably time at the institute of harsh realities (that is, living life in the real world), I do know enough that to begin finding some semblance of balance in your life, you have to begin looking at yourself from within. Thus, by utilizing our first game plan principal, you need to seek knowledge, not about how to play Mel's harmonized scales, but concerning better comprehending yourself, understanding who you really are, and how to improve by honestly analyzing your physical, mental, and emotional well-being issues (along with your strengths) and candidly assessing your needs.

Are you severely overweight or obese? Ill? Depressed? Do you have too many responsibilities, or not enough? Do you have difficulty getting along with other people, or on the other end of the spectrum, too kind to others to a fault and can't seem to say no to anyone? Does your elevated ego prevent you from thinking you need to change anything about yourself? Or is your lack of self-esteem dredging you through the depths of despair and bleakness? The better you know yourself, your problems, and your requirements, the more efficient your path forward to a better, healthier, and more balanced life will be.

Prioritize.

Once you critically assess your issues, your strengths, and your requirements, along with evaluating your have-to-dos with your want-to-dos, prioritizing your solutions to your problems is an unbending requirement in order to help bring better balance into your life. To paraphrase a former famous bike rider person, if you pursue everything, you will achieve nothing. That's why my guitar had to sit in the closet for 40 years. Thus, establish your priorities to move forward in your life the best you can (and with help if necessary) to begin bringing your life into better balance.

Also, a note to you younger reader people, as you proceed through life, your priorities will constantly change due to where you are in life and what happens on your journey. Believe it or not, your children will grow up one day, giving you some extra time for yourself. After hitting that pothole, my only priority in life was to lie as motionless as possible to prevent searing pain from coursing through the entire left side of my body. Hopefully, your future priorities will gravitate toward a healthier and more balanced lifestyle as you progress through your precious life.

Yes, life can be, and normally is, chaotic and confounding. I think it has something to do with Mr. Einstein's quantum theory of entanglement. I have no idea, I'm not that smart. But I do know that finding balance in your life will always be a work in progress. At least, it has been for me. Only having those 14 days off all year back in 2013, my life was definitely out of balance between what I had to do and what I wanted to do because my life had not quite turned out the way I had it planned.

How did I survive? First of all, starting with all those carrots and that fiber book from way back when, I had always taken care of myself by providing my body and brain with the essential nutrients and building blocks they required to perform their affairs at least well enough to please Voltaire. And of course, as a kid and continuing into adulthood, I enjoyed running, playing sports, riding my bike, and engaging in other physical activities such as walking and gardening.

My last gig at the grocery store was, in effect, comparable to extended gym workouts as I traversed all over the store, putting those cases of corn, eight-packs of sports drinks, and gallons upon gallons of milk and water on the shelf. Plus, I met so many new friends, both work associates and customers, who enriched my social realm.

Mind you, my time in Restorationville was a bit out of balance, but because of my overall health, I survived the year. However, I was being drained and more than likely could not have carried on much longer without experiencing degradation in my health. But again, I survived to live another day because of my healthy diet, having many friends, and being in good physical condition going into that year.

And that is an excellent starting point for you to find balance and stability in your life between doing what you have to do and what you want to do in your precious life, that is, by prioritizing taking care of yourself physically, mentally, and emotionally as we have discussed over the past three chapters. And of course, by spending the requisite, but not excessive, time here in our Repair Shop.

Regardless of where you have come from, or what you have been through, taking better care of yourself facilitates stabilization in your life, allowing you to then improve yourself and your situation and move forward. And recovering and bolstering your health and well-being enhances your ability to balance your "gotta do" matters with your "wanna do" affairs, plus, more than likely, will improve your quality of life.

Now, you may be perfectly pleased with, after doing what you "gotta do" during your day, gobbling down your ultra-processed, fat-laden, preservative-rich [insert four-letter word] that you just microwaved, and then, without any thought of exercising and strengthening your body, sinking into your favorite comfy chair until bedtime, mindlessly keeping up with those people who live in some far-off wilderness place, or those housewives from wherever, while snacking on empty-calory salt and sugar treats and imbibing a fizzy drink or three.

Meanwhile, your heart, lungs, and arteries are probably *not* resonating melodies of harmonic bliss with that latest round of gunky junk you just bombarded them with, not to mention your waste removal crew screaming for some fiber to facilitate their responsibility of moving things along. Thus, despite your contentment illusion, not taking care of yourself will lead to a revolt, or simply a nondramatic accelerated deterioration from within, and the possibility of you reaching your expiration date long before you anticipated exponentially increases. Father Time may have you locked down by halftime if you don't push back.

I hope you have not been inflicted with any serious health shocks and traumas, but if your waistline is increasingly expanding while your muscles are turning to mush, again it's only a matter of time before perverse health outcomes will occur. Thus, now is most definitely the time to begin passing the ball to all four of your teammates. They all need to be as optimally engaged as possible in your perpetual effort to fend off Father Time and his unremitting accomplices. The base and pillars of your well-being structure all need to be as equally strong and balanced as you can construct them to protect you from their erosive schemes. So again, now is the time to shore up your structure.

No, despite life being a blessed gift, it is not all fun and games, nor will it ever be. Finding balance and equilibrium in your life will always be a work in progress and constantly shifting. Start with assessing your strengths and weaknesses, then prioritizing your "gotta dos" with your "wanna dos," because as one our game principles states, you will have conflicting goals (I still think that one should have been on Mr. Franklin's list). Use tools that work for you and promise yourself to stay on your journey with the goal of incremental and continuous improvement despite how erratic your progress may be. Because the healthier you are, and better balanced your life is, the better you can respond to those major pothole events in your life.

———

So, as those NASCAR people (not to mention The Who) told us long ago, we cannot go full gas, non-stop and do everything all the time, or we will blow a gasket or two, and perhaps our entire engine way before the end of the race. We most definitely need to find an off-ramp to Restorationville and quite regularly visit our beloved Repair Shop denizens, Recovery, Resilience, Risk, and Balance throughout, and particularly at the end of our day.

Yes, we all need frequent moments of respite during our day from pausing for that deep breath when dealing with a stressful situation, to longer timeouts such as a stopover in the breakroom to breathe our engine for a few minutes, or to come into the pits for a midday meal, or if we are lucky, a short nap, to recover from our mental and physical toils and in order to delay total exhaustion until bedtime.

And we all need lengthier recovery sessions, including our cherished weekends and periodic vacation getaways, for some needed rest and recreation. Hopefully, you will not need any prolonged periods of recovery due to significant illness, injury, or other acute or chronic incidents of infirmity. But fortunately, our Recovery colleague can renovate most anything if allowed the time to do the necessary revitalization.

Our Resilience associate, as we have learned, provides us with the ability to counter our setbacks and struggles in life, adapt, and carry on in some manner despite our misfortunes and difficulties. But if we lack resilience, we must not withdraw from life, dwell on our misfortunes, and possibly sink into the quicksand of unworthiness, victimization, substance abuse, and addiction. We must seek support from trusted family, friends, workmates (or all of the above), and if all else fails, professional guidance to grow our steadfastness. Developing our bounce-back capabilities is doable though may take a while, perhaps quite a while, but we must engage in this vital endeavor and always continue the quest.

Whether we are fortunate enough to possess compelling resilience capacities or not, we must not ignore our problems and difficulties (especially the vengeful wrath of Father Time), or they will certainly become worse, perhaps much worse. We must face our predicaments in pursuit of a path forward, get help if needed, and move on. Life is always ahead of us, not behind us. Cultivating our resilience facilitates our ability to rebound and overcome (or at least cope with) Father Time's insidious and unremitting assaults on our health and well-being.

Despite our final two Restorationville dignitaries Risk and Balance lacking significate recovery and regeneration skills, ignoring them can positively lead to extensively requiring the services of our Recovery and Resilience assistants. As we all know, undertaking any activity involves some level of risk of harming our bodies, but we have options. We can choose to live in that padded room and avoid all risk, although that would perhaps be exceptionally boring, and our novelty-seeking brains may have a few words with us.

We can also choose to accept undertaking riskier experiences but endeavor to mitigate adverse outcomes by wearing our helmets while riding our bikes (as Mr. Brady does when challenging Ponce and his conquistadors), always holding onto the handlebars, or wearing our seatbelts while driving.

Finally, we can accept activities involving risk because the benefits of the pursuit far outweigh the possibility of bodily harm such as swimming at my shark-infested beach. Thus, always chose your Risk undertakings wisely to lower the possibility of adverse outcomes in your chosen pursuits.

Finding balance and equilibrium in your life will always be complex, a work in progress, and constantly shifting, but vitally important. Assess your strengths and weaknesses and prioritize what you have to do with what you want to do. And please remember, though our lives may never be as harmonious as Beethoven's famous sonata, always strive for a more balanced, less stressful tomorrow.

Okay, let me offer you an apology here. I know you are probably disappointed that all of those letters in this chapter's title are not the initials of the Fifth Dimension band members, Mars and Jupiter have not quite aligned just yet, and the age of Aquarius is still not upon us with all its peace and love. Sorry about that, but at least you have now met our beloved and astutely beneficial compatriots of the Repair Shop: Recovery, Resilience, Risk, and Balance. Please get to know them well. Restorationville is a vital place to pass the ball to daily and consistently. And please, continue to build that third pillar of your structure strong.

———

We have now met all four of your teammates: Fuel, Hardware, Software, and the Repair Shop. Quirky names yes, but all highly valuable players on your well-being squad. And we have almost completed constructing your new house of health using those breathtaking blueprints to preserve your well-being.

Again, eating a healthy diet, engaging in appropriate exercise, learning, and constructively connecting with family, friends, workmates, and others, and spending the necessary time in our recuperative hamlet of Restorationville will take us a long way down the boulevard toward better health. But there is more to the story. Let us head on to the closing segments of our journey through this book, and a new beginning for you!

CHAPTER 10: PURPOSE, MEANING, HOPE

I ALMOST WANT to start this chapter out with one of our regular timeouts. We have all been through so much these past few years. With the worst pandemic in a hundred years, severe supply chain issues due to the disruptions, extreme weather, the rising cost of living, hatred, anger, fighting, and war all around the world, it seems there is no place to hide. I think I can speak for many of us that it may be time to jump off Ozzy's crazy train for a while.

All of this madness we have been experiencing here and abroad is the main reason I have theorized that Jupiter and Mars have not yet quite aligned, thus delaying the dawning of the Aquarius age as the Fifth Dimension postulated. How we all could use some peace, harmony, and understanding these days! NASA recently collided a vending machine sized satellite into some far-off asteroid in an attempt to change its course. Perhaps they could send another rocket up there to nudge Mars into better alignment with Jupiter.

But despite all this crazy train confusion going on these days, I can always hope for some improvements in our collective lives, and I hope you will, too. More on hoping for that improvement, but meanwhile, we have now met all four of our well-being teammates: Fuel, Hardware, Software, and the Repair Shop.

However, this chapter is not about them, it is all about us. We are the team captain of our personal health squadron. As I mentioned back in Chapter 2, I began to think about always staying healthy (though I had no idea how) in my very early teens after seeing how much weight one of my childhood baseball heroes had gained in the few years since he had retired from my beloved sport. I still cannot recall who he was, but I do still remember to this day what a significant transformation his body had gone through in such a short period. And again, I promised myself way back then I would never go there!

I actively began working with my well-being crew after moving to the college town when I discovered that fiber book (and though I didn't know it, eating all those carrots as a kid and running around outside all over the place every chance I got). Yet, it took me decades to learn the skills we will deliberate in this chapter, and I am still trying to master them toward being a better, healthier person and team leader.

As I mentioned in Chapter 4, you and I are the point guards of our individual health squadrons, and our responsibility requires that we connect with our well-being mates and orchestrate our team's offense (and defense) in our game of life. Our main job is to distribute the ball to all of our colleagues and let them make healthy plays against Father Time and his menacing marauders to keep us in the game for as long as possible.

Perhaps we may not become the greatest point guard ever, but we can become a much-improved performer and team leader in our life. We can't all be like the ultimate team maestros Magic, Isaiah, Mr. Stockton, or the Big O back in the day, or play as well as Steph or Ms. Bird today, but we can become quite acceptable at increasing both our healthspan and lifespan by performing as fluently as possible with our four well-being colleagues.

Also, as I stated back in Chapter 4, the glue that keeps our team together is our common purpose, meaning, and hope toward living as long and as healthy as possible in our game of life. Back in the cavepeople days, I'm guessing the common purpose for the clan was to stay alive considering all those saber-tooth tiger creatures roaming around looking to make them their next meal. Now that those cavepeople have spread all over the planet and we are them, I would have a difficult time articulating the common purpose of our entire clan, consisting of all eight billion of us. As you know, I am an athlete, not a philosopher person.

Thus, we will only focus here on growing our own sense of purpose, meaning, and hope in our own lives in order to be a better captain and team leader of our well-being crew with the goal of staying alive and healthy for as long as possible and living a more meaningful and worthy life.

We will explore each of these three subjects individually in a moment, but first, though I'm not a mystic mind reader (just an ancient athlete), I suspect all of my non-sports-fan readers are tired of all these sports terms, and you are impatiently sitting on the edge of your seats in fixated anticipation of the final unveiling of the complete blueprints for building that new, robust, and heathier you.

Purpose, Meaning, & Hope (You)		
Physical Activity (Hardware)	Mental Activity (Software)	Three R's & B (Repair shop)
Nutrition (Fuel)		

Just take a moment to behold the elegance of the design and the ornateness of the structure. Examine the exquisiteness of each of the tiniest details! Okay, so again, maybe it's not the fanciest or most ornate edifice ever conceived in the history of the world, but it is highly functional depending on your effort in constructing your gazebo of good health.

There you are at the top, supported by your foundation and three load-bearing columns. I hope you have built (or at least in the process of building) your well-being structure sturdy and strong. The sounder and more balanced your assembly is (and for you sports fans, the better your leadership and cooperation is with your teammates), the longer you will live and with a higher quality of life.

So let us explore these three gems of enrichment in our lives.

PURPOSE

Since I do not have a PhD in Biology (or Archaeology) from one of those high-level university places, I have no idea whether the chicken or the egg came first. Likewise, since I do not have a medical degree in Psychiatry (nor Antiquity), I also have no idea whether purpose or meaning came first into the lives of our cavepeople ancestors after they escaped the shackles of sheerly responding upon instinct like the other creatures they found themselves living among.

And truth be told, much deliberation abounds whether the concepts of having purpose and meaning in our lives are identical notions or are very differentiated from each other. Scanning published research, some very perceptive people say they are absolutely different, while other published individuals and organizations use the terms interchangeably. To be honest, I do not even thoroughly understand what my beloved dictionary is trying to tell me what each concept truly represents (more on this below).

So, since I do not know which concept came into our cavepeople ancestors' lives first, nor if they are the same or different, let us arbitrarily begin our discussion here with purpose from my perspective. As mentioned above, I'm only speculating that our cavepeople predecessors' main purpose in life was to stay alive (cue up those saber-toothed tiger creatures) which, fortunately for us, they finally managed to achieve.

WHAT IT IS

According to those NIH scientist people we met in Chapter 8, living a purposeful life is exceedingly beneficial to us for many reasons we will discuss in a moment. But what does having a sense of purpose in our lives entail and encompass? In highly non-scientific terms, our purpose in life is the motivational reason we get out of bed each day, other than just satisfying our physiological needs, like eating breakfast.

A primary example is rising most days to perform our job, occupation, or profession in support of ourselves, our family, our employer, and our community. No rocket science going on here, unless, of course, you are one of those NASA scientist people trying to figure out how to get Mars and Jupiter into closer alignment. By the way, a note to all of you NASA scientists and all you other smart people out there, I hope you have been paying attention particularly over the last four chapters. Father Time and his band of well-being bandits don't care how smart you are, they will still brutally attack you if you ignore your well-being teammates.

I have always had some sense of purpose in my life, and I think if you check your memory banks, you have, too. Despite wanting to become an MLB player, an Olympic marathon runner, a world champion tennis player, a high-level corporate executive (I could go on), etc., I knew deep down early on what I genuinely wanted to accomplish in life was to raise a family of my own (and of course, be healthy). And for a vast majority of people, family is the essential reason they rise out of bed every morning and proceed through their day.

For many others, the primary commitment in their lives is nurturing their jobs and careers, whether it be saving the world, acquiring wealth and prestige, or just surviving from day to day. Other motivations that get people out of bed are learning, taking care of others, pursuing adventures and hobbies among others.

And by the way, having more than one purpose in life is perfectly normal, though we should employ our Balance colleague from our Repair Shop, prioritize our endeavors (and perhaps eliminate a few), and not load our boat too extensively, else we risk sinking into various nightmare situations of stress overload. Remember what our former famous bicycle rider said in the last chapter about trying to do everything and accomplishing nothing.

YOUR PURPOSE IS?

I have to ask, do you know (given your age) what your purpose in life is right now? By the way, my beloved dictionary defines *purpose* as having an intention of doing something. Do you know what you intend to do with your life today, tomorrow, next year, or over the course of your entire existence here on Mother Earth? And do you know why having a purpose rather than merely existing with no particular focus or direction in your life is so important? Let us take a look.

As you may recall from Chapter 3, when I went to see my primary care doctor for my annual well check appointment a few years ago and divulged to her that I was preparing to soon retire from the widget factory, she anxiously asked me if I had solid plans in place upon my retirement? She didn't insert the "purpose" word into her question, but that is principally what she was drilling down to.

She knew not having any purpose in my life going forward, having nothing to do all day (and perpetually keeping up with those Kardashian people, internet influencers, and wilderness survival people doesn't count), and not regularly doing anything physically (getting up off the couch to go to the kitchen or bathroom does not count either) is an express ticket to many of the ill outcomes we discussed in that chapter.

And her concern does not just apply to just us boomers who are retiring, but particularly to you young millennials and zoomers (and everyone else in between and beyond) who want to spend all your time meandering through the metaverse, unceasingly staring at your phone, or camping out on your couch mindlessly gazing at your widescreen. Trust me (and my insightful doctor) on this, Father Time is licking his lips if you are guilty of these charges and have no meaningful purpose in your life. More on finding your purpose momentarily.

BENEFITS

Having a focused sense of purpose spawns many beneficial outcomes for our physical bodies and, particularly, our cranial computer. According to several studies I have perused from our NIH scientist friends and several major universities, having a sense of purpose in your life lowers your cognitive decline as you proceed through the years and approach my age and beyond. Your chances of developing Alzheimer's disease diminish when you possess a constructive sense of purpose.

Also, people with the north star of purpose guiding them through life are usually happier and less lonely. They are able to better manage pressure, anxiety, and other emotional distresses than those who do not have a guiding light of purpose. Plus, those with a positive purpose in their lives tend to maintain better health habits, enjoy better sleep, and stay within healthy weight ranges, helping them to stay stronger longer and increase their healthspan as their lifespan lengthens.

Possessing a powerful sense of purpose can give us explicit direction in our lives, guide our major life decisions, and shape our goals that genuinely mean something to us. And like that little knob on my electron microscope, having a sense of purpose will bring our lives into better focus, allowing us to make better decisions moving forward on our expedition into the future.

Additionally, having a sturdy perseverance toward effecting our purpose can help us through the tough times. Harsh times will happen to all of us eventually. However, possessing a steadfast purpose in our lives will help us bounce back, get through the sad, bad, and stressful times, and continue on down the road throughout our lives.

And just so you know, it doesn't matter what culture, race, sex, or age group you fall into (again, we are all human beings), the benefits (and there are many more than I have listed above) you receive from living a purposeful, and of course healthy, life are the same.

FINDING YOUR PURPOSE

Being an archaic athlete and former widget factory worker who spent most of his time putting numbers into little boxes, I am not the world's leading authority concerning how to find purpose in your life. However, an entire universe of books, articles, and online content has been written (and spoken) by people with exceedingly more credentials than I have. Of course, Ponce has sponsored many of those communiqués out there, so beware.

Thus, concerning how to find purpose in your life, as I have maintained throughout our time together in these pages discussing other aspects of your well-being, if you need help to uncover your true purpose in life, seek assistance to uncover your reason for rising from your sheets every day if you feel constantly bored, seem to be aimlessly drifting through your days without that proverbial paddle, and believe you have no sense of purpose in your life.

Begin with yourself. Ask yourself questions about why you feel so directionless. And, as I mentioned above, search your memory depositories for a time when you felt focused and motivated, and then ask yourself what has changed. Talk to your family and friends for clues concerning how you wound up without a compass and how to find a new (or old) purpose for living your life. And of course, if all else fails, seek qualified, professional counselors for assistance.

And just so you know, our purpose can, and normally does, undergo a series of subtle or sometimes dramatic metamorphic phases during our expedition through our days, particularly when one chapter ends, and another begins in our lives. You will recall my doctor's concerns when I was preparing to retire from the widget factory. She knew that I would suddenly lose a major reason for rising from bed most mornings and a significant portion of my social structure.

And particularly for you young zoomers, finishing and leaving school (and all your scholastic comrades, most of whom you will never see again) and transitioning into the working world can be a stressful, often traumatic experience. Thus, be prepared with all the support needed to maintain and grow your purposeful living, which again will help you through those stressful phases, regardless of your age. The earlier you begin discovering the new world of living with a purpose (and parents, help your children out here the best you can), the better and more focused (and resilient) your life should be.

Sadly though, and what breaks my heart, is that for apparently far too many people, their health is not an imperative reason they rise to seize the day (not even on their weekends). Too many humans these days attempt to get through each 24-hour period with as little effort as possible (both physically and mentally) and eat considerably more than their calorie expenditures necessitate, which mostly explains why three out of four Americans weigh way more than they should. Sigh.

Another fascination that dismays me these days is how nonchalant so many people (again across all age categories) are concerning their nutritionally desolate diets and physical expenditures of a rock. Just the other day, I heard a young radio announcer and his co-host laughing about his, to paraphrase, delicious and convenient diet of corn dogs and candy bars. As that longtime sports announcer person used to say, come on, people. It may be funny now, but Father Time is smirking and will get the last laugh more than likely sooner than later.

So, even if you genuinely are living a life driven by a just purpose, please include improving (or maintaining if you are already there) your health and well-being as a supplemental reason to get out of bed every day as we have discussed over the last four chapters. And as mentioned back in Chapter 6, take the advice of our old buddy Mr. Franklin that an ounce of prevention (nutritional food, regular exercise, positive social connections, adequate rest, and recovery) now is worth a pound of cure (massive medical bills and misery) later.

Again, improving and maintaining your health and well-being doesn't have to be your major priority and purpose in life, but should be among your top few. And if you are aimlessly drifting through your precious days here on Mother Earth (or someday on Mars so those NASA people say) without a compass, sextant, or roadmap app, improving your health is a most excellent locale to launch your mission toward living a purposeful life with all of its benefits we have discussed above.

And inaugurating your new mission toward improving your health is especially straightforward to commence and maintain. Begin with a tranquil walk down the street, down the hall, or around the block. Swap a carrot for a candy bar as a between-meal snack, a cup of tea for a fizzy drink, and dare I suggest partaking in a salad for lunch. Smile (or at least nod) to a stranger at the store. Build upon your early successes (our continuous improvement game plan principle), and most importantly, always keep your budding well-being vessel in the wind and never halt your purposeful journey.

Okay, pull your chair up a little closer. I have a secret to tell you. When I suggested above to smile at that stranger in the store, I had some inside information from those NIH scientist people (actually, it was on their website). When we perform a random act of kindness to help or cheer up someone, we fortify our well-being more than if we had treated ourselves.

Now, that is not to say, be kind only to others and not to ourselves. Again, we need to employee our Repair Shop's Balance associate to help us appropriately distribute our performances of kindness between us and others. But in general, studies show being compassionate to ourselves and especially to others increases our self-esteem and our overall happiness, not to mention generating an entire bouquet of advantageous physiological benefits for our brain and body. And who knows, perhaps those two planets will draw a little closer into alignment if more people sign up for this important mission.

Thus, in summary, I urge you to have a wholesome reason for rising from your place of rest each day. Having an explicit, positive sense of purpose provides us with a more focused sense of direction, helps us to make better decisions on essential affairs, and strengthens our resilience during our "hard times" (my grandmother always said were coming).

Also, possessing a guiding light of purpose in our lives helps us to be happier, less lonely, and better able to manage and maintain better health habits, enjoy better sleep, and stay within healthy weight ranges. Yay! And performing genuine acts of kindness to others (including your puppy dog) and ourselves also increases our well-being. And do not forget to periodically assess your purpose throughout your life when transitioning from one major stage to another.

Last, if you feel you have no sense of bearing and purpose in your life, beginning a mission to improve your health is a simple, straightforward, and enormously beneficial place to begin your quest toward living a purposeful life. Being healthy gives you so many more options to enjoy the one life that you are blessed with.

MEANING

As I mentioned, I had a difficult time deciphering the differences between *purpose* and *meaning*, according to my beloved dictionary. Purpose, it says, is an intended result and defines meaning as what is intended. Is my dictionary trying to tell me that purpose and meaning are the same thing? Am I missing something here, or am I just not that bright? As my famous sweathog neighbor just up the road a few miles used to say, I'm so confused.

So, I went to my bookcase and retrieved my other dictionary (I think I received as a gift upon my graduation from high school from the fifth-grade teacher I mentioned back in Chapter 3; note to self: everything you have is old, dude) and pulled out my detective's magnifying glass from my desk for an in-depth search for some clues as to exactly what our two concepts precisely mean.

That dictionary stated that purpose was something to be aimed for, that is, something intended to be done, as my beloved dictionary declared. Turning the pages over to the definition of meaning (and using my detective's magnifying glass to shift through all of the manifestations of the term), my high school graduation gift said that meaning was something that is significant or important to us and gave as an example, "health is everything." I could not have agreed any more with that assessment.

From my perspective, purpose and meaning are slightly different, but work in tandem with each other. That is, our reason for getting out of bed each day should be pursuing something significant, or meaningful, to us. You know, that rise and shine thing to achieve grand and mundane accomplishments each day, both of which are vitally important. And let me particularly emphasize those routine (often tedious and mind-numbing) achievements such as performing chores and doing the little things that connect all of the dots which, by the way, is the bedrock of our monitor and maintain game plan principle.

All the benefits we discussed above in our Purpose section will be supplemented by adding meaning to your purpose in life and will further sharpen your focus and path forward through your days here on the third planet. And again, with meaningful purpose in your life, you should become more incentivized to maintain better health habits and better able to cope with emotional distresses as our NIH scientist people articulated, not to mention being better able to bounce back after a major pothole incident occurs in your life. Hand raised in that scenario!

Searching for meaning and significance in your life is virtually the same process as discovering your purpose, as we discussed above. Again, begin by asking yourself what is genuinely important and meaningful to you, and what do you want to accomplish today, tomorrow, next Thursday, next year, and in 20 years that will be genuinely significant and gratifying to you.

You can also talk to your spouse, your family, and your friends for suggestions concerning meaningful routes to venture upon, but just make sure their suggestions are meaningful to you and not to them. And, of course, if all else fails, do not be ashamed to talk to a qualified, professional counselor for assistance in uncovering what is truly significant and important to you.

And let me say this, if you feel your life is meaningless and not significant, that is not a totally a ruinous obsession. It could be (if you do not seek assistance), but at least you know the difference between having meaning (and purpose) in your life and not. You know that something is missing, and now, you just have to search, again with all the help you require, to find your meaningful reason to get out of bed every day.

As I have suggested, if you do not know which path to begin your meaning-seeking journey upon, head down the road in the direction of improving your health; because again, having your health opens up a wider array of options for you to pursue in your search for a significant reason to rise each day. And nurturing your health is a simple and straightforward place to begin.

And now hear this! I have a special memorandum for you young zoomers (and all other age categories, for that matter). I do not think it is a big secret that a large percentage of you have regularly felt anxious, depressed, and shrouded by unhappiness (not to mention hopelessness) recently. But trust me on this, those feelings are not new and more than likely have been around since our cavepeople days.

They certainly were 50-something years ago when I moved to the college town as I mentioned above (and back in Chapter 2) and was working at that grocery store. Being so lonely and away from home and living in a strange town for the first time, I call that time my life's Great Depression era. But then I found that fiber book, met some new friends, and my path forward was rejuvenated, and the dark clouds of despair slowly dissipated, although they do return from time to time today. That is just part of life, though with the breeze of a meaningful purpose in your sails, they normally don't linger.

However, I will grant you this, in today's always-on, social media driven world, those feelings of anxiety and loneliness are more intense, and the cards are stacked against you, me, and most everyone else with so many distractions, internet influencers, the metaverse, and bad food that abounds. If you feel you are perpetually running into a brick wall, or have fallen into the dark bottomless abyss, may I suggest you call a timeout.

Perhaps you are focusing more on what you think you are missing out on rather than being thankful for what you are blessed with. You feel your life doesn't measure up to the lives of all those glorified social media influencers, and you are becoming even more depressed and disengaged in life. Again, please call a timeout! And please, make a genuine effort to find a meaningful reason for rising from your place of rest each day.

And during your search for a meaningful purpose in your life, recall my cycling friend's mission and just take care of your own little bubble (your schoolwork, your family, your job, your health, etc.) the best you can. And with any luck, you rise to the point where you feel confident enough to begin performing a random act of kindness or two for someone in your life or a random stranger.

I have been riding with a new group of cyclists lately, quite honestly, because I cannot keep up with the other group I used to ride with before the pothole incident. Instead of hanging on by my fingernails until I couldn't with that group and not being able to help them out, I can now be significantly more beneficial to my new friends during our rides by taking long turns on the front, breaking the wind for them, and that means a great deal to me as our NIH scientist people said it would.

Okay, so as with the chicken and the egg conundrum, I still don't know if purpose or meaning came first into the lives of our cavepeople ancestors. But if I had to guess, I would postulate they both dawned on our ancient, cave-dwelling forebearers at approximately the same time as they are basically the same concepts and serve to complement each other toward benefiting our health, well-being, and happiness. Please make an authentic effort to truly find a reason to rise and shine every day that will mean something to you! I think you will thank yourself.

And now, on to hoping for the best.

HOPE

Way back in Chapter 2, I was telling you that my favorite MLB team when I was a kid was the Pittsburgh Pirates. And to this day 60-something years later, I still check every morning during baseball season to see if they won last night. However, if you are a Pirate fan these days, you know that come April, we don't have much hope that our beloved Pirates will ever get back to the World Series again in our lifetimes. After all, they do hold the record for most losing seasons in a row.

So, when springtime rolls around here on the peninsula, instead of hoping for a return to the playoffs, I just hope that they don't lose 100 games in their 162-game season. It gives me a reason to keep checking on them every day. For the first half of the season this year, they fought valiantly to win as many ball games as they lost. But soon after the MLB all-star game in mid-summer, they began to fade. And now, deep into August with a month to go in the regular season, apparently yet again, they have given up hope, and are now expeditiously marching toward yet another 100-games-lost season. Update: they yet again "managed" to accomplish losing (exactly) 100 games this year. Sigh.

Perhaps when Mr. Brady finally retires from football, he can come pitch for the Pirates. Note to TB12, 300-plus pound beasts won't be trying to pummel you when you get on the pitcher's mound, unless, of course, you buzz one of those 200-plus pound sluggers in the batter's box with a high fastball under their chin. Heck, at this point, we would love to have Mrs. Super Model come join our Pirates. With those two playing for us, perhaps we may be able to get a few more fans in the stands. That would at least help out the popcorn-selling people.

Anyway, enough about not having much hope for the Pirates. And sorry, non-sports fans, you more than likely have no idea who the Pittsburgh Pirates are, but don't even bother looking them up. Although, they do have a picturesque ballpark nestled along the Allegheny River, which merges just downstream from the venue with the Monongahela to form the mighty Ohio River. Our country does have much beauty to behold, and more on beholding beauty momentarily.

However, even if you don't know much about the Pirates, you probably do know a little something about the sky-high cost of everything these days. Can anyone afford a small house or apartment anymore, or a full tank of gas, or even something to eat? And let's not even talk about the wars, weather calamities, those increasing tragic incidents-that-must-not-named, and widespread hatred issues happening here and abroad. Yes, the long-awaited alignment of Jupiter and Mars seems to be hopelessly far off in the distant future these days for most everyone, young and old, and for the world in general.

———

BUT BEFORE WE fall too far down into depths of hopeless depression, let us take a timeout for a happier story. As I was loading my bicycle into my vehicle after a long morning ride with my friends today, E-bike Mike pulled up to greet me. He is one happy fellow and astutely inquisitive! We conversed for almost half an hour as lunch time was rapidly approaching and my stomach was reminding me just how empty it was after 50 miles in the saddle.

He saw the front wheel of my bike sitting there and just had to inspect it. He was marveling over the precision construct and lightness of the wheel. He even counted all of the spokes! Just so you know, each of my wheels has 18 spokes. I had no idea. To me they were just an "economical" set of wheels that the bike shop mechanic had recommended, but to E-bike Mike, they were articles of splendid engineering because he understands those things unlike me.

Then, he gave me the total rundown on his new E-bike. And I am telling you, E-bike Mike has that thing tricked out. He has installed so many gadgets (including a pair of dice) on that machine, as well as some kind of apparatus that allows its electric motor to tell him how it's feeling. I'm not sure how all that works, but of course, he had his phone seamlessly controlling everything. And speaking of engineering, that piece of machinery was a study in sturdiness. He laughed as he admitted that maybe he had broken the frame of his old e-bike because of his girth. You cannot help but being filled with joy when seeing this man.

After listening to some of his greatest hits (come to find out, he is an accomplished musician and singer), he began telling me of a recent incident he and Mrs. E-bike had on another paved trail we have up the road a few miles. He allowed as how he may not have been paying attention as Mrs. E-bike began a left-hand turn and he did not. Henceforth, a collision ensured, and she "fortunately" landed in the grass as opposed to the unforgiving tarmac.

As you may recall from Chapter 5, Mrs. E-bike is approximately the same size as Mr. E-bike, and when he tried to help her to her feet, he pulled some muscles in his arm admitting he had not utilized the free gym membership he had available to him. I have not asked him why he has not put the same emphasis on his diet and muscle-strengthening routines as he has with his aerobic competences. I do get it; it is a ton more fun zipping along our beautiful trails both off-road and on our paved pathways rather than lifting a dumbbell (and no, that is not my nickname).

But as a reminder, you have to utilize each of your well-being teammates and allow them all to employ their skills in your game of life. You cannot (or should not) leave one or more of your colleagues without the ball for long periods of time, or worse, sitting on the bench. Trust me on this, Father Time will not hesitate for one micro-moment to promptly and reprehensibly exploit that weakness in your strategy.

And you need to build all of the components of your well-being structure as equally sturdy and robust as you possibly can. If your nutritional base is weak, the weight of you and your health pillars will deteriorate your foundation and you will teeter into that miserable space between your healthspan and your lifespan with endless pain, pills, and doctor visits well before perhaps even halftime (that is, as a reminder, reaching 50 years old). Or worse, you and your entire struc-ture could collapse upon your faulty foundation, ending your game of life well before it had to.

If one of your outer well-being columns is weak and crumbling, you could slide from your perch into the depths of Miseryville or again breakdown your entire structure. And if your main load-bearing Software post falters, you will implode from within, game over. There seems to be an epidemic of that particular phenomenon in America these days. So again, employ all of your teammates with equality as well as you can. And build your well-being structure stout and balanced and live long.

Okay, the referees are signaling this timeout is over, but one more quick item. I have noticed an uptick in the number of articles in the news media lately concerning the acceptance of people living with obesity, like Mr. E-bike. Over the years at the widget factory, I had several friends who were in the overweight and obese categories. I loved them all. However, as we all proceeded through the years performing widget-assembling stuff, I witnessed what that excess weight can physically do to a human body and the misery it can bestow.

Also, when I was a kid, my dad (who stood 6' 3" and weighed less than 200 pounds all through my childhood) had a short, stout friend who looked a lot like how the Jolly-man used to look before losing all of that weight. As I have told you, my dad made it all the way to 92 with an above average healthspan; his friend was gone before he reached retirement age.

No matter how well severely overweight people are accepted, having excess weight on their bodies is taking its structural toll on their hip joints, knees, ankles, and feet (not to mention all those other medical issues we discussed in Chapter 3). It is just a matter of physics. E-bike Mike could explain Sir Isaacs's laws of motion and gravity way better than I ever could, so let me just say this, please double-down on your efforts to be more like Jolly-man and employ all of your teammates.

He didn't want to be on pills for the rest of his life when his doctor proverbially punched him in the face, thus his extraordinary discipline to put distance between himself and those pharmaceuticals. And along with his exemplary diet, he gets abundant exercise at his job and gets to interact with many people. And you will remember, he does have those 43 clocks he has to wind up and work on periodically as his creative outlet. Thus, he is covering all of the bases (he told me he goes to bed early and gets up early) and his efforts are paying off with his improving health. He told me the other day about how happy his doctor was.

Okay, okay, okay, we are getting back out on the floor now! Sorry, the refs are yelling and threating us with a technical foul. For my non-sports-fan readers, that means Father Time gets to take a free shot at us, and that is the last thing we should be offering up to that menacing Force of Devastation. So, let us get back out there to our regularly scheduled chapter. And again, please re-marshal your efforts toward improving your health and well-being regardless of where you are on the weight spectrum.

———

So, back to hope seemingly fading from the scene these days for so many people (not to mention the Pirates). As I mentioned several times now, circumstances got so appalling in my life, particularly just after the first decade of this new millennium, I distraughtly typed something resembling "how to find hope" into my browser one day. Of course, as you have guessed, I got about 4,706,132,598 results in .6 seconds.

I perused through the first few pages of those commentaries (many of them of course written by you know who) and I distilled what I read down to a five-point strategy to promulgate a path forward that helped me through my darkest hours and days. Perhaps my strategy can also aid you with finding some hope in your life and a path forward during your grimmest periods. But if not, as I have said all along and will continue to say, seek professional help and guidance if you are struggling and sinking deeper into despair.

HOPE: CONSIDERATION ONE

The first hope strategy I settled upon for my journey through the badlands of despondency was to realize, and accept (which is the difficult part), that life doesn't always turn out quite the way we have it planned as we have spoken. Furthermore, despite the many we have had in this book, life has no timeouts; and for most affairs, we have no (or dreadfully little) control over its twists and turns. Life incessantly goes on and does not and will not halt over our misfortunes. I had to face this reality squarely in the eye, and I acquired a trophy black eye or two (or three, I lost count) along the way. Father Time is absolutely relentless.

It was during this period when our game plan principal to focus only on what we can control was beginning to be conceived in my tortured mind. I had to realize, I could not change what had happened, and I could not change what was going to happen for the most part. Thus, the only logical path forward was for me to set sail toward focusing on what I could control and persisting in doing what I had to do in order to navigate toward gentler waters on my voyage through life.

Also, as I mentioned in the last chapter when we were discussing resilience, I found a trusted colleague, my cubicle mate at the widget factory during those depressing days, to converse with about what was happening. As you will recall, he was also navigating through a particularly arduous strait in his life, and though our dialogues did not fix our problems, airing our tribulations out with each other definitely helped us (at least for me) to cope with them. So as the chorus reminds us, do not be ashamed to reach out to a helping friend, family member, workmate, or again, if all else fails, a professional to talk to as I did back during that particularly taxing windward leg of my life's expedition.

Thus, the best you can, focus only (or at least mostly) on what you can control in your life, learn from your misfortunes, endeavor to let them go, and strive to rise above your tribulations (with as much help as you need). My parting gift when I got voted off that mountain was a picture of the Himalayan guru (sitting cross-legged of course) with the inscription saying, "Let that [insert four-letter word] go." My token souvenir was rather humiliating and embarrassing, but it did unmistakably get the point across. Letting [insert four-letter word] go is a most demanding mission when life does not turn out quite the way we have it planned and keeps hammering us in the face, but is vitally necessary for our well-being.

HOPE: CONSIDERATION TWO

The second approach I decided upon in my quest to find some hope for brighter days in my future, was to cut off the what-ifs, or at least, the best I could. What if this happens? What if that happens? Worrying about all possible appalling outcomes in your situation can drive you to drink before lunch (hand reluctantly raised as I have mentioned), or much worse self-destructive behaviors. I am not saying ignore all of your potential threats and perils, you should be prepared to face (the best you can) your worst nightmares should they occur, but don't let your dire what-if possibilities eat you alive.

Another type of what-if to squash is wishing you had done something differently: why didn't I do this, what if I hadn't done that, etc. Again, like caterpillars on tender green leaves, continuously hashing these second-guessing scenarios through your mental processor can devour you from within and lead you into dark dungeons of despair.

As with accepting the fact that life doesn't always turn out the way we have it planned, squelching our negative what-ifs bombardments during grim stretches is also an arduous assignment. However, instead of chewing your fingernails off worrying about what could happen or beating yourself up over something you did or didn't do, again, try to learn, find strength, and grow from your depressing prior experiences and woeful missteps so that you will be better prepared for life's hard knocks in the future. And learning and growing through life helps to let [you-know-what] go and brings the temperature down on you what-if wildfires.

And to swing back briefly to our discussion in the last chapter, like risk, our what-if scenarios can turn out to be positive if we exercise our brain into conjuring up a few. Thus, in the thick of thinking up all those adverse what-ifs that can happen to you, try to also summon some positive (and realistic) outcomes that theoretically could transpire.

If our cavepeople ancestors had only worried about all the injurious what-if possibilities, they would never have pursued hunting those wholly mammoth beasts that provided months of food, tons of tools, and years of fur coats. Fortunately, they learned from Og and Bog's debilitating and mortal wounds, came up with better strategies, and here we are today though we don't have to hunt wholly mammoths any longer. Phew!

So again, try the best you can to cut off your pessimistic what-if scenarios, learn and grow from your unhealthy experiences and deeds, in the pursuit of cultivating more bountiful fields of hope for brighter days in your future. As that old saying goes, prepare for the worst (by assessing your most likely negative what-if scenarios) and hope for the best (those positive what-if results you conjured up). Life generally settles somewhere in between.

HOPE: CONSIDERATION THREE

The third plank of my budding hope platform I formulated during that dire period in my life was to seek inspiration from others who had been inflicted with even more devastating and grave events in their lives yet had rebounded and gone on to morph into something better than they were before. Or they created a foundation, an agency, or some type of service that helped many people who had been through the same thing they had. That is, seek heroes who were knocked to the canvass by one of those thunderous right crosses of calamity we spoke of in the last chapter and then bounced back to display exceptional (or even common place) levels of courage and resilience.

So many examples of people who have created so much good after experiencing catastrophe abound among us to aspire to, some famous, most not. Perhaps you know a friend or family member who has recovered from a traumatic event. Seek them, learn how they overcame their trauma, and grow your resilience as we discussed in the last chapter to begin scaffolding your hope for better days in the future.

HOPE: CONSIDERATION FOUR

Now, swinging back to our first hope tenet for a moment, when life doesn't quite turn out the way we have it planned, and given we have very little control over life, when something damaging, injurious, or prejudicial happens to us, we basically have two choices we can make. We can choose to play the victim's role, *or* we can put on our big person pants, try to overcome the situation (or at least make the best of it), and possibly, like those people we just discussed, rebound, and create something better from the situation.

During that dismal and dark period in my life, I could have played the victim's role and walked around all day with the back of my hand across my forehead, muttering "Oh, woe is me." Truth be told, there were moments throughout numerous days I did, prover-bially of course. But the last thing you want to do is lock yourself into your "poor-little me" closet and whine and whimper.

And just so you know, numerous triggers throughout your day can set you off and push you further into the cubbyhole of victim-hood, but as Mr. Petty always advised, stand your ground, and don't back down to your feelings of affliction and victimization. Thus, our fourth beam to build our hope for brighter days is to try to perform something good during those tortuous and catastrophe phases, rather than choosing the victim's role.

And again, just so you know, we don't necessarily need to become a hero or save the world. Accomplishing something good can simply mean continuing to do what we "gotta" do to uphold our responsibili-ties, taking care of those we have to take care of (including ourselves), and continuing to move forward in our lives instead of checking into Victimhood Village. But trust me, this is easier said than done, there-fore as always, seek help if you need to, but do not resort to groveling for too much attention and sympathy which only serves to lock you more securely inside your poor-little me closet.

HOPE: CONSIDERATION FIVE

Finally, while traversing through my darkest days and in search of some ray of hope for better days in my future, I learned to be thankful for what blessings I had, and there were many. Most importantly, I still had my health, and I had a good job at the widget factory (and the one at the grocery store). And, of course, I had my family and friends. And though I lost my ability to run during those dark days, I at least had those aerobic machines at the gym to stay physically strong, and I went for those long walks in the park. My time in the Repair Shop was a bit sketchy back then (which, of course, is not recommended), but I survived.

In addition to being grateful for the simple positive factors in my life, I also learned one dreary morning back then to proactively seek and cherish beauty to strengthen my assurance that the hope of brighter days was conceivable in my life. As I mentioned above, our country has much beauty to behold, and I have seen much of that magnificence from the Keys on the peninsula to the rocky shores of Rhode Island, not to mention the two crown jewels of Yellowstone and the Grand Canyon (there is a reason they call it that).

However, experiencing these beautiful vistas is not necessarily the type of beauty I am speaking of (though seeing those gorgeous national wonders counts). As I mentioned, I lost my ability to run during those dismal days, thus losing my go-to release valve. One gloomy weekend morning (weather wise and mentally), I was out riding my old fat tire bike (my beloved bicycle was not yet a gleam in my eye) just trying to spawn some of those feel-good endorphins inside my body for some relief.

As I rolled through the misty and overcast countryside, a bald eagle (a rather rare sighting in my area of the peninsula) flew by and perched in a tree above, as if protectively watching over me as I passed. As I ascended a slight incline with that magnificent bird looking on, the sun briefly broke through the clouds and shined majestically down upon me as I crested the hill. The road sparkled as if studded with diamonds. It was a sight to behold!

The sun (and the eagle) then quickly disappeared on my short descent down, never to be seen again that day, but there was that magnificent moment. That scene persistently played through my consciousness for the duration of my ride and led me to realize that despite my life's current gloom and doom, good things, beautiful things could still occur if I only kept living and doing what I had to do. That experience made me feel much better, and I have never forgotten it.

So yes, to spawn some hope for happier days, be thankful for the positive aspects of your life. And try to regularly pursue stoking some splendor up in your own life and appreciate such wonder when it does randomly occur. Beholding the crescent moon speaking to Venus (with Mars and Jupiter listening on nearby) just after the sun has bid adieu for the day, relishing the warmness of a deep friendship, or appreciating the adoring eyes of your devoted pooch lovingly looking up at you–all those blessed moments count toward building a stronger sense of hope in our lives.

In summary, yes, we all need to have a reservoir of hope on our life's journey. Along with having purpose and meaning in our lives, hope gives us a reason to get up in the morning (or afternoon, or night). So if you find yourself locked deep inside your "poor-little me" closet (and screaming to get out) for whatever reason, be it physical, mental, or emotional, hopefully my simple strategy I used a decade ago (and still do) can provide you with a key or two to help you escape from your dungeon of desolation and despondency.

When life doesn't turn out quite the way we have it planned and all those negative what-if arrows are piercing our brains from all angles, focus on what you can control, learn from your misfortunes, endeavor to let them go, and rise above them best you can. Seek help and inspiration from others who have been through deep valleys of despondency and despair yet survived and perhaps eventually prospered.

And please don't back down to your feelings of affliction and victimization, as Mr. Petty advocated. Strive to engage in worthy actions, or at least do what you have to do to carry on with your life productively and honorably. Be thankful for the blessings you have and seek and cherish beauty to strengthen your assurance that the hope for brighter days is conceivable in your life.

———

OKAY, we need to take a timeout here with a minute or two left in this chapter, because I have to tell you something. Now truth be told, upon reviewing my notes from those turbulent years in order to write this section on hope for you, I feel as if I have been forcefully dragged against my will into Mr. Wells' time machine and been taken back to bear all those appalling emotions and anxious moments once again.

I'm not going to lie to you. I have had a few rough and ragged days emotionally stretching into a couple of weeks now.

Reality is screaming at me that a second verse of those horrific years could actually play out in my life reasonably soon. Yet another menagerie of nightmare what-if scenarios has ravaged my time worrying about future possibilities, most of which are beyond my control, and I have lost precious time in the Repair Shop agonizing over that reality. It has not been a fun voyage recently.

Additionally, I do not turn on a dime like those racecar-like zero-turn mowing machines those lawn maintenance people zoom around on, but more like a large ship in open, turbulent seas. But all along, during this latest tour through the dark side, I have been attempting to channel Mr. Petty's advice and have been trying to stand my ground the best I can in this latest, intense battle for my own well-being.

I have constantly been reminding myself that when those days of difficulty (or brand-new nightmares) do come around in the future, to remember that all I can do is handle the situation the best I can in the moment, and in the meantime, try to relax and prepare.

Given my past track record, those are not the most comforting words I have ever heard, but that is all I have. And that may be all you have in your darkest moments. None of us (that I know of) has a magic wand (except perhaps Mr. Potter), so again, all we can do if we see stormy weather headed our way on the radar, is to prepare for the most likely worst outcome and hope for the best and keep telling ourselves that we can manage our setbacks (with help if needed) when they do come.

Meanwhile, I have continued to ride my beloved bike with my friends, to eat nutritiously, and attempt to get enough rest (some nights are better than others). I have continued to hammer away at writing this book for you, and I have continued to pluck away at my attempt to produce ear-pleasing sounds to emanate from my guitar, although Mel just keeps shaking his head.

Then this morning (at last), I woke up with a text message on my phone conveying some good news. Later in the day, I received another text from another person also bringing a morsel of good tidings, then yet another, thus apparently, the tide is headed back toward the brighter side in my life, at least for now.

And that is the point of this timeout. Even if you recover from a chronic illness, a mental (or emotional) crisis, or a social miscue, I can assure you that eventually, setbacks will spring up (and possibly abound) in the future just as the tides always come back in after they have gone out. Father Time and his cruel cult of crusaders will always be planning and executing counter offensives to spring upon us when the sun is shining in our lives. That is what they do. Expect those blitzes and prepare best you can to fend off those barrages by continuously maintaining and improving your health and well-being.

OKAY, in the closing moments of this section concerning having and cultivating hope in your life, let me give you an exemplary example of having vast quantities of hope. Now at the tender age of 92, my mom recently promised her great-grandson that she would come to his high school graduation. If she makes it to his ceremony, she will be 102 years old. So yes, my mom does possess plenty of hope bearing off into the future, and I hope you do, too, even if you are 92 or 22.

And by the way, I hear from reliable sources that my Pirates made some front office hires a while back who have made some significant upgrades to the team which may soon begin to pay dividends. My favorite player (minus his long, flowing braids) is back with a new crop of young (and old) talent by his side. Perhaps come springtime next season, there may be hope that we won't lose 100 ballgames again next year, and dare I say it, we could actually win as many games as we lose. No, I won't go quite that far, but trust me on this, if there is some semblance of hope for brighter days ahead for my beloved Pirates, there is hope for all of us!

Yes, we are the team captains of our personal health squadron, and we have focused in this chapter on growing our sense of purpose, meaning, and hope in our lives in order to become a better player and team leader for our well-being crew. Hopefully, along with me, one of your meaningful goals, that is, the reason you get out of bed every day, is to stay alive and healthy for as long as possible and live a worthy life.

The deeper your sense of purpose is in your life, the more meaningful it is to you, and the better you are at always hoping for the best, that is, living life as optimistically as possible, the stronger you will be as your structure's roof protecting your health from the erosive onslaughts of Father Time and his caustic crew. And the more you cultivate your sense of purpose, meaning, and hope, the better team captain you will be managing your competitive (and cooperative) colleagues in your game of enjoying a healthier, longer, more enjoyable life.

Few of us can change the world, or nudge Mars and Jupiter into better alignment and spawn the age of Aquarius for all eight billion of us. But we can focus inward on what we can control as one of our game plan principles suggest and nudge our own personal health planets into better alignment one bite, one step, one friend, and one good night's sleep at a time, over and over again each day until we can't.

So please study, and more importantly, activate and embed these three gems of enrichment we have discussed here, purpose, meaning, and hope, into your own life, along with persistently utilizing the talents of all your well-being teammates in your lengthening and prosperous game of life. And if you haven't already (and more on this in the next chapter), please take that proverbial (and literal) first step toward aligning your own personal planets by improving your health and well-being as we have discussed here and over the last several chapters.

————

BACK IN CHAPTER 2, I told you all about my story, when I decided to always try to stay healthy, how I learned over the years to accomplish that (at least well enough to please Voltaire), and thankfully, my long and winding journey (potholes, bike crashes, and all) is still healthily (for the most part) continuing.

But now, it is time for us to head on down Grandma's river and focus on your story. Where are you along your long and winding pathway through your life? And where do you want to go from here? Can you still run that 5k in 30 minutes? Are you carrying a little extra freight on your frame? Are you suffering from a chronic illness? Are you always sad? Okay, just call a timeout, relax, and breathe. It is not game, set, match just yet. I am sure you still have plenty of competitive fire in you and more life to live and enjoy.

So let us now head on over to the next chapter and talk about your continuing story. I have some matters I need to emphasize to you, and I hope you will promise me that you will take care of them the very best you can, or at least well enough to please George.

There it is! The green flag just flew, so let us now go talk about you!

CHAPTER 11: YOUR STORY

Yes, it's been a while now since we went on our virtual bike ride together way back in Chapter 1, and we then read all about my mostly healthy, long and winding (and again, thankfully still continuing) journey in the second chapter, but now, it's all about YOU!

It is time for you to go out there, get healthier, and live! I hope you have been paying attention. Life is too grand and too short to not pay attention to your health and well-being. As I said in the beginning, we all know what the outcome will be in our game of life, but so many wonderful activities, fascinations, and joy can occur between the opening bell and the final buzzer.

Along with the inevitable setbacks, difficulties, and tragedies that you will encounter along the way, goodness, delight, and glory can also be yours to behold and adore. Learning to read, obtaining your first job, watching your child discover the world, being laid off from your job, remembering Grandma's river freely flowing (for me), experiencing your parent dying, seeing your child in a cap and gown, plodding through mind-numbing task of toil; as one of my cycling friends says, "It's all good." And as our singer-sailor person once said, some of it's tragic, some of it's magic, but again, it's all good and we have all been blessed with life.

And depending on your level of effort, your story can continue for many more interesting, exciting, and meaningful chapters! So please ask yourself, how do I want my life story to turn out? If I had to guess, I think you would prefer to be more healthy than not and (cue up Mr. Spock) live long and flourish (or is it prosper?). Therefore, let us now take a few more moments to review, reemphasize, and rehearse what you "gotta" do (along with many other assignments) before you head out onto the floor to face Father Time and his misery mercenaries.

EFFORT IS REQUIRED

Yes, as I just mentioned and have said all along, and please do not forget this, effort is required on your part (despite what Ponce says) to mesh as tightly with your teammates as you feasibly can toward becoming a formidable force to fend off Father Time and his notorious gang of mayhem makers for as long as possible. And hopefully (and again, this is doable), you put in the energy and determination to make it to the century mark in your life. And a note to you young zoomers and millennials out there, that period of 100 years is significantly shorter than you think, particularly when you, with any luck, get to be my age.

Build your well-being ramparts strong to withstand Father Time's insults and corrosive assaults for as long as possible. It all starts (but more importantly doesn't end) with consuming one serving of nutrient-rich green beans from a can (or preferably fresh) instead of throwing [insert four-letter word] into the microwave, with one tranquil (or spirited) stroll around the block preferably with a loved one or cherished friend, with engaging in a candid problem-solving conversation with a work associate deciding which nails to use to attach shingles back upon someone's roof after a hurricane blew through, and with getting a good night's rest and enjoying your weekend.

Build upon this simple start by employing our game plan principles and by remaining firmly grounded in a reality mindset. Fabricate your health and well-being structure sturdy and continue fortifying it until Father Time and his insidious team of erosive elements eventually topple your stout fortress. Even Mother Earth herself probably will eventually succumb to Father Time, whether it be from humans, aliens, or some unknown force that even our friend Einstein (or E-bike Mike) could explain. However, I wouldn't lose any sleep over that possibility. Just stay focused on your own mission to better your health and well-being.

YOUR JOURNEY WILL BE UNIQUE

I have introduced and acquainted you with Jolly-man Stan and E-bike Mike and spoke of how dissimilar their journeys have been since getting to know them over the past year. The Jolly-man has now lost over a third of his body weight in less than twelve months after his doctor proverbially punched him in the face by telling him to change his dietary ways or die.

With herculean self-restraint, Jolly-man Stan has maintained his astonishingly austere diet over the past year, which has resulted in his vast weight loss of nearly 100 pounds. Even with my ample endurance athletic discipline, I could not maintain his dietary protocols. And apparently, like me, E-bike Mike doesn't have the Jolly-man's extreme disciplinary resolve regarding his nutrition, either. But he does hammer that e-bike for miles upon miles while the Jolly-man only gets passive (but adequate) exercise.

So, the imperative message to remember is that we do not all start from the same train station in our recovery projects and protracted reclamation efforts. Some of you will begin your revitalization endeavors considerably deeper inside the dark forest of affliction and unhealthiness than others and face significantly lengthier trails to traverse to more scenic venues of well-being.

And of course, we all have different competences. We are not all blessed with the Jolly-man's extreme disciplinary skills concerning the quantity (and quality) of his nourishment. Again, I do not, but we do all have some level of capabilities and restraint. Use your own abilities, attitudes, and whatever else you can muster to stay the course to Healthyville. Be steadfast and patient on your trip, and as Confucius said many millennia ago, it doesn't matter how fast you go, or how slowly, it only matters that you do not stop. And please, do not be distracted or surrender to your self-doubts and setbacks, as one of our game plan principles articulates.

Thus, your journey will be unique. Do not critically compare your excursion to anyone else's adventure. Your maintenance or recovery expeditions will perhaps be similar, but inescapably distinctive and diverse from anyone else's drive to betterment and healthy sustainability over the years. Your recovery journey will not be like mine, nor the Jolly-man's, or E-bike Mike's. Enjoy being distinctive and unique.

A LONG AND WINDING AFFAIR

Additionally, as one of our reality checks from Chapter 5 states, your revival expedition and your survival voyage will not be linear like a beeline down the drag strip at 300 miles per hour like Jolly-man Stan's weight loss. Again, as Sir Paul told us long, long ago, it will be a long and winding affair. And your expedition will more than likely resemble routing your path forward through a mystical interwoven labyrinth. But that is not necessarily a totally dreadful experience. I am sure you have heard of taking the scenic route.

On one of our family trips off the peninsula up to New England one summer to see family, I planned a stop for the kids to explore a living maze of over 1500 hedges to break up the boredom of the two-day drive. We were in there quite a while navigating and searching for each avenue of progression and often having to reroute our bearing due to the multiple dead ends we came upon, before finally reaching the completion of our long and winding expedition. The kids had so much fun on that excursion through that living web of hedgerows, and that family adventure definitely qualified as one of those precious moments for all of us to recall and smile about.

And your recovery journey back to Healthyville can be just as entertaining and rewarding (particularly if you set sail with some of your family or friends) despite the many setbacks, potholes, and dead ends you will encounter, detours you will have to overcome, and lane changes you will have to execute. Again, remember to employ all of our game plan principals (particularly not being afraid to change course) along with our reality checks from Chapter 5.

YOU MUST BEGIN

Speaking of our family excursions off (and upon) the peninsula, as the youngsters were growing up, I began formulating a plan (when they were still quite young) for the vacation they would never forget which involved making a beeline to the gateway city to the west (to see old friends) and then visiting several of our country's most breathtaking venues including, as I have mentioned, the Grand Canyon and Yellowstone.

I meticulously planned that two-week escape down to the minutest detail (don't worry, there was plenty of room left for adventure), and for the most part, everything went according to plan. Of course, there was that one hotel-than-must-not-be-named, but not being afraid to change course, I procured another place to stay that evening (which cost me nearly a week's pay) where the kids would feel safer. Otherwise, the trip went mostly as planned.

Now let me ask you this, how long have you been planning your long anticipated excursion to Healthyville? A month? A year? Since forever? Well, let me just tell you this but I'm sure you already know, the only way you will ever enjoy the wonderful spectacles of Healthyville is to load up in the van, pull out of the driveway, and head on down the road toward well-being. You will never get there if you don't ever leave the station of unhealthiness.

Yes, absolutely the most important imperative to accomplish on your way to revitalization and to the enjoyment of the refreshing sites in Healthyville is to simply get started (if you haven't already). Beginning your journey to recovery, health, and well-being could be your greatest life achievement, or at least, one of your most important.

Again, you don't have to try to be like Jolly-man Stan and lose weight at the speed of light. Remember it took me, Mr. Athlete Guy, over a decade to lose those 20 pounds. Your results and accomplishments will be unique, but again, your most important achievement will be to begin your journey to Healthyville and always continue on your voyage toward better health, well-being, and enjoyment of life. Life in Healthyville can be, and is, so worthy of your efforts, and so are you to your loved ones.

MUNDANITY OF PRACTICE

Okay, if you had me strapped to a board and were holding a needle-sharp nail millimeters from a giant water balloon suspended over my head and asked me which of our twelve game plan principles is the most important one or else, I might tell you to go ahead and burst my bubble because it gets hot down here on the peninsula. All of that water spilling across my body would be refreshing. However, if it was December (yes, at least for me, it does get cold down here), I would probably shout out that our second game plan principle, that is practice, is our most important tenet that most definitely needs to be adhered to.

But I get it. Selling you on the mundanity of practice is a hard transaction because of all of Ponce's enticing (and expensive) fountain of youth products and alluring (and ensnaring) nothing-for-something services. But I have to be brutally honest here, most big achievements in life are the culmination of countless ordinary undertakings and recitals over, and over, and over, and over again and again and again.

One salad every Friday is not going to get you to Healthyville.

And skipping one fizzy drink for a glass of water every other Tuesday will not decrease your proximity to there, either. Nor will just one walk in the park every few weeks. Playing 4,384 renditions of "Sor's Waltz" over the last year will, or at least, make you better as I am slowly becoming with that particular piece and with the guitar playing endeavor in general.

By now, you know where to begin your journey to a healthier vista and lifestyle by first seeking knowledge and direction from reliable sources on how to get there; and then practicing and practicing and then practicing that advice some more and from now on (whether you have Mel shaking his head at you or not).

Build your nutritional base by consuming one healthy meal after another over time (years, not just days or even weeks), that is, continuously practicing good dietary habits from now on and for the rest of your life. Shore up your Hardware column by engaging in recurring episodes of aerobic, muscle-strengthening, flexibility, and balancing activities. Run, maintain, and continuously update the code inside your cranial computer by habitually striving to learn something new and staying socially engaged. And of course, spend the requisite time in the Repair Shop.

Working on all of these small skills during practice time with your teammates and then drilling them into habit will take you a long way toward Healthyville (and keep you there upon your arrival for most of your game) when you and your well-being colleagues are out on the floor and start performing flawlessly together (or at least well enough to please Voltaire). Strive to progress incrementally and to always, always, always continuously improve your health by practicing and practicing good health habits most every day until the final buzzer sounds.

MONITOR AND MAINTAIN

Just before I blurted out "practice" as you were about to plunge that needle-sharp spike into my bubble, I almost exclaimed that our monitor and maintain principle was most important. That principle is only a few electrons behind our practice principle in terms of its importance. You would have to use my electron microscope to see just how close both principles actually are in their significance to your well-being.

And I know, just like practice, selling you on the essential and necessary effort of continuously monitoring and maintaining your health is also problematic and nearly futile again given all of Ponce's magical maintenance pills and effortless procedures he will sell to you for a hefty ransom. But again, I cannot overrate the importance of constantly monitoring and steadfastly performing the countless recurring (and often boring) preservation activities toward the perpetuation of your well-being structure beginning with maintaining your personal hygiene, keeping your living spaces clean and safe, and routinely visiting your health care providers for any signs of danger (and premature deterioration) ahead.

When our good friend Jeanne, the French lady who lived to be 122, was about to turn twelve, the magnificent and iconic jewel of Paris, the Eiffel Tower, was completed. As you will recall from Chapter 5, she told me one day just how much maintenance effort was required to preserve that grand steeple of magnificence. For instance, it takes two to three years (depending on the weather) to paint the entire structure and Mr. Eiffel recommended that those Eiffel Tower painter people paint his masterpiece every seven years. That is a fair amount of painting, otherwise known as maintenance. But that magnificent monument is still in its glory when I see it every year while watching the Tour of France on television.

Now I am not recommending hiring any of those Paris painter people in order to get yourself painted every seven years, but it is just as imperative to consistently perform your maintenance protocols as it is practicing your beneficial nutritional habits, exercising, mental calisthenics, and recovery efforts to maintain your physical and mental mansion of glory. Again, the importance of practicing your healthy habits and constantly monitoring and maintaining your well-being structure are only nanometers apart.

Also, as you progress through your life, your standard maintenance procedures will need to evolve. Living down on the peninsula all these years and spending so much time out in the sun working, exercising, and having fun, I now annually go see my skin doctor, who checks my epidermis for any early signs of melanoma and other skin diseases. Over the past couple of years, he has removed several precancerous anomalies on different parts of my body. Again, routine maintenance is far more palatable than enduring any major restoration endeavors.

Speaking of watching all those Tour of France races, half of the fun of viewing those telecasts is seeing all of the majestic sights France has to offer. However, those television helicopter people often fly over once majestic ancient castles, many of which have now crumbled into disrepair (though many are now being preserved) due to not having been properly maintained over the centuries. Yes, Father Time goes after everything, including your own well-being citadel.

So again, I cannot overemphasize the significance of persistently performing those numerous, often mind-numbing (but frequently gratifying) maintenance activities and constantly monitoring your well-being structure to preserve it in as stellar a condition as possible over the decades. Sorry, we are not actual castles, so I cannot wish you centuries of long life.

But if you have let your castle of well-being fall into disrepair (like my childhood baseball hero did), do not fail to embark upon your refurbishment project like I did with my dental restoration (back in Chapter 5). And once you renovate your fortress of health back to some semblance of splendor, continuously monitor its condition and reliability spend the requisite time to maintain it. And as a reminder of one of our other game plan principles, use tools and health apps (not to mention your bathroom scale) that best work for you to achieve your monitoring and maintenance efforts.

The more consistently you maintain your original or newly

reconstructed house of health, the longer you will enjoy this wonderful blessing we call life. And when you continuously maintain and strengthen your well-being structure, you will have a sturdy shelter from the storm when a hurricane of illness and affliction blows through your life. The perpetuation of your physical and mental mansion of glory is truly the culmination of countless routine monitoring undertakings and ordinary maintenance task.

IT MUST BE A TEAM EFFORT

As I said way back in Chapter 4, in any kind of team sport, coordination and collaboration with your colleagues is essential to presume any semblance of success, particularly in your well-being endeavors. Just as it does in the effort to win a ball game, execute a business plan, implement a rescue operation, or assure your personal journey to well-being, meshing with your teammates is of the utmost importance.

And as the team leader of your well-being squad, your associates will only be as productive as the level you involve them in your health-improving mission, so embrace and engage *all* of your teammates so they can play up to their potential and bestow their particular talents toward your success. Encourage, motivate, and employ them as equally as you feasibly can.

Yes, as your well-being construction team's foreperson, you must strive to build your nutritional base durable and robust, your Hardware, Software, and Repair Shop columns sturdy and secure, and you, as your well-being structure's roof, resolute and steadfast. Becoming an integral unit working in a balanced manner to share the load will be the difference between succeeding and failing toward accomplishing the objective of improving (and maintaining) your health and increasing your healthspan (not to mention your lifespan). You can do this. You need to do this to reach your potential.

PURSUE A HARD THING AND USE YOUR FOCUS KNOB

In Chapter 8, I spoke of doing a hard thing to consistently engage our cognitive functions, that is, our cranial computers, with new and reasonably challenging endeavors like learning to play an instrument, learning a new language, or other new demanding activity as we move through our game of life.

If you remember, those Harvard and NIH scientist people told us that in addition to eating well and exercising, habitually practicing a demanding skill you are interested in goes far toward maintaining and improving our cognitive skills as we age and helps to keep our brains healthy. Again, that is why (other than having always wanted to) I am learning to play the guitar now after spending so many decades on Mother Earth, not to mention undertaking this hard thing of writing this book.

I also mentioned the importance of having a focus knob to increase your attention span, relax your neurons, and lower your stress levels from the constant multitasking, screen-switching, and addiction to social media that consumes the lives of so many people today. I also delineated how your challenging hard endeavor activities could double as your focus knob, as Jolly-man Stan has found with his 43 non-electric vintage clocks that he joyfully winds up and also works on when one falls ill.

And my guitar training is my double-edged sword to keep my brain working across all (well, most of) its trillions of neurotransmitters. After spending an amount of time on technique drills and scales, I begin learning some new material during my practice sessions. Mel is now torturing me with a three-page composition he put together called "Adventures in B-Flat."

After months of practice, I can almost get through the first two pages of the piece, and the good news is, at the bottom of page two and into page three, the composition more or less is a repeat of the opening measures. Of course, Mel being Mel, put in several variations and then went off in an entirely different direction further down page three. I suppose he did name the piece "Adventures in B-Flat" for a reason. He wasn't kidding about the adventure part.

However, I also spend a certain amount of time during my sessions playing material that I have thoroughly memorized, and my fingers know where to go, such as Mel's dumbed-down version of "Sor's Waltz." After performing those four thousand and something renderings of the waltz, I am getting to the point where I can close my eyes while my fingers flit across the fretboard, and I can actually listen to the music I am playing and feel the nascent and emergent commencement of the flow. I still have a way to go to receive a thumbs-up from George, but it's all good. I am getting there.

Now, just so you know, your challenging endeavor does not necessarily have to double as your focus knob. One of my stress relievers during all those years I worked at the widget factory (and to this day) was to engage in activities pertaining to my fondness for plants. I have always loved verdant foliage for whatever reason. I have several plants that are decades old, and I just repotted one today that spent decades happily sitting upon my desk at the widget factory. That plant was my little piece of nature inside four solid concrete walls, and I have passed its offspring on to my offspring, who are also fond of foliage and greenery.

So turn off your phone and television, get up off the couch, and engage in a demanding activity in which you are interested, increasing and maintaining your cognitive capabilities, whether it be mastering the game of chess (good luck with its trillions upon trillions of possible board positions), writing a memoir (without a ghostwriter), or learning how to draw portraits of people (or pets), in an effort to keep your neural transmission lines as free of gunky junk and potholes as possible. And if you would like to color along with Mr. Spock, be my guest (just don't interrupt him).

Your brain is the heart of who you are, and you most definitely want to protect your cranial computer by routinely exercising that most complex entity found in the universe. You also want to give it time to engage in something it enjoys, relieving stress. As I said earlier, no rocket science is required or the use of Ponce's products.

LIVE MOSTLY IN THE REAL WORLD

Okay, I know this is going to shock you, but please allow me to tell yet another story. You remember our young lady back in Chapter 3 who, as I was relaxing on the beach, came solely to take all of those glamorous selfies of her beauty? I am fairly certain that her trip to the beach that day had something to do with her virtual world, as I mentioned back then.

Recently, a young (and very healthy, by the way) couple I know were on holiday hiking some high, rolling hills in a faraway magical locale. They summited one of those mythical mounds, and standing atop the scenic vista, they overheard another sightseer there exclaim, "Wow, look at this view! It looks just like the metaverse!" Sigh.

Now as a cyclist, I could get on a stationary bike, strap on some augmented reality googles, and cycle the same routes (though computer-generated) as those Tour de France people ride in real life. I could pedal up the Alpe d'Huez, down the terrifying descent of the Col du Galibier at more than 60 miles per hour (cybernetically, of course), and through the cobbled streets of Paris on the Champs-Élysées. And I think I could then post those virtual rides online like I had actually cycled them in real life (one cyclist I know said she actually did this; I have no idea if it's doable).

Nevertheless, I would not feel the bone-deep chill at the moonscape top of Mont Ventoux, I would not feel the howling wind screaming by my face as I descended the Col du Tourmalet at highway speeds, *and* I can most definitely assure you that I would not feel the excruciating pain when I hit the virtual tarmac when losing control of my bicycle on one of those death-defying descents in my augmented reality world (as you know, I have some real-life experience in that crashing category).

No, life happens in the real world. You can only kiss and hold your baby daughter or son in that world. You can only watch your children grow taller than you in the real world. You can only scratch your puppy's belly in that tangible domain. And that is the only realm in which you can get and stay healthy. So please, eat your healthy meals in the real world (even if you have to heat your nutritious leftovers (instead of you know what) in the microwave) and walk through your (safe, but not necessarily scenic) authentic real world park.

I will grant you this, however: strapping on your other world googles would make your stationary peddling effort (which is beneficial) much more interesting. Riding on a stationary bike is not the most exciting thing to do without moving through that time and space thing (and feeling the wind in your face) that Albert used to lecture about.

Now, just so you know, I'm not totally dismissing the digitally coded virtual reality realm. Way back in prehistoric times, when I was earning my real degree at the university, I was part of a simulation business team that competed against teams from other colleges in our conference. Each week, the different teams had to make cost, production, and marketing decisions, and then enter them into the computer on a nerve-racking deadline schedule.

I don't remember exactly how we did all that, but I do remember using a punch card machine and processing those cards through a card reader. You Zoomers probably have no idea what I'm even talking about, but if you type "cavepeople computers" into your search engine, you may find some images of those stone-age processing tools we used in college back then.

Now truth be told, participating in that antediluvian business simulation competition did teach me numerous lessons (many of which were quite germane when I began working at the widget factory) regarding the general decisions businesses have to make to survive, how to work with teammates with various backgrounds, and how to negotiate life in general. So again, virtual reality and the metaverse are not something to be totally avoided if that is your fancy, but it is most definitely not the real world either. Thus, like anything else, use it responsibly.

WORKS FOR EVERYONE (INCLUDING YOU)

Okay, a couple more points to review here before we go, and these are important. As I have said, it doesn't matter who you are, it doesn't matter what color your skin is, it doesn't matter what gender you are or identify with, it doesn't matter what nationality you are, it doesn't matter which side of the political aisle you stand (or sit); you, I, and everyone else on this planet are all human beings, and our bodies all require basically the same fundamental ingredients we have discussed: consumption of a mostly respectable and nutritious diet, adequate exercise, engagement in meaningful social interactions, and procurement of sufficient rest and recovery.

And as I have repeatedly stressed to you, you don't have to be perfect, just good enough to please George and Voltaire, but making them happy does require some effort, as mentioned above. Remember, no shortcut exists for a long run of health and well-being, despite what you know who says.

Strive for incremental and continuous improvement on your way to Healthyville and rejoice in the mundane chores of practice and maintenance required to get there (and stay there) by listening to good music while performing those tasks or recruiting a willing partner or friend to keep you company and help you (and themselves) out. I most definitely prefer to ride my bike with friends rather than by myself and I do have a good time when consuming (and preparing) a healthy meal with friends or family.

And despite the inevitable setbacks, focus on only what you can control, and employ all of our game plan principles, including not being afraid to change the road you're on. But again, the absolute most important affair for you to accomplish is to cross that proverbial starting line toward improving your life. And again, as Confucius advised us all those many millennia ago, don't worry about how fast you are improving, just never furlough your efforts to the sideline and sit on the bench.

Yes, no matter who you are, we are all human beings, and consuming a mostly nutritious diet, getting proper and sufficient exercise, learning new things, engaging in meaningful social interactions, and procurement of sufficient rest and recovery will render your arrival in Healthyville favorably possible.

SEEK HELP IF NECESSARY

Just the other day, I completed a ride with two of my very best cycling friends. As we often do as I mentioned way back in Chapter 1, we hung around for ten or 15 minutes, reflecting upon our ride, socializing, and basking in the glow of our just completed flow. We said our goodbyes, and as my friends were leaving the parking area, I began backing out of my parking space when I heard a horrible scrapping noise emanating from underneath my car.

My first thought was that a branch from one of the surrounding trees must have blown underneath my vehicle (it was a very windy day that afternoon) and lodged there, thus producing the worse than hideous sound of fingernails scrapping across the chalkboard. I pulled into a safe area a short distance from the parking lot at the entrance of the camping area, stopped my car, set the brake, and looked underneath. Even I (an athlete, not a mechanic) immediately diagnosed the problem.

A protective metal plate covering the bottom of the engine was hanging to the ground, fastened to the vehicle by only one remaining plastic grommet and I had no car-working-on tools on board. Driving the few miles home would have been hazardous possibly to me, but particularly to other motorists if that metal plate suddenly became detached, went air board, and flew through someone's windshield. I couldn't risk that scenario.

As miracles go, a fellow cyclist that I did not know and a visiting camper within seconds appeared upon the scene, fortunately more than willing to help non-mechanically inclined me out. As the cyclist handed us tools, the camper and I operated on the obstinate piece of metal hanging from my vehicle's undercarriage, and finally, after 20 minutes of toil, we pried the stubborn metallic plate free.

I got exceedingly lucky that day as the help I needed suddenly and miraculously materialized. As all of you know, in the normal sphere of reality, this phenomenon does not typically happen if seemingly ever. In most instances, assistance for your struggles when genuinely required has to be proactively pursued.

So please, always remember if you cannot escape the meandering maze of your well-being challenges and pitfalls, do not procrastinate to seek qualified advice and guidance, and not Ponce or any of his conniving cohorts out to make a buck off you. And please, never, ever be ashamed to ask for that help if you genuinely need it.

OKAY, with three seconds left in this section, let us take a timeout here, and this is a very important one, as most last-second timeouts are. A few days ago, I was in the produce section of the grocery store where I used to work, selecting my fruits and vegetables to consume during the upcoming week.

Just before my weekly greeting to my friend, the busy (and very healthy) produce clerk I used to work with who is usually behind the counter frantically cutting up fresh fruit when I visit the store, I saw another former store employee that I had trained to put those cans of corn on the shelf when he and I used to work in the grocery department. Of all the part-time stock clerks I trained, he was one of my most challenging souls, but I also knew I would never forget him.

He was a breezy, seemingly jovial young fellow with a mischievous wit about him, but I could sense some deep, underlying anxieties roaming freely inside the dark corridors of his consciousness. I asked him how he was doing and where he was working. He was basically okay and does now have an honest, respectable job, and has already gotten a promotion off the bottom of the workshop food chain.

And fortunately, I sensed another positive development in him. I could see in his eyes and hear in his voice that though he didn't particularly adore this job, he somehow knew at this point in his life, he had to stick with this occupation for now, which was a positive tell that his maturity was now finally kicking in. I have been there and have witnessed that maturing phenomenon in myself and others during our first decade of adult life. So overall, he is doing reasonably well.

He then asked me how I was currently doing, which I responded, "Very well." I then elaborated on why I was doing so well, first, so he would believe me and not think I was just engaging in "small talk," and second, to hopefully, knowing him the way I do, plant a small seed of optimism in his mind that life could be enjoyable if he kept "doing what he had to do."

I started by telling him I was still riding my bicycle all of those crazy miles, and that after all of these years, I was finally learning to play the guitar which I let him also know is not the easier activity I have ever immersed myself into. And I then told him I was writing this book, and naturally, he asked me what the tome was about. After giving him a brief synopsis of its subject matter, he then asked me a shrouded, but formidable question.

"So, it is possible for anyone to be happy?"

Knowing him the way I do; I understood the gravity of his question, and I was honest in my answer to him. I told him something approximating, "That is a hard question because we don't all start from the same place. Some of us are born with enormous advantages, talents, and, well, just plain luck. And some of us are born with major impediments to overcome, huge roadblocks to somehow circumvent, and major health and mental issues from day one. Now, most of us are born somewhere in between, but we do not get to choose our parents whom we are born to, so we just have to do the best we can with what we are born with."

Now I am sure I was not that grammatically correct or sagely sounding (if it even sounds that way). I think you know me well enough by now that I'm an athlete, not a great orator, much less an intelligent one. However, I can read people fairly well and I could see a look of disappointment come over his face when he realized that I didn't have a Ponce endorsed solution. When I pressed him to see if he truly was doing okay, he began to open up and give me some of the details of his life that were troubling him, again a sign of his growing maturity.

He told me he had gained a bunch of weight, but fortunately, had eliminated most of the superfluous mass he had been carrying. He could stand to lose another pound or two, and shore up his muscle definition a shred, but he was essentially in the proximity of being considered physically healthy. He then began to reveal some mental issues he has been grappling with specifically involving depression. His revelation was confirmation of what I had surmised years before. He then went into more detail about his current struggles.

Paraphrasing, I told him as compassionately as I could, "Look, if you need some help, go get it whatever it takes, and I cannot emphasize that enough." I let him know that I have repeatedly stressed that in this book. I then continued, "Go see your human resources people. Or go out and find a counselor, again whatever you need to do, and talk to them. Get some help. And most importantly, do not be ashamed to seek that assistance and to accept it. Please do not try to go it alone and overcome your serious problems by yourself if you are sinking further into despair."

He nodded with a painful, but I think appreciative, look on his face. I think he was at least now contemplating my suggestion and giving some serious thought toward initiating my suggestions. I mentioned this back in Chapter 3 but moving from not having any intention to move toward healthier behavior to at least thinking about it, is a positive step in the right direction according to a high-level behavioral theory (which is way above my head) known as the Transtheoretical Model/Stages of Change. I am positive those scientist people could explain that theory far better than I ever could.

Anyway, after a few more words of encouragement, I then allowed as how back when we toiled together at the store, he was always one of my favorite work associates. He responded with a sly grin. "Really? I always thought I was a pain in your [insert three-letter word]." Again, to paraphrase, I told him, "Well, you were, but I always knew you had some cards under the table that you weren't showing, so I always let you slide a bit." He sheepishly smiled, and I again told him to go get some qualified help and support if he needed it.

I don't know if he will actually go out and seek any assistance, but I could see that he was now at least mentally scrutinizing that maneuver. And, if you can relate to my friend, please do not hesitate to also seek competent support whether you are suffering from mental issues, physical difficulties, isolation, loneliness, or all of the above. If you have made it this far in this book, you have also indeed been contemplating positive changes in your life.

––––––––

To wrap up this section, as the message of our timeout above implies and as our refrain continuously reminds us, if you sincerely need help and guidance toward resolving your most difficult problems at any time during your long and winding journey through your blessed gift of life, do not hesitate to seek that assistance, and do not be ashamed to receive it.

However, let me say this. Endeavoring to solve our own problems is what we humans have always done since back when our cavepeople ancestors roamed around seeking food, shelter, love, and happiness, while avoiding all those saber-toothed tigers. Overcoming our own difficulties is the preferred method and should definitely be pursed in most cases when physical and mental challenges are presented to us.

Also, as we spoke of in the last chapter, sulking inside your poor-little-me closet and eternally seeking attention by perpetually crying coyote (is that the right animal?) is not in your best interest. Nor is masking your demons with humor (as my breezy friend above always tried to do), adult beverages, magical mushrooms, or perilous pharmaceuticals in search of a gilded thoroughfare to nirvana.

Therefore, stand up to your adversaries of pain, affliction, and disease, and do your best to incapacitate them. And by the way, the healthier you are, the better your chances of improvising and overcoming your antagonists. However, again, if all else fails and you are irreversibly succumbing to your fiercest foes, do not hesitate or be ashamed to seek reasonable, qualified, and professional help and care.

———

THE BUZZ of the crowd is rising to deafening decibel intensities and anticipation is rising to electrifying heights as it is almost time to get out there on the floor with all of your remarkable teammates. And hopefully, your well-being structure is coming along quite nicely according to those breathtaking blueprints and being built with the sturdiness of granite.

You can do this. You may not win a bunch of Super Bowl rings like Mr. Brady, or Wimbledon tennis tournaments like Ms. Serena, or WNBA championships like Ms. Bird, or be famous like those Kardashian people or internet influencers, but that's okay. Your goal, and mine, is to wake up tomorrow and face the new day with a sense of purpose, a sense of determination, health, and a sense of anticipation that the new day will be better than yesterday. Let us all make the most of this exquisite affair we call life.

I have tried to ground you in reality throughout this book, and I have given you a strategy and a dozen important game plan principles to get you started and implement. It's your story now! So please, cross that starting line toward improving your health and well-being, stay the course the best you can, and continue on your journey for as long as you have breath in your lungs.

Just as I was mounting my bike yesterday for a lovely afternoon ride, I saw E-bike Mike just coming off the trail. He told me he had been out for precisely an hour and 47 minutes and that more than half of his ride was on the off-pavement trails that, I can tell you, are exceedingly more difficult to ride on than our paved trail. When I told him to keep up the good work, he responded enthusiastically, "Absolutely!"

I am not a world-class athlete telling you to be perfect like me (I am seriously not flawless) and then you will be absolutely great and wonderful. No, I'm just a humble athlete with maybe a little talent as my long-ago running friend once said, and all I am again, and again, and again saying to you is please, cross that start line toward making yourself a little (or a lot) healthier and perhaps a little happier. That mission is most definitely worth the effort.

And, before we move on to our final chapter together, think about where you are on your own long and winding pathway through life. Where do you want your story to proceed from here? And how do you want the chronicle of your life to turn out in its final passages? As a reminder, for most people, seeking opulence and acclaim will be a futile endeavor, but setting a steadfast course to Healthyville is doable and will give you an exceedingly better chance to end your story with a sense of satisfaction and commendation.

CHAPTER 12: SHOWTIME

LET us now have a moment of silence, please.

Thank you for that moment, for you see, I had another very special friend for decades at the widget factory that I briefly mentioned back in Chapter 4. He was the gentleman who would periodically proclaim certain widget matters truly a thing of beauty. I repurposed his famous phrase back in that chapter to describe how your life could also authentically be enhanced and become a thing of beauty depending upon your level of participation with your well-being teammates and the construction quality of your well-being house of health.

We have now properly met those health-enhancing colleagues and gazed upon the complete breathtaking construction blueprints of your new well-being fortress (aren't they a thing of beauty?). I hope you are exceedingly eager to start (and continue) building the new you from the foundation up. I sincerely hope so!

My dear friend had another famous saying. Every three months, several high-level Mothership people would come visit our facility (along with many other elevated senior manager people via the primordial teleconferencing system we hoped would function back then) for a huge quarterly appraisal of our widget-construction progress. Just before we walked into those major summits, my dear friend would always say, "It's showtime!"

And now my friends, it is showtime for you to begin (if you haven't already) toward improving your health and well-being. Are you prepared? Are you ready? Please say you are. Please say you have been paying attention and at least have been thinking about getting healthier.

GETTING YOU OVER THE START LINE

Everyone truly loved my dear friend, and when he looked you squarely in the eye, you would believe anything he said. Rumor has it he once even sold Ponce some magical mermaid oil to clear up his battered skin and make him look young again. He was that good. Incidentally, I'm not sure if Ponce got his maltreated skin from exposure to the peninsula's searing sun rays or battling Mr. Brady and his buccaneers.

Anyway, I know I am not nearly as convincing as my dear friend once was, but I do truly hope I have somehow persuaded you into improving your health so you can better enjoy that glorious gift of life you and I have so fortunately been bestowed. My entire (meaningful) purpose for doing this hard thing of writing this book is to just get you over the start line and on your way to a healthier and more enjoyable (and meaningful) life. Again, you are so worth it not only to yourself, but to your friends and loved ones!

You don't have to go out and try to win Super Bowls, or ride in the Tour de France, or become famous like those movie star/social media personalities. Trust me on this, those people have their own problems just like you and I, and many will die way too young because they did not physically, mentally, and socially take care of themselves being too absorbed in becoming rich, powerful, and famous. That is why you should not compare yourself with anyone else and feel woefully inferior, insecure, etc. You are you and hopefully healthy. That is what is genuinely important!

Although I have been to the Rocky Mountains, I am certainly not a guru like the one who rescued the widget factory from the Wild West days of fabrication folly. And I can't check on you every three months like those Mothership people checked on us at the widget factory. However, I have tried to ground you in reality throughout this book, and I have given you a strategy and a dozen important game plan principles to get you started, toward a healthier life good enough to get a thumbs up from George (and Voltaire).

Yes, here we are life fans and participants. It's getting close to game time. You have now met and practiced with (yes?) your new teammates. And your new healthy well-being structure is in the finishing stages, or at least has begun. But if you haven't begun your journey to (or back to) Healthyville, it is now time to get started toward that healthier destination. As I said in the last chapter, you must begin your expedition to actually get there. So please, cross the start line!

STAY IN THE GAME

As I rolled out of bed a few days ago, settled down to read my digital paper, and drink my morning coffee, I turned 70 years old. How did that happen? Yes, I have now been aboard the good ship Mother Earth for seven short decades. Most of those 70 years have been in the real world, and it's been a decent ride, potholes and all. But I still have 30 years to go until the end of regulation in my game of life and more than 50 years to catch Jeanne, so I will most definitely keep doing what I "gotta do" to get there.

I may not be as young as I used to be, but then again, I'm not nearly as old as most people my age. However, if I stopped working with my teammates, if I stopped maintaining my well-being structure,

I could very well be a very old 75-year-old if I even made it that far. Father Time is always lurking in the shadows and ready to pounce when you let your guard down.

You must stay involved and cooperating with all of your teammates in your game of life for as long as you possibly can to fend off that stealthy stalker. And, you always have to continue maintaining and fortifying your well-being fortress in case a major Category 5 health hurricane is on the horizon and blows through your life. The stronger your structure, the better your chances of survival and recovery.

I was purchasing my weekly groceries the other day when I saw one of my very favorite millennial friends working there, and I pointed out to her, a sadly bent over, unhealthy guy supporting himself with a walker in the next checkout lane. I let her know that I had graduated from high school with the gentleman. Her eyes got as big as the cookies they sell over in the bakery, and I told her, and I am telling you, please stay healthy because that is where she, and you, could be if you spend most of your time on the bench and not in the game with your teammates. So please, stay in your game of life and live long (and healthy)!

HAVE FUN DOING THIS

As I also mentioned back in the last chapter, selling you on the mundanity of healthy practices is a most difficult transaction. I would guess most people are not as hard-headed (I've been called worse) as me and sit there and play those 4,384 renditions of "Sor's Waltz" by myself. I think Mel just nodded in the affirmative. I'm not sure if he was nodding positively about me being hard-headed or that most people wouldn't play that many renderings of the waltz.

Anyway, to mitigate the mundanity of practicing particularly when you are building your nutritional base or shoring up your physical activity column, most people have more fun when they embark upon these well-being missions when they participate with family, friends, and work colleagues. I know I earnestly have significantly more fun when I am riding my bike with my friends than when riding solo. Not only is it safer (we are there to help each other in case something goes wrong like yesterday), but we are also strengthening our mental activity center post as we socially engaged with each other while pedaling (and changing that flat tire) and particularly after the ride as I have mentioned.

Now truth be told, I don't mind practicing my guitar by myself (for now) because it has always been something I have longed to do, and also at this stage, no one would have to hear my million mistakes. As I explained in our reality checks in Chapter 5, I still have feelings of awkwardness and unworthiness in my endeavor to make my six string sing. And I would still feel extremely awkward if I got up on stage with my rock and roll buddy. But who knows, maybe someday?

Eventually though, I would like to find someone more advanced than me to practice with so they could show me some new techniques and ways to play (don't get mad, Mel, you will always be my most treasured teacher) so to continue to improve my proficiency with the instrument. And it would be more fun than practicing by myself all the time.

So whether you chose to head out on your journey to the fertile fields of healthier venues alone or with friends, family, etc., or a combination of both depending upon the terrain you are traversing, have fun doing it.

As I have mentioned before, when I got to toil with those people in the widget factory maintenance department, we worked hard, but we did have some fun! Likewise, with my workmates at the grocery store. So, as I told you in the last chapter, your journey to Healthyville will be unique, but try your best to have fun along the way, no matter which way you chose to get there.

SENDING OUT SOME NOTES

Okay, before we go, I would like to send out some messages (but not in a bottle) to all of you, beginning with you millennials and zoomers. Your particularly important note is that you are now right in the thick of this wonderful affair we call life. Plus, you are bringing up the kids today who are tomorrow's hope, a particularly important task! Teach them well as those Woodstock singer people from long, long ago once sang.

Also, you are just reaching or have already arrived at your physical peak here on Mother Earth. In general, we reach our physical crest somewhere around 25 years of age and then more or less stay on that plateau for about ten years before then beginning to descend back down into the valley of physical limitations and inability. There is a reason why very few professional athletes are still performing in the professional ranks as they near 40 years of age. That is why Mr. Brady is such an anomaly.

Beginning somewhere during our mid-thirties, the inevitable erosion of our muscles and physical ability starts to manifest (not to mention weight clandestinely creeping upon us if we do not monitor it as those 30 pounds did on me during that era in my life). That degeneration begins slowly at first and then commences to pick up speed like a snowball down a steep hill (not that I, the peninsula dwelling person, would have any experience with that) as we head into our fifties.

However, depending on how well you cooperate with your teammates, your physical decline can be (and hopefully will be) barely discernible as mine was (and Mr. Brady's) as I headed into my forties and fifties as illustrated by my 5k racing chart from back in Chapter 2 and again presented here.

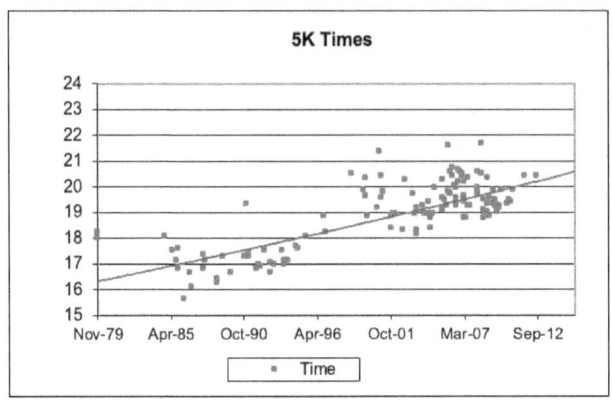

After a couple years of not racing in my late forties (though I continued to run those 20 miles per week and eat a healthy diet), and then taking a while to get back into racing form, when I launched into my fifties just after the turn of the millennium, there was no exponential upsurge in my 5k times, only a modest, straight-line rise as you can see (aided by steadily offloading that extra freight I was carrying aboard my frame). As I said way back in Chapter 2, I was determined that Father Time was going to have to fight for every tenth of every percentage point of my physical decline for as long as I am alive.

So, to you young millennials (and no, I am not going to call you middle-aged), and particularly to you youthful zoomers, I am stalwartly urging you to start now (if you haven't already) to fend off Father Time and his destructive forces of degradation! Begin and, more importantly, continue building your bastion of well-being sturdy and steadfast.

And depending how robust and resilient you fabricate your protective edifice, perhaps you and your agile teammates can keep Father Time and his dilapidation militia scrambling for the upper hand for years, decades, or perhaps even an entire century, and then head into overtime in the pursuit of Jeanne's longevity record.

And one more quick word of guidance for you zoomers and millennials. Do not waste your enviable youth away wishing you could retire. Too much life happens between becoming old enough to vote and old enough to sign up for Medicare. Despite seemingly being at your ragged edge all day, every day, all the time, embrace the grind.

Pursue your meaningful purpose, hope for the best, and bring those children up well despite these tough times we all live in since apparently Mars and Jupiter still have not quite aligned. And hopefully, somewhere in the midst of all your labors and endeavors, you will increase your happiness and your satisfaction of life; and then when the time comes, head on into retirement contently and with a plan when that chapter of your life begins.

And speaking of Retirementville, I have a special note for you Gen X people thinking about finally moving to and residing there, now that the kids are grown and on their own. As I just expressed to those up-and-coming zoomers and millennials, you most definitely need to have a plan before moving there, and I am not just talking about a financial strategy.

My word of advice is that when you punch that time clock for the last time and formally retire from your main vocation, you must not retire from life. I am sure you remember my doctor being so concerned as I headed off into Retirementville about my plan. Retirement is grand if you are healthy enough to enjoy it (remember that millennials and zoomers) and have prepared yourself physically, mentally, and financially for that chapter in your life the best you can and have a definite plan moving forward.

I recently had lunch with a friend who is still working at the widget factory and within a decade of moving to Retirementville. Upon asking her if she had a relocation plan, she said she would more than likely do volunteer work, which, knowing her the way I do, she probably will and would be perfect for that. And of course, she has all of her children, grandkids, and friends to harass, I mean interact and socialize with. I know she is out there somewhere laughing right now because that is also one of her favorite pastimes (laughing and socializing with her kids, grandkids, and friends, not harassing people) and part of her plan.

So my Gen X friends, please have a well-defined map prepared (and get help if you need to) before you begin your journey into that delightful land of retirement because you never know when, and this is why I am emphasizing this to you, a physical (or mental) calamity will transpire that suddenly incapacitates you and forces you into residency there before you are prepared for the stay.

Father Time can strike at any time, particularly if you haven't taken care of yourself. So please, improve (if required) and maintain your health, and have your relocation plan to Retirementville prepared long before you actually plan to commence your relocation there, just in case a tornado of affliction or accident strikes.

Between my book writing endeavors, bike riding, and learning to play "Sor's Waltz" (and Mel's long and winding "Adventures in B-Flat"), I am enjoyably "working" 30-40 hours per week and staying fully engaged in life. That was my plan to stay in the game, and so far, I have been fortunate enough to enjoyably remain there despite various pothole skirmishes.

I have known several people who got so bored (because they didn't have a plan) when retiring that they went back to work just to have something to do. As much as I enjoyed working at the widget factory and particularly at the grocery store, I cannot imagine reengaging in either of those two endeavors. Life is too grand! So, as I did, please have your retirement plan up to date long before relocating to that leisurely hamlet of potential enjoyment!

And a sincere note to you boomers and beyond. At this point, simply do the best you can to remain or move closer to Healthyville. A lot of water from Grandma's river has now flowed under the bridge my family and I used to cross before continuing through the woods to see her when I was (and you were) a kid a long, long time ago.

And judging by my 50+1-year high school class reunion, not to mention being anywhere out in public, many of you have not exactly engaged in stellar protocols of health maintenance and practice since our grade school days. I just lost two more former high school class-mates (that I know of) in the past few weeks. It breaks my heart because better outcomes were within our reach even back then. Not that I am that smart, but I had that mostly figured out shortly after graduation after seeing my former baseball hero and not ever wanting to go there.

I know many of you have some serious health issues to manage, but do not give up. Despite the passage of time (and water in Grand-ma's river under the bridge) since our high school days, most of you can still maintain, perhaps even improve your health, maybe elimi-nate a few prescriptions and save some money, not to mention, becoming a little happier if you begin performing more regularly with your well-being colleagues and begin some restoration projects on your health fortress.

Even my former high school classmate I mentioned earlier still gets out there and walks with his walker when he is shopping for groceries instead of opting to ride around the store on one of those motorized vehicles. I was in a grocery store a while back and I liter-ally witness a traffic jam of those vehicles in progress, where else, but on the snack aisle. I just shook my head and moved on to the next aisle.

Anyway, I do see my high school friend in the grocery store fairly regularly, so he is still out there getting around and he is a funny dude! If he would work more closely with his Fuel teammate, he more than likely could lose a generous portion of his excess weight, thus making his getting about a little easier. So please, my boomer mates and our parents' generation, get out there the best you can and do what you can do to improve your health while you are still able. Most all of us can, to some degree, and yes, including me, still improve our health by cooperating more closely with our well-being teammates. As we used to say, go for it!

Now, since it has taken me awhile to write this book, I have a special note to three very recently retired athletes that we have come to know in these pages (and mentioned above), Ms. Serena, Ms. Bird, and Mr. Brady (are you sure you are retiring?). Please, please, please do not take the same route through your retirement years as my boyhood baseball hero did.

Perhaps you don't have to work quite as hard as you did during your athletic careers, particularly with your Hardware teammate, but Father Time and his team of stealthy exploiters don't care if you were a GOAT (greatest of all time) or not. Please, stay in your game of life with your well-being teammates and continue to monitor and maintain your extraordinary houses of health. And a shout out to Mr. Kareem, job well done, Sir, since launching your last NBA skyhook (and airplane flying days) all those decades ago!

And a note to all of you, I have for the most part (despite those moments I wanted to pull my hair out) enjoyed doing this hard thing of writing this book for you, and I truly hope that, in some way, this tome will get you over the start line and help you improve your health so you can better enjoy the one life you have. And a note to Dr. Duckworth, this book writing endeavor has certainly been hard for me. Somewhere in there, I think my grit thing grew!

MY PARTING GIFT TO YOU

Now that we are near the end of our journey through this book together, let me bestow upon you a parting gift strikingly similar to the one I received after getting voted off the mountain. As you move through life, *please do not* embrace the hate! And because those two planets we have discussed so many times now have still not synced up quite yet, sadly, there is a lot of it about. But please, let that [insert four-letter word] go.

When you are harboring hate, animosity, and resentment, you are taking minutes and hours away from your life. You are only killing yourself from within! I cannot emphasize this point enough. And like pennies adding up to dollars, embracing the hate is adding up to months and years off your life.

A while back, I went to get my hair cut. As I sat there waiting for my barber to finish cutting the millennial's hair sitting in his chair, an older gentleman (and yes, he was actually older than me, I think) came in, and when our barber asked him how his vacation went, the gentleman began talking about how wonderful his trip with his wife was to see the fall leaves up the coast.

Now I cannot exactly recall how the conversation turned, but when the older "gentleman" noticed the millennial not paying attention and saw his worried mind turning over a mile a minute, the dialogue quickly descended away from those beautiful vistas on our eastern seaboard and down into the dark side of disgust.

Apparently the young man owned a lawn maintenance business, and responding to a leading question from the older guy, began agitatedly complaining about the high price of gasoline for his mowers and how parts for his machines were also sky-high, how he couldn't find people who wanted to do an honest day's work, etc., etc. And the older dude just kept gleefully pushing his hot buttons, dramatically raising the young man's stress levels.

The conversation then turned to places where it should not have gone. I will simply leave it there, but the millennial was becoming more and more steamed with loathing. I should have called a timeout and tried to bring the conversation back to the autumn leaves. Sadly, I watched a called third strike go by.

I am guessing the young man lost an hour and a half of his life during that fifteen minutes it took to get his hair cut due to the increased stress coursing through his body generated by that older man. As you will recall our discussion of purpose and meaning in our lives back in Chapter 10, working together is exceedingly more beneficial and healthier than harboring hatred toward others, or for yourself, for that matter. I'm not sure what the elder man's motives were.

I wish I could say there will not be a next time, but I know conversations like this transpire every day, everywhere. Too many people today (and more than likely since the days of our cavepeople ancestors) enthusiastically embrace the hate bombarding us. I suppose, unfortunately, it is part of our DNA.

Living life with civility seems to have gone the way of the passenger pigeon and dodo bird these days for too many people. But I have to tell you, sheltering, and more sinisterly, abetting and participating in rage and detestation, is doing your body and mind no good. You may win a battle or two, perhaps many, but you will likely lose the war to Father Time much sooner than you are anticipating.

I have always tried to get along with everyone from the prince (not that I know any) to the plumber, from the queen (and no, I don't know any queens either though I've known a few people who thought they were) to the cleaning people. That is, I always at least try to find the good in all people I come across. Sometimes I come up empty with certain people, but like our singer-sailor friend once said (and this just in, may you rest in peace Mr. Jimmy), it doesn't take any more time to see the good side of life (and people) than the bad.

So again, embracing and particularly engaging in the hate only increases your stress levels, killing you from within and possibly actually getting you killed. So please, please remember, lighting us up with rage is one of Father Time's more sinister deceptions, not to mention one of Ponce's main money-making endeavors. Just shut it down. Turn it off. And, as my parting gift from getting voted off the mountain so articulately proclaimed, just let that [insert four-letter word] go. Again, you are only killing yourself from within if you do not.

Please do not embrace the hate!

And here is an additional trinket in your parting gift bag for you to ponder over. For most of you (including me), longing for and seeking fame and fortune will be fruitless, and if you manage to achieve it, typically it is only fleeting. And normally, as those famous Rush singer people told us long ago, it's all just a grand illusion anyway, and down deep inside, we are all just human beings. We all require basically the same subsistence and activities (you know what they are by now) to remain healthy. Your health will always (or should) be the most important treasure you will ever possess.

So be thankful for what you do have and absolutely do not focus on what you think you are missing out on and yearn for what others hold and possess. Those famous people have their issues, too. Every pot of gold comes with its own particular array of complications. So again, appreciate what you do have in life and always be optimistic about the future and hope for the best. Seek memories and those moments of beauty that only life, including yours, can provide. Life (mostly in the real world) is always there waiting for you to immerse yourself into and appreciate.

———

So, let's conclude this book with one more story. Did you honestly expect it to end any other way? Back when I was getting my real college degree before I began my long tour at the widget factory, a movie came out starring my favorite actor back then (I don't have one now), Robert Redford, and his co-star was Jane Fonda (more on Ms. Fonda in a moment).

Mr. Redford was playing the role of a famous, but aging, rodeo cowboy. Now, I can't remember exactly how all this happened, but somehow, he became acquainted with an enormously famous horse being treated by Ponce and owned by some greedy people. Mr. Brady was still in diapers back then and of no help, so Mr. Redford, since he didn't want to be a famous cowboy any longer, decided to rescue the famous equine himself from the perilous care of Ponce and turn him (the horse, not Ponce) loose in the high mountains where the grass was green and the air was clean, so he could again run free and be with other healthy mares and stallions.

Somehow Ms. Fonda, who was playing the role of a famous investigative reporter, found out about Mr. Redford's caper, and decided to follow him to the highlands in her high-heel boots. Trust me, I not making this up. Anyway, somewhere on their journey, Mr. Redford found out that the greedy people were after him because they obviously wanted their famous horse back under the care of Ponce, so he decided to go off road with the horse.

Ms. Fonda, being a city lady, was understandably having a diffi-cult time keeping up with Mr. Redford, especially lugging around 14 pounds of microphones and camera equipment (smart phones were not a thing back then) for her exclusive reports. So as all good Holly-wood movies do, in the end, the horse ran free and healthy, Mr. Redford was off the hook for absconding with the famous equine but still needed a job because he didn't want to be a famous cowboy any longer, and the greedy people fired Ponce.

In the famous, final scene, Mr. Redford and Ms. Fonda were sitting in a coffee shop, having one last cup of coffee before saying their goodbyes because the movie was about to end. Since he didn't have his job being a famous cowboy any longer, she asked him, "What are you going to do now?" Mr. Redford thought about it for a second and said, "I don't know. I'll find something simple. Hard maybe, but simple."

And that, simply, is the moral and message of this book. Improving your health and well-being is, for the most part (depending on your starting point and underlying conditions), a relatively simple, straightforward process, though of course, it may be a little hard, or as I like to say, doable with sustained effort like that learning to play the guitar for non-musically talented people like me. And more than likely, roadblock after discouraging roadblock unquestionably will litter your path forward to better health and an improved quality of life. But do not despair and do not give up!

Back in Chapter 2, I mentioned the fitness craze going on during the eighties a few years after that Mr. Redford movie came out about that famous horse. Ms. Fonda, not wanting to be a famous investiga-tive reporter any longer, got into the fitness obsession back then and made several extremely popular fitness videos (YouTube wasn't a thing that long ago). I think she made more money doing that fitness gig than continuing her investigative reporting job in the movies. I have no idea.

Anyway, according to my search engine (keeping up with famous people as you probably have guessed by now is not my preoccupation), Ms. Fonda, now in her mid-eighties, still partici-pates in those exercise sessions, geared down these days as appro-priate for her age, along with consuming a Voltaire-approved diet. Though Father Time and his caustic cohorts are incessantly taking their toll on her body (apparently, she has some after-birth parts in her body like I do), and she is battling a serious disease, she is still well enough to make a new movie these days about Mr. Brady (now that he is all grown up). I don't think Mr. Redford is in that one.

So, if consuming a healthy diet, exercising, and staying engaged in life works for her, and me, I am fairly confident it will work for you, too. We are all human beings. Your life is too precious, and the effort you put forth will be worth it! Please begin and continue your journey!

I have tried to be honest with you and ground you in reality. No quick fixes are in existence to achieve better health (despite what Ponce says), and steady progress is not realistic, nor guaranteed. It will be a round-about journey of three steps forward, a couple back-ward, and one here or there off in some angled direction, you know, the scenic route.

Also, your homeostasis partner can and probably will be at times difficult to work with but does have your best interest in mind (always remember that). And yes, feelings of awkwardness and unworthiness, and quite frankly, demoralization, are part of the process and a part of life in general. But please channel Mr. Confucius and always continue upon your well-being journey.

And let me say this once again in plain English and in the interest of reality, depending on where you start, your journey to good health and well-being, like Mr. Redford's new job, is more than likely going to be reasonably (perhaps profoundly) difficult. But as I prefer to say, doable with sustained effort and with a little help from your friends, family, and health care providers if needed and you should not be ashamed to ask for that assistance if required. Your journey to or back to Healthyville may very well be the most difficult task you ever undertake, but it will be one of your most important life achievements and so worth the effort.

I have countless times felt like throwing my guitar as far as I possibly could because I was so frustrated with my less-than-mistake-free renditions of "Sor's Waltz" (I won't even mention those "Adventures in B-Flat"), but I am not going to back down as Mr. Petty preached, and most days, I continue to practice that melodious (at least on paper) piece of music by Sor along with several other melodies and compositions. And every now and then, and more and more often, I am beginning to experience the ethereal sensations of the flow while playing. So please, promise yourself that you won't back down either, and that you will always stay on your journey toward better health, come what may.

—————

HERE WE ARE in the final moments of this book. We have no timeouts left, and showtime is upon us. Showtime for you to begin improving your health, your well-being, and more than likely, your happiness. I have given you a strategy (the four corners offense), a set of breathtaking blueprints for your well-being fortification (aren't they truly a thing of beauty), a dozen game plan principles for you to employ, and a couple of parting gifts to guide you on your journey to Healthyville. Life is truly a blessed gift! You can do this! Now is the time to get out there and cross the start line on your expedition to Healthyville!

So, as my dear widget factory friend would always say, "It's showtime!" Please go out there (mostly in the real world), improve your health and well-being, and live!